Contents

Outdoor Play, Every Day

Innovative Play Concepts
for Early Childhood

Karyn Wellhousen

DELMAR

™

THOMSON LEARNING

Australia   Canada   Mexico   Singapore   Spain   United Kingdom   United States

DELMAR
THOMSON LEARNING™

Outdoor Play, Every Day:
Innovative Play Concepts for Early Childhood
by Karyn Wellhousen

Business Unit Director:
Susan L. Simpfenderfer

Executive Production Manager:
Wendy A. Troeger

Executive Marketing Manager:
Donna J. Lewis

Acquisitions Editor:
Erin O'Connor Traylor

Production Editor:
J.P. Henkel

Channel Manager:
Nigar Hale

Editorial Assistant:
Alexis Ferraro

Cover Design:
Tom Cicero

Library of Congress Cataloging-in-Publication Data

Wellhousen, Karyn.
   Outdoor play, every day: innovative play concepts for early
childhood/Karyn Wellhousen.
      p.cm.
   Includes bibliographical references and index.
   ISBN 0-7668-4061-1
      1. Play. 2. Early childhood education—Activity programs.
3. Outdoor recreation for children. I. Title.
LB1139.35.P55 W45 2001
372.13'84—dc21   2001048856

NOTICE TO THE READER

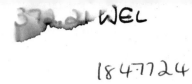

To my loving and devoted family:
my husband Jeff,
our children Katy Jo and Jackson,
and Maggy the cat

Preface

Outdoor play has long been considered essential to the overall growth and development of young children. For centuries, pioneers of early education and related fields have recognized the benefits of fresh air, large motor play, and exploring natural environments. Jean Jacques Rousseau, Johann Heinrich Pestalozzi, Friedrich Froebel, Patty Smith Hill, and Rachel and Margaret McMillan each validated the need for outdoor play and learning. Their individual provisions for learning and playing outdoors made this experience a tradition in early childhood education.

Today, outside play remains a component in most early childhood curricula, but the time appropriated for outdoor experiences has declined steadily. Playing outdoors was once considered an essential part of childhood. Now it is viewed as a *recess* from the more important tasks of the school day. *Outdoor Play, Every Day: Innovative Play Concepts for Early Childhood* explores the historical and political reasons for this unfortunate shift in attitudes and provides a plan for reinstating outdoor play to its original, intended level of importance.

TARGET AUDIENCES

The text is written with four groups of learners in mind:

- *students* of child development and early childhood/elementary education
- *professionals* practicing in these fields
- *parents* of young children
- *community leaders*

Members of these groups will gain a basic understanding of the need for outdoor play as well as learn specific methods for implementing appropriate outdoor learning experiences in preschools, child care centers, elementary schools, backyards, and community playgrounds. Like its companion text, *A Constructivist Approach to*

Foreword

Advocacy of the importance of play in all domains of young children's development has never abated over the decades and centuries of early childhood education in this country. Throughout the historical swings in thought and practice, belief in the necessity of play in the lives of young children has persisted. At times, these voices have been muted in the face of trends toward structure in school reform movements; nevertheless, early childhood educators have maintained their position that young children need play as part of their daily lives in an early childhood center.

Research on the benefits of play for later achievement in school continues to document the positive relationship between play and learning. The large number of scholars pursuing topics in play research has resulted in an accumulation of evidence of how young children play as they proceed through stages or levels of development in the early childhood years and how play both facilitates and reflects development and learning.

The overwhelming evidence on the benefits of play seems to be at odds with the current forces of school reform and its effect on education in preschool and primary grades. Concerns about academic achievement and preparation for standardized testing have diminished or excluded opportunities for play as part of the curriculum and school day, even for young children in many settings. The possibility that play can enhance achievement rather than interfere with learning seems to be incongruous to policymakers. As a result, the play movement and school reform efforts resemble two ships passing in the night without any effort to communicate with each other.

Wellhousen's book is a welcome addition to play literature in its focus on how to infuse learning into outdoor play. Many teachers in early childhood settings want to incorporate the outdoor playground as an extension of the indoor classroom. Wellhousen describes how outdoor play can have a direct connection with objectives and strategies for learning that are appropriate for the developmental progress of young children. She begins with how outdoor play benefits infants and toddlers, proceeds with preschool and primary-age children, and includes information on how the teacher can bridge theory and developmental progress with outdoor experiences that use play as the vehicle for learning. Many activities and anecdotal stories of children's and teachers' experiences throughout the text support her position on the blending of play and learning.

The challenge for early childhood educators to be able to include play, particularly outdoor play, in the young child's school experiences will continue in the foreseeable future. Wellhousen not only presents strategies to successfully manage outdoor play and learning, but provides teachers with information to articulate to parents and decision-makers how play will advance rather than retard achievement.

Sue C. Wortham

Preface

Outdoor play has long been considered essential to the overall growth and development of young children. For centuries, pioneers of early education and related fields have recognized the benefits of fresh air, large motor play, and exploring natural environments. Jean Jacques Rousseau, Johann Heinrich Pestalozzi, Friedrich Froebel, Patty Smith Hill, and Rachel and Margaret McMillan each validated the need for outdoor play and learning. Their individual provisions for learning and playing outdoors made this experience a tradition in early childhood education.

Today, outside play remains a component in most early childhood curricula, but the time appropriated for outdoor experiences has declined steadily. Playing outdoors was once considered an essential part of childhood. Now it is viewed as a *recess* from the more important tasks of the school day. *Outdoor Play, Every Day: Innovative Play Concepts for Early Childhood* explores the historical and political reasons for this unfortunate shift in attitudes and provides a plan for reinstating outdoor play to its original, intended level of importance.

TARGET AUDIENCES

The text is written with four groups of learners in mind:

- *students* of child development and early childhood/elementary education
- *professionals* practicing in these fields
- *parents* of young children
- *community leaders*

Members of these groups will gain a basic understanding of the need for outdoor play as well as learn specific methods for implementing appropriate outdoor learning experiences in preschools, child care centers, elementary schools, backyards, and community playgrounds. Like its companion text, *A Constructivist Approach to*

Block Play in Early Childhood, this book is intended to preserve a great early childhood tradition and serve as a complete resource for adults who care for and teach young children.

⚘ORGANIZATION OF THE TEXT

Chapter 1 explores the fascinating evolution of the role of outdoor learning. The pioneers—whose ideas, writings, and practices formed early educational practices—are introduced with an emphasis on their philosophy of outdoor play. Even though much disagreement among these historical figures is apparent in other curricular areas, there is an underlying consensus that outdoor play experiences are essential to children's growth and learning.

Chapters 2 through 4 focus on the developmental nature and appropriate experiences of three different age groups: infants and toddlers, preschool and kindergarten, and primary grade students. Each of these chapters opens with an overview of the cognitive, language (and literacy where appropriate), social-emotional, and physical development of children in the three broad age categories as they pertain to outdoor experiences. (Readers are reminded that the development of children varies widely within these age groups.) The developmental overview is followed by age-specific recommendations and guidelines for providing appropriate outdoor learning experiences. Collectively, these include play zones, music and movement experiences, complexity and variety of play experiences, outdoor learning centers, physical arrangement of play areas, quick ideas for adding interest, integrated learning units, play equipment, games, and field trips. The role of the teacher in outdoor play is explored along with suggestions for dealing with inevitable conflict. Specific suggestions for making provisions for children with special needs during outdoor play and learning periods are discussed in Chapters 2 through 4.

Providing safe outdoor play areas for *all* children, regardless of ability, is the foremost responsibility of adults. Chapter 5 presents a comprehensive overview of safety and accessibility requirements associated with playgrounds. Technical information supplied by playground safety organizations is explained in simple terms using tables and illustrations. Also discussed are current guidelines for designing and refurbishing playgrounds to meet criteria established in accordance with the Americans with Disabilities Act.

Emphasis is placed on the value of outdoor play by devoting all of Chapter 6 to observing and assessing children's outdoor play. An overview of the assessment process is given along with suggestions for designing specific assessment plans. Various methods of recording observations are explained, including anecdotal records, observation guides, checklist/rating scales, and photographs/videotapes. The controversial role of standardized evaluations is also addressed.

Children's outdoor play experiences reach far beyond the school setting; therefore, Chapter 7 examines the role of residential and community play areas. Backyard playgrounds are much safer when guidelines suggested by playground safety experts are followed. Supervision, age-appropriate design, fall surfacing, and equipment are all elements that deserve attention if children are to be kept safe from injury in their own backyard. Many communities are recognizing the value of public play spaces for children. Recommendations for organizing a community-built playground are made along with two successful case studies.

FEATURES

Each chapter contains specific features to help the learner focus on pertinent content. *Guiding Questions* are listed at the beginning of each chapter. Readers can use these as a pretest to determine their current level of knowledge, or the questions may serve as a focal point before reading the chapter.

Chapter-Ending Material   *Key Terms* are listed near the end of each chapter. (They are **boldfaced** in the text and are defined in the *Glossary* at the back of the book.) The *Theory into Practice* section invites readers to apply newly learned information. These activities may be completed in the college classroom, at a field experience site, school, or public setting. *Related Web Sites* and *Related Resources* direct the reader to additional information. These can be used to research in greater detail topics related to each chapter.

Instructor's Manual   An *Instructor's Manual* is available to teachers using this book as a classroom text. Features of the *Instructor's Manual* include chapter overview, student objectives, student activities, and testing suggestions. When used in conjunction with the pedagogical features provided in the text, instructors can plan effective lectures and execute comprehensive lesson plans.

ACKNOWLEDGMENTS

I gratefully acknowledge the many individuals whose time, talents, commitment, and confidence made this project possible. Many thanks to colleagues at Delmar, expressly Erin O'Connor Traylor, Alexis Ferraro, and J.P. Henkel for their insight, dedication, and patience.

I express much gratitude to the following reviewers who went far beyond their role of critic and whose kind words inspired me to be a better author: Linda Aiken, Southwestern Community College; Pamela Davis, Henderson State University; Martha Dever, Utah State University; Meryl Glass, San Francisco State University; and Katherine Wilder, Nash Community College.

A heartfelt thanks to four individuals who made noteworthy contributions to this textbook: Dr. Sue Wortham for providing the Foreword and for continuously setting a higher standard for all writers; Dr. Melinda Sothern for her invited essay in Chapter 4; Dr. Steven Sanders for designing a new checklist (Chapter 5); and Tina Covington for her explanation of the community-built playground (Chapter 7).

Thank you to the individuals who assisted me in obtaining model releases, permissions to reprint, reproducible artwork, and photographs. I express gratitude to the adults who agreed to be photographed as well as the parents who allowed their children's beautiful faces to appear in this book.

I would like also to thank a select group of professors whose encouragement early in my career has been pivotal to my success as an educator and author: Drs. Gerry Brudenell, Robert Doan, Virginia Green, Belin Mills, Janet Taylor, and Charles Wolfgang. Finally, I thank my parents for refraining from placing sensible boundaries on my aspirations.

Learners, instructors, and all readers are encouraged to contact me with questions, suggestions, or comments about *Outdoor Play, Every Day: Innovative Play Concepts for Early Childhood* or its companion text, *A Constructivist Approach to Block Play in Early Childhood*, through Delmar, a division of Thomson Learning, 3 Columbia Circle, Albany, NY 12212-5015 (tel. 800-998-7498, Web site *www.delmar.com*).

Karyn Wellhousen

About the Author

Karyn Wellhousen has over twenty years of experience working with children and teachers. She began her career in Early Childhood Education in child care centers and university lab schools. After receiving her Bachelors and Masters Degrees in Education, she taught kindergarten and first grade in Mobile, Alabama. She completed her Ph.D. in 1988 and has served on the faculties at The University of Texas at Tyler, The University of Texas at San Antonio, and The University of New Orleans.

Currently, she divides her time between her two greatest loves: family and writing. As a teacher and stay-at-home mom, she has spent hundreds of hours observing young children at outdoor play. It is her hope that the teachers, parents, and community leaders who read this book will keep the tradition of outdoor play alive for future generations.

CHAPTER 1

The Evolution of Outdoor Play in Early Childhood Education

Guiding Questions

1. *What are the primary similarities and differences between the Froebelian kindergarten and the progressive kindergarten?*
2. *Is progressivism still evident in the primary grades of today's schools? Explain your position.*
3. *What was the original purpose of the first nursery schools?*

INTRODUCTION

The value of outdoor play has been recognized in some capacity since childhood was first recognized as a separate period of life. Since then, opportunities to play and learn in an outdoor setting have been an integral part of educating young children, although the extent of the perceived worth of outdoor play has fluctuated. At present, outdoor play is not valued as it was during the periods of the Froebel kindergartens, progressivism, and early nursery schools. In fact, today the basic need to play outdoors is largely overlooked and the multitude of opportunities to learn from the outdoors is underestimated in most early childhood programs serving children from infancy through third grade.

EARLY INFLUENCES

The concept of educating young children emerged in the 19th century when childhood was first recognized as a unique period of life. Prior to this time, children were regarded as miniature adults and often endured harsh and cruel treatment (de Mause, 1974; Graves, 1990). Under the best circumstances, they labored alongside parents to help provide food and clothing needed for the family's survival (Wortham, 1998). As conditions in society changed and a greater understanding of children surfaced, more positive attitudes and ideas concerning their care and education became accepted and, at times, popular (Maxim, 1985).

Martin Luther, a religious reformer, and John Comenius, a bishop and educational theorist, were influential in changing ideas toward childhood. However, Rousseau is credited with influencing Pestalozzi and Froebel, the first educators to implement practices designed specifically to suit the nature of young children. According to Graves, Gargiulo, and Sluder (1996), Rousseau's work and influence designates the dividing line between historical and modern periods of education.

Jean Jacques Rousseau

Jean Jacques Rousseau (1712–1778), a philosopher and social theorist, is credited with distinguishing childhood as a separate stage in life. His novel *Emile* (1762/1911) chronicled the life and education of a fictitious young boy who was educated in a rural setting by a tutor. Emile learned from nature and his own exploration rather than from books and formal practices. Rousseau's novel was a vehicle for criticizing the educational practices of his day as well as a way to present his views on the natural development of the child. Rousseau believed sending children (boys) to a remote rural area where they could learn from nature was of greater benefit than formal schooling. He emphasized both the influence of nature on learning and the need to balance intellect with physical well-being (Corbett, 1979).

Rousseau proposed a stage theory of child development, with four stages encompassing growth and changes that occur from birth to twenty years of age (Frost, 1947). The first two, infancy and childhood, dealt specifically with young children. Infancy is the first stage and includes children from birth to five years of age. In this stage, Rousseau advocated that children learn through natural physical activity and their independence be encouraged. Early education for children in this stage begins in the home where mothers allow their children to explore nature and encourage learning through discovery. Children from five to twelve years of age were in the childhood stage. They learn best from direct experience from the environment rather than from books. According to Rousseau, education came from three sources; nature, people, and things (Graves, Gargiulo, & Sluder, 1996).

Rousseau wrote about his educational ideals and prescribed practices, yet never implemented them personally. Perhaps Rousseau's greatest contribution was the powerful influence he had over educators who attempted to translate his ideas into actual educational practices.

Johann Heinrich Pestalozzi

Johann Heinrich Pestalozzi (1746–1827), a Swiss educator, is "credited with establishing early childhood education as a distinct discipline," (Graves, Gargiulo, & Sluder, 1996, p. 85). His first venture as an educator came when he converted *Neuhof* (meaning new house) into an orphanage. This allowed him to explore educational theories emphasizing the importance of learning through nature. After the school closed due to financial failure, Pestalozzi decided to follow Rousseau's vision and became a tutor for two boys whom he took into the country and gave the freedom to learn from nature. He concluded the experience was impractical because the boys did not learn as he thought they would (Corbett, 1979). But this did not deter his belief that nature was vital to learning. Pestalozzi later directed two boarding schools where he refined his educational beliefs and practices. He concluded that learning only through a child's own exploratory behavior is not sufficient. In order to create a balance, he designed the *object lesson* in which a teacher presents an object for study (often from nature) and allows each child to use their senses for exploration (Frost, 1947). This teaching strategy offered a concrete and meaningful way to introduce concepts and information to young children. Pestalozzi also advocated children taking nature walks because they afford an opportunity to observe and appreciate things in a natural setting, assist in learning the names of plants and animals, introduce natural science and geography, and engage children in healthy outdoor exercise (Corbett, 1979).

Friedrich Wilhelm Froebel

Like Pestalozzi, Friedrich Wilhelm Froebel (1782–1852) was also strongly influenced by Rousseau. The emphasis he placed on nature was in keeping with Froebel's own boyhood experiences and training. As a child, Froebel spent hours outdoors exploring plants, flowers, and living creatures. As a young man, he became an apprentice to a forester where he had the opportunity to formally study vegetation and other elements of nature. These experiences left a lasting impression and were a formidable part of the theory used to devise the concept of the kindergarten.

In order to continue his education at a university, Froebel earned money by working as a classroom teacher. He enjoyed teaching and in 1807 took on the responsibility of tutoring three boys. Abiding by Rousseau's philosophy, Froebel took them to the countryside where they could learn from nature while being sheltered from the problems of society. Like Pestalozzi, Froebel abandoned the experiment in favor of a more organized approach to teaching and learning (Corbett, 1979).

In 1808, Froebel and his three students went to visit Pestalozzi's school in Yverdon, Switzerland. The new *object lessons* methodology was innovative and receiving a good deal of attention. Froebel saw he had much to learn from Pestalozzi and his intended two-week visit lasted two years (Corbett, 1979).

Froebel reflected on Pestalozzi's method and examined its strengths and weaknesses. While recognizing the value of Pestalozzi's innovative teaching methods, Froebel thought the overall approach lacked a fundamental philosophy with direction and organization. Froebel took what he learned from Pestalozzi and added a highly symbolic philosophical foundation described as *unity* (or harmony). His philosophy was based on a Christian perspective of God, undoubtedly influenced by Froebel's father, a Lutheran minister. A focal point of this philosophy was the reciprocal relationships between God, humans, and nature.

At age 55, after much thought and deliberation, Froebel created the first kindergarten in Blankenburg, Germany. Two years later, he opened a second kindergarten in Dresden, Germany, and for the next eight years traveled and opened several more kindergartens in Germany. The popularity of this unique idea of educating young children grew gradually and the first English kindergarten opened in 1851 in London. By 1870, private kindergartens had spread rapidly throughout England. Mothers were eager to have their children exposed to an educational setting designed especially for the young, and community-minded women fervently seized the rare opportunity for a career.

The influx of immigrants coming to America from Eastern Europe during the mid-1800's (Maxim, 1993) introduced the kindergarten to the United States. Many of these early immigrants were well-educated and wanted their children to attend kindergartens like those established by Froebel in Germany. However, schools for children under age six were not available. As a result, German women who had trained under Froebel and immigrated to America established private kindergartens in their homes. The concept of this revolutionary idea known as the kindergarten became extremely popular (Maxim, 1993). Margarethe Schurz is credited with opening the first kindergarten in the United States in 1855. It served German-speaking immigrants and was privately operated. The first English-speaking kindergarten was established by Elizabeth Peabody in 1860. The first public school kindergarten in the world was opened in 1873 in St. Louis, Missouri, under the guidance of Susan Blow.

Another wave of immigrants arriving from Europe in the late 1800's and early 1900's continued to influence the establishment of American kindergartens (Freedman, 1995). Unlike those arriving earlier, many of these immigrants were poor and did not assimilate into the perceived typical way of life for Americans. The majority lived in dire poverty where disease, crime, and delinquency escalated and children were neglected and expected to fend for themselves. In an effort to reduce the strain of poverty, young children were targeted as the hope for resolving problems associated with immigration. Religious and philanthropic groups quickly opened scores of kindergartens throughout poor immigrant neighborhoods (Hill, 1941/1999).

One of the most fascinating aspects of these first kindergartens established in Germany, the United States, and other countries is that each and every one followed an identical, prescribed curriculum. Because Froebel's practices were learned first-hand by apprenticing in his kindergartens or through kindergarten training centers, every teacher was taught the same philosophy and methodology. These precise, fixed methods were then relayed to educators in different parts of the world and implemented in newly established kindergartens. Some variation in practices began occurring in the United States at the turn of the 20th century because teachers were unable to directly study Froebelian practices as their predecessors had. It was no longer possible to travel to Germany, observe Froebel at work, and see firsthand how kindergartens were operated because by 1852, German kindergartens were banned for political reasons and Froebel was deceased. But, for six decades there were no competing philosophies on how kindergartens should be operated. The term *kindergarten* brought to mind only one set of practices, those devised by Friedrich Froebel. Compared with today's myriad of philosophies, curricula, and teaching strategies, it is alluring to reminisce about a time when there existed only one, unified, clearly prescribed kindergarten.

Froebel's Kindergarten Curriculum   Froebel's kindergarten was a planned, specified program in which the teacher tenderly nurtured the developing child. His kindergarten was based on the child's inherent need to play, a radical idea for his day (Maxim, 1993). For Froebel, providing opportunities for play in the kindergarten was "the engine that propelled the system" (Brosterman, 1997). The kindergarten activities were designed around the idea that children learn best through playful endeavors. This philosophy applied to both indoor and outdoor activity.

Froebel's early love for and study of nature influenced the foundation of the first kindergarten curriculum. Rather than sitting at desks, enduring rote memorization exercises, children moved with ease as they interacted with specially-designed materials. Outdoor activities were as carefully planned and implemented as those done indoors. Kindergarten children were introduced to nature study, not only to teach about plant life, but also as a way to introduce the sacredness of living things. Each child was given a designated plot to grow a garden. They planted and watered seeds, observed the changes as the seeds sprouted, and cared for the growing seedlings. Froebel intended this activity to teach children scientific principles of nature as well as instill a sense of responsibility toward living things (Brosterman, 1997). Object lessons, a methodology adopted from Pestalozzi, were often centered around articles of nature such as a pinecone, an orange, or flower. Nature walks in which the children and their teacher explored natural surroundings were also routine. Frost (1992) interpreted Froebel's (1887) description of outdoor play in this way:

> Froebel's outdoor playgrounds were nature itself. Children built canals, dams, bridges, and mills in the streams; cultivated gardens and fruit trees; tended plants and flowers; observed beetles,

butterflies, and birds; explored old walls and ru-
ined vaults; and cared for pets. Open areas were
provided for running, wrestling, ball games, and
games of war (p. 115).

Froebel describes the unified spirituality and prac-
ticality of outdoor play as:

Everything must submit to his [kindergarten student's] formative instinct; there is the heap of
earth [from which] he builds a cellar, a cavern,
and on it a garden, a bench. Boards, branches of
trees, laths, and poles are made into a hut, a
house; the deep, fresh snow is fashioned into the
walls and ramparts of a fortress; and the rough
stones on the hill are heaped together to make a
castle: all this is done in the spirit and tendency
of boyhood, in the spirit and tendency of unifica-
tion and assimilation (p. 106).

Froebel's instinctive understanding of the child's
need to freely explore the outdoors is obvious.

The unified acceptance of Froebel's principles
began to dissipate around the turn of the twentieth
century. Misconceptions regarding Froebel's theory resulted in a more rigid use of materials than he originally intended (Maxim, 1993). Because there was no
original source to look to for verification of his ideas
and practices, the Froebel kindergarten became diluted.
During this same period of history, a new wave of
thinking regarding the education of children was
emerging. This new philosophy based on scientific
study left little room for the symbolism of the Froebelian kindergarten.

PROGRESSIVE EDUCATION MOVEMENT

Progressive education or **progressivism** emphasized
the importance of planning curriculum around the interests of children. These ideas were a radical departure
from teacher-directed, memorized, rote learning practices. The **child-centered curriculum,** as a concept
and term, became known during the progressive education movement (Graves, 1990). Several educational
leaders who significantly influenced many contemporary teaching practices emerged during this era.

John Dewey

John Dewey (1859–1952), a philosopher with an intense interest in education, is considered the founder of progressivism. His innovative ideas were based on democratic principles and the scientific method. Teachers of elementary students were encouraged to integrate subjects and design curriculum around meaningful events in the lives of children rather than teach isolated academic disciplines. He believed the purpose of schools was not only to prepare children for the future, but to prepare them for the realities of the present. He stated, "education, therefore, is a process of living and not a preparation for future living" (Morrison, 1998, p. 75).

Dewey established an experimental elementary school at the University of Chicago in 1896. Along with activities such as carpentry, cooking, and sewing, an emphasis was placed on the need for physical exercise during the school day. *Gymnasium work* was considered a means of developing moral and intellectual control. "He [the student] gets healthy exercise; for the child demands a much larger amount of physical activity than the formal program of the ordinary school permits" (Dewey, 1899/1999, p. 162). The need for physical movement was both recognized and validated by Dewey.

Progressive schools following Dewey's philosophy sprang up throughout the country. Educators were excited about a theory that capitalized on the interests and needs of children as opposed to forcing students to learn dictated subject matter that offered no meaning to them. Some of these early progressive schools are still in existence today, determined to continue the practices begun over eighty years ago. The City and Country School founded by Caroline Pratt in 1914 is located in New York City and continues to educate children using principles established by Dewey. The School of Organic Education was established by Marietta Johnson in 1907 in Fairhope, Alabama. Today the school continues to educate children from kindergarten through the twelfth grade by nurturing children's innate interest in learning. (See Figure 1–1.)

Figure 1–1   The statue of Marietta Johnson, founder of the
Organic School, and her students was designed
from a photograph taken by John Dewey in 1919
during his visit. Ms. Johnson is delivering a science
lesson to her students outdoors. The school is still
in existence.

CHILD STUDY MOVEMENT

The child study movement that emerged around 1890
is characterized by a scientific approach to studying
the unique characteristics of young children. Scientific
study included formal observations of children and
data collection. G. Stanley Hall (1844–1924), recognized as the "father of the child study movement,"
and his prominent student Arnold Gesell (1880–1961)
both made significant contributions to understanding
child growth and development. As a result, the two influenced dramatic changes in early childhood education, specifically the kindergarten (Puckett & Diffily,
1999; Graves, Gargiulo & Sluder, 1996). Although the
Froebelian trained kindergarten teachers rejected these
new ideas as irreverent, Patty Smith Hill emerged as a
reformer of the kindergarten.

Patty Smith Hill

Leading the reformation of the kindergarten according
to new scientific findings on children and a progres-

sivism philosophy, was a kindergarten teacher by the name of Patty Smith Hill (1868–1946). Hill was trained under the Froebelian system but recognized that, as practiced, the kindergarten was too rigid. After studying the work of John Dewey and G. Stanley Hall, she became perhaps the best-known leader of the progressive kindergarten movement (Maxim, 1993; Graves, Gargiulo, & Sluder, 1996). Hill used her understanding of progressivism along with the scientific findings on children's development to devise her own kindergarten curriculum. She exchanged the materials created by Froebel for larger construction apparatus and traded the symbolism of the Froebelian kindergarten for scientific knowledge. Children's need to play freely was fundamental to her philosophy for the progressive kindergarten (Graves, Gargiulo, & Sluder, 1996). As a result, outdoor play became increasingly important and greatly valued. Hill (1941/1999) describes the benefits of equipment designed for the progressive kindergarten while criticizing Froebelian practices.

> Manufacturers have responded to the demand for these larger materials, providing slides, *jungle-gyms* for climbing, swings, see-saws, teeter boards, and merry-go-rounds, adapted to the size and maturity of the children. Kindergartners have also introduced many home-made materials of their own invention, such as loaded kegs for rolling, and large, hollow blocks for reaching, stretching, lifting, pulling and pushing. These are all normal modes of exercise essential to growth. Through such innovations as these the sedentary habits developed by chair and table, which the former small materials cultivated, have now been excluded. Large, soft balls stimulating vigorous rolling and tossing on the floor or in the playground are now substituted for the tiny ones formerly used for table play (p. 85).

In 1898 when Patty Smith Hill wrote a program manual for the progressive kindergarten, most early educators still believed fervently in Froebel's principles and methods. The philosophical differences between the Froebelian ideology and the progressive education movement created a great division in the kindergarten community (Paciorek & Munro, 1999). Susan Blow, Hill's greatest adversary, was a staunch Froebelian who directed the first public school kindergarten in 1873.

The two debated their conflicting positions both publicly and privately for decades.

Patty Smith Hill's progressive kindergarten eventually became recognized as a **traditional approach** to teaching young children and was practiced until the 1960's. A 1959 publication verifies that Hill's practices were still in place more than 60 years after she blazed the new trail. In a publication aimed at parents and teachers, Anne Hoppock (1959/1999) explains the importance of each element of the traditional kindergarten. Concerning outdoor play and the study of science and social studies, she writes:

> Dressed for the weather, he spends a generous period of time out of doors. He uses his imagination in the use of such equipment as boxes, hollow blocks, and boards. He gains further bodily strength and skill as he climbs, balances, lifts, pulls, and pushes in the process of his imaginative play. He doesn't have courses in such *subjects* as science and social studies but through field trips, people and things brought into the classroom, stories, pictures, and other active experiences, he gathers and uses a great deal of *subject matter* about the natural, physical, and social world of home, school and neighborhood (p. 95).

Patty Smith Hill and other reformers had a strong understanding of the needs of children and aptly devised a curriculum to suit their unique characteristics. Unfortunately, Hill's philosophy and methodology (once considered progressive and later traditional) did not withstand the forthcoming era of significant economic, political, and social change in America.

CONTEMPORARY KINDERGARTENS

For more than 120 years, kindergarten could be defined according to two specific, distinct philosophies; the Froebelian method or the progressive (eventually referred to as the traditional) kindergarten. During the period of the Froebelian kindergarten, teachers were trained as similarly as possible and children all over the world followed the same schedule and used identical materials as they worked and played. After the debate between the two philosophical camps subsided, all children in progressive kindergartens followed a daily schedule that included story time, music time, outdoor play, work period, circle time, rest time, and snack time (Hoppock, 1959/1999). During the mid to late years of the 1960's however, every facet of society and education became susceptible to upheaval and change. Unfortunately, the kindergarten was not immune to these changes.

Since the 1970's many aspects of the traditional kindergarten have gradually disappeared or become extinct (Golant & Golant, 1997; Wellhousen & Kieff, 2001). Outdoor play ranks high among the vanishing activities. Kindergarten children of the early 1960's regularly enjoyed outdoor playgrounds, organized group games, music and movement experiences, nature hikes, and walking field trips. Children entering school even a few years later, however, were met with a very different experience, including less time devoted to playing and learning in outdoor settings. The reasons for such drastic changes can be explained in terms of political, social, and economic trends that continue to the present day.

A defining moment for kindergartens and primary grade schools occurred when the Russian government preceded the United States in successfully launching a satellite into space. When Sputnik was launched in 1957, education became the target for blame. The response was to provide more federal money to develop new models of early education and a restructuring of math and science curriculums (Henniger, 1999). Regrettably, an overriding emphasis was placed on the intellectual development of young children, while neglecting (for the first time in the history of early education) other, equally crucial areas of growth. This period was a significant turning point in the dissolution of outdoor play in early childhood programs.

The emphasis on intellectual development of young children and math and science teaching for older students led to a new era of accountability. During the 1970's, behavioral objectives and other rigid educational practices were implemented with the idea that all concepts could be dissected, taught, and the degree of understanding measured (Cowles, 1996). Also problematic in this era was the downward push of primary grade curriculum and methodology into the

kindergarten (Spodek, 1982/1999). Standardized testing for children of all ages (as well as beginning teachers) became the fashionable educational trend for the
1980's and has continued to the present, although
with increasing criticism (Elkind, 1982). Testing is
viewed as a remedy to a perceived decline in students'
academic performance. The result of this trend is more
time devoted to teaching content (often focusing only
on subjects to be tested) and less time for outdoor play
and other activities valued in traditional early childhood classrooms. Cowles (1996) summarizes the constant upheaval in educating children in this way:

> Every time that society got in trouble, policy-
> makers thought the school had to be rigid to pre-
> pare children to save the country. Catching
> children in time through those years and, yes,
> even now, meant reverting to mind-dulling me-
> dieval practices, which did not work for all chil-
> dren and a total revocation of the abundant
> knowledge about children that has been gener-
> ated through centuries (p. vii).

In other words, proven educational practices for
young children are consistently dismissed in effort to
find a quick fix to society's latest tribulations. In some
cases, this includes mandating outdated, obsolete
practices.

THE NURSERY SCHOOL MOVEMENT

The nursery school movement cannot be completely
detached from the evolution of the kindergarten; however, the two did develop separately (Frost, 1992). The
most obvious distinction was kindergartens were serving children who were at least five years of age while
nursery schools were intended for children younger
than five years old (Wortham, 1992).

Rachel McMillan (1860–1931) and her sister Margaret established the first nursery school around 1911
in a slum area of London, England. Their objective was
to compensate for the neglect experienced by poor
children living in a highly industrialized area. Their
program was the first to offer more than the custodial
care government-sponsored day nurseries supplied.
The McMillan sisters emphasized self-care responsibili-

ties including cleanliness (small groups of children were bathed at once in waist-high tubs and their clothes were laundered), health (daily inspections by nurses to control the spread of disease), nourishment, fresh air, and outdoor play and exercise (Maxim, 1993; Puckett & Diffily, 1999). The facility was referred to as an *Open Shed* or open-air nursery school because the structure was a shelter completely opened on one side to the outdoors. The McMillans understood that sunshine and fresh air were essential for children's health and well-being. Maxim (1993) describes the nursery school as follows.

> The building had one side that opened into a garden or play area; children were encouraged to play in that outdoor area for most of the day. They romped in herb, vegetable, or flower gardens as well as in nontraditional play areas, such as *junk piles* containing mounds of ashes or nuts and bolts. McMillan valued these play activities not only for their physical benefits but also because she saw them helping children to control their muscles and develop sensory images (taste, touch, smell, hearing, and sight), as well as to acquire basic intellectual skills (pp. 38–39).

Abigail Eliot, an American social worker, trained for six months in the McMillans' open-air nursery school. In 1922, Adams became director of the Ruggles Street Nursery School in Boston, making it one of the first nursery schools in the United States. The nursery school concept quickly gained popularity, and many nursery schools were opened as private schools or with funds from colleges and universities. Regardless of the funding source, the McMillans' open-air nursery and subsequently the Ruggles Street school served as models (Graves, Garguilos, & Sluder, 1996; Maxim, 1993).

Bank Street School in New York City is among the early nursery schools still in existence today. The school, originally named the Bureau of Educational Experiments, was established by Harriet Johnson and Lucy Sprague Mitchell in 1916. Because the school was located in a heavily populated, crowded area, the children's playground was established on the roof of the school. Although this idea sounds startling by today's licensing standards, the roof often served as the primary play area for children living in New York City in the 1920s (Paciorek & Munro, 1999). Today the school retains its original philosophy, "to understand through study, experimentation, and research the complex development of children, and to create environments that support and promote their development" (Mitchell & David, 1992, p. 5).

As the federal government became involved in providing funding for nursery schools, the number of schools established for children under the age of five increased significantly. These programs include the Works Progress Administration in 1933, the Community Facilities Act (also known as the Lanham Act) in 1942, and Head Start in 1964.

The McMillans' open-air school remained the primary model for nursery school education until the 1960's. Government involvement, along with other factors, contributed to the development of a variety of different *models* of contemporary early childhood programs (Graves, Gargiulo, & Sluder, 1996). The value placed on outdoor play experiences varies according to the theoretical perspective and developmental appropriateness of each model (Epstein, Schweinhart, & McAdoo, 1996). However, none of these contemporary models assign outdoor play the same degree of importance as did the original nursery schools.

AN OVERVIEW OF TRENDS

Reference has been made to the social, political, and economic trends of the last forty years that have influenced early childhood education. Wortham (1992) addresses the following examples in context of the time period in which they occurred: increase in divorce rate, technological advances, medical advances, environmental protection, declining birth rate, increase in women entering the workforce, fast food, television, disease, greater need for child care, homelessness, exposure to drugs and violence, compensatory education, special education, war, fluctuating federal funding for social services and education, inflation, and poverty. As new trends inevitably occur, efforts are made to address society's needs through early childhood education. Sometimes the results are positive and successful, such as changes that have been made to address children with special needs. Too often, however, quick fixes are implemented as solutions to long-term problems. Young children benefit most when sound research is integrated with tested practices consistent with child growth and development.

CONCLUSION

The outdoors has been incorporated into early childhood education since its beginning. Even though Rousseau never implemented his philosophy, he inspired others such as Pestalozzi and Froebel who respected the benefits the outdoors has to offer young children. Froebel designated outdoor learning and play as a central theme of his theory and it survived as an important element even throughout the reformation of the kindergarten. Patty Smith Hill and other kindergarten reformers used scientific findings to give credibility to the value of outdoor play. Dewey's progressivism offered support for outdoor experiences in the elementary school as well. Finally, outdoor play was the nucleus of the early nursery schools. Social, political, and economic influences over the last forty years provided motives and funding for exploring new models of teaching young children. While progress is to be embraced, the cost should never be the dissolution of a tried and true element of education. Sadly, this is the case with outdoor play.

KEY TERMS

progressivism
child-centered curriculum
traditional approach

THEORY INTO PRACTICE

1. Develop a timeline including the following events:
   a. first kindergarten
   b. first U.S. kindergarten
   c. first public school kindergarten
   d. progressivism
   e. child study movement

    f. kindergarten reform
    g. first nursery school
    h. early U.S. nursery school
    i. launching of Sputnik
    j. standardized testing movement
    k. early education programs receiving government funding
2. Select one of the people discussed in this chapter who influenced early education and either:
    a. read and summarize a selection of their original published work, or
    b. research and report biographical information.
3. Interview an adult who attended kindergarten prior to 1960. Observe a kindergarten and compare the two experiences.

RELATED WEB SITES

www.froebelgifts.com
Web site for a nonprofit foundation disseminates information on the life and work of Froebel. Includes a bibliography of books related to Froebel's work.
www.hum.ou.dk/center/kultur/exhibitE/index.html
Odense University's Department of Cultural Studies Web site includes five articles about the historical origin of objects designed for children including the sandbox, tricyle, and pram (stroller).

RELATED RESOURCES

Elkind, D. (1988). *The hurried child: Growing up too fast too soon* (Rev. ed.). Reading, MA: Addison-Wesley.
Kindergarten messenger: The official newsletter of the Froebel Foundation. Available through: Kindergarten Messenger, 407 Richmond St. NW, Grand Rapids, MI 49504-2061. 888-774-2046.
Weston, P. (1998). *Friedrich Froebel: His life and times.* Grand Rapids, MI: Uncle Goose Toys.

REFERENCES

Brosterman, N. (1997). *Inventing kindergarten.* New York: Harry N. Abrams.
Corbett, B. (1979). *A garden of children.* Mississauga, Ontario: The Froebel Foundation.
Cowles, M. (1996). Introduction. In M. Johnson, *Organic education: Teaching without failure.* Fairhope, AL: Marietta Johnson Museum of Organic Education.

de Mause, L. (Ed.) (1974). *The history of childhood.* New York: Psychohistory Press.

Dewey, J. (1899/1999). Three years of the university elementary school. In K.M. Paciorek & J.H. Munroe (Eds.), *Sources: Notable selections in early childhood education* (2d ed., pp. 159–163). Guilford, CT: Dushkin/ McGraw-Hill.

Elkind, D. (1982). The hurried child: Is our impatient society depriving kids of their right to be children? *Instructor, 91*(5), pp. 40–43.

Epstein, A.S., Schweinhart, L.F., & McAdoo, L. (1996). *Models of early childhood education.* Ypsilanti, MI: High/Scope.

Freedman, R. (1995). *Immigrant kids.* New York: Puffin Books.

Froebel, F. (1887). *The education of man.* New York: D. Appleton & Company.

Frost, J.L. (1992). *Play and playscapes.* Albany, NY: Delmar.

Frost, S.E. (1947). *History of education.* Woodbury, NY: Barron's Educational Series.

Golant, S.K. & Golant, M. (1997). *Kindergarten—It isn't what it used to be: Getting your child ready for the positive experience of education.* Los Angeles: Lowell House.

Graves, S. (1990). Early childhood education. In T.E.C. Smith, *Introduction to education* (2d ed., pp. 182–219). St. Paul, MN: West.

Graves, S.B., Gargiulo, R.M., & Sluder, L.C. (1996). *Young children: An introduction to early childhood education.* Minneapolis, MN: West Publishing Company.

Henniger, M.L. (1999). *Teaching young children: An introduction.* Upper Saddle River, NJ: Merrill.

Hill, P.S. (1941/1999). Kindergarten. In K.M. Paciorek & J.H. Munroe (Eds.), *Sources: Notable selections in early childhood education* (2d ed., pp. 81–90). Guilford, CT: Dushkin/McGraw-Hill.

Hoppock, A. (1959). What are kindergartens for? In K.M. Paciorek & J.H. Munroe (Eds.), *Sources: Notable selections in early childhood education* (2d ed., pp. 91–100). Guilford, CT: Dushkin/McGraw-Hill.

Maxim, G. (1985). *The very young* (2d ed.). Belmont, CA: Wadworth.

Maxim, G. (1993). *The very young: Guiding children from infancy through the early years.* New York: Merrill.

Mitchell, A. & David, J. (Eds.). (1992). *Explorations with young children.* Mt. Rainier, MD: Gryphon House.

Morrison, G.S. (1998). *Early childhood education today* (7th ed.). Upper Saddle River, NJ: Merrill.

Paciorek, K.M., & Munro, J.H. (Eds.). (1999). *Sources: Notable selections in early childhood education* (2d ed.). Guilford, CT: Dushkin/McGraw-Hill.

Puckett, M.B., & Diffily, D. (1999). *Teaching young children: An introduction to the early childhood profession.* New York: Harcourt Brace.

Seefeldt, C., & Barbour, N. (1998). *Early childhood education: An introduction.* Upper Saddle River, NJ: Merrill.

Spodek, B. (1982/1999). The kindergarten: A retrospective and contemporary view. In K.M. Paciorek & J.H. Munroe (Eds.), *Sources: Notable selections in early childhood education* (2d ed., pp. 101–111). Guilford, CT: Dushkin/McGraw-Hill.

Wellhousen, K., & Kieff, J. (2001). *A constructivist approach to block play in early childhood.* Albany, NY: Delmar.

Wortham, S. (1998). *Early childhood curriculum: Developmental bases for learning and teaching* (2d ed.). Upper Saddle River, NJ: Merrill.

Wortham, S. (1992). *Childhood: 1892–1992.* Wheaton, MD: Association for Childhood Education International.

CHAPTER 2

Outdoor Play for Infants and Toddlers

Guiding Questions

1. *In what ways do infants and toddlers differ from preschoolers?*
2. *How should the outdoor physical environment for infants and toddlers be different from that of preschoolers?*
3. *How will the outdoor play area reflect the differences between children who can be described as "no mobility, low mobility, and high mobility"?*
4. *What are the four zones appropriate for high mobility children?*
5. *How can teachers appropriately respond to the challenging disposition of toddlers during outdoor play?*

INTRODUCTION

Infants and toddlers are unique in many ways. They have a great capacity to learn but are in constant need of supervision and attention. Their extremely affectionate yet sometimes difficult temperament makes caring for and teaching very young children both a demanding and rewarding job. Thoroughly understanding infant and toddler development can alleviate anxiety about their somewhat unpredictable nature and provide motivation to create an enriching outdoor play environment.

Brain Development

Since the 1980's, scientists have made great progress in their study of the human brain (Shore, 1997). This is due primarily to new technological advances that allow for noninvasive methods of collecting information about the brain. Prior to these new technologies, brain research was limited to animal studies and human autopsies. Scientists now know the brain is a complex network based on neurons (brain cells) and synapses (connections between brain cells) (Shore, 1997). Signals are rapidly fired between neurons that create vital connections (called *synapses*) between brain cells. The number of synapses created multiplies most rapidly during the first three years of life. In fact, a toddler's brain possesses about twice as many synapses as needed for cognitive functioning throughout an entire lifetime. Brain development is so rapid during the first three years; this time span is considered the *critical period* for learning, perhaps because brain development is more productive from birth to age three than it will ever be again. After age three, synapses, which have not been stimulated through environmental experiences, begin to deteriorate and brain development slows. The greatest threat to brain development during this critical period is cortisol, a hormone that reduces the number of synapses made between neurons. Cortisol is released when babies are in stressful situations such as feeling fear, pain, discomfort, or neglect. Therefore, the quality of care and the types of experiences children receive during the first three years of life impact brain growth and development. Emotional security and stimulating experiences ensure that brain cell connections are developed, protected, and preserved.

During this critical period of brain growth, attention should be directed toward making infants and toddlers feel safe and successful. The physical environment where children spend their time must contribute to feelings of security. However, Lowman and Ruhmann (1998) have found that this is not always the case. In fact, many young children do not receive these types of experiences. Even though the National Association for the Education of Young Children (Bredekamp & Copple, 1997) recommends that programs for infants and toddlers be distinctly different and *not* a *scaled down version* of a preschool classroom, there is an alarming trend to treat toddlers like smaller preschoolers. This pushdown phenomenon is obvious in the equipment and activities (Lowman and Ruhmann, 1998), as well as the physical environments, for this age group (Dodge, Dombro, & Koralik, 1991). Attention to physical environments and planned experiences helps teachers meet the unique developmental needs of infants and toddlers.

COGNITIVE DEVELOPMENT

Infants naturally engage in different forms of play activities that evolve as they become older and have more experiences interacting with adults and older children. It is their play with objects and people that stimulate brain development and subsequently cognitive growth (Piaget, 1962). One of the earliest forms of infant play is repetitive motor activity such as bouncing one foot on the crib mattress while lying on his back, banging a rattle, or batting at an object within reach. Infants may also play by making sounds, either because they find them pleasurable or to draw attention and provoke a playful response from caregivers. These sounds are typically in the form of cooing or babbling repeatedly. Piaget (1962) and others (Johnson, Christie, & Yawkey, 1999) referred to these types of activities as **functional play,** suggesting infants are actually practicing for some meaningful function they will need later in life. He argued the reason infants are so fascinated with repetitive actions such as opening and closing the playhouse door, crawling up and down a set of three steps, banging and throwing toys, and repeating the same nonsense sounds over and over is because they will use these skills in some manner as they grow older.

Infant play is very different from the play of older children and adults who use play as a recreational activity. For infants, functional play is the means to learning important concepts and skills. Therefore, playing with a caring adult is essential to their intellectual development. Parents are the ideal first playmates because their response to playful infant behavior involves warm contact. This combination of responding to an infant's need for playful activity and providing physical contact promotes healthy attachments and growth. As adults engage in games such as "Peek-a-boo" and "Patty Cake," babies' brains are stimulated. Caregivers can take clues from parents' natural willingness to play with babies by offering activities that stimulate intellectual development. These activities include rhyming games, singing, offering toys that respond to manipulation, and other experiences that stimulate the senses.

A significant milestone in intellectual development is a fascination with **pretend play** or transforming objects and one's self into make-believe roles. Vygotsky (1976) believed that pretend play is a toddler's way of practicing how he will use symbols in later childhood. This is important because understanding symbols is necessary for learning to read, write, and solve mathematical equations. Signs of pretend play with objects may emerge as early as twelve months of age and become more elaborate as infants make the gradual shift into toddlerhood (Trawick-Smith, 2000). Younger toddlers typically pretend to be animals, objects, or people. Later, they use available objects to act out a familiar action (Watson & Jakowitz, 1984), such as pretending to eat with a spoon even when there is no food nearby. Next, toddlers begin using two or more different objects or props to play out a scene (McCune, 1995). This demonstrates growing intellect because it requires the toddler to think of a familiar scenario, then choose, locate, and use the appropriate objects. For example, a toddler, age twenty-four months, was observed wearing a bicycle helmet and swim goggles as she peddled a small tricycle across the playground making racecar noises. With more experience at pretend play, toddlers will reenact a sequence of familiar behaviors or routines. A thirty-month-old toddler was also observed as she sat on a wheeled toy. She pretended to secure a seatbelt, carefully studied and selected a plastic key from a toy key ring, acted out inserting the key into the *ignition,* and then made the sounds of an engine starting. Using her feet to push the toy along she *drove* down the trike path.

As toddlers mature and draw on previous pretend play experiences, they begin substituting realistic objects with more abstract ones. An example is the child galloping around the play yard on a *stick* horse and corralling it under a slide. A stick doesn't resemble a horse and a slide does not look like a barn, but the toddler's developing imagination is capable of turning these abstract objects into something meaningful. Using abstract, substitute objects in place of the real thing is considered an important step intellectually because toddlers are using available objects to symbolize something completely different.

It is important to toddlers' growing imaginations to provide materials that can be used outdoors for dramatization. An observant teacher quickly realizes that pretend play experiences occur spontaneously outdoors and are unpredictable and limitless. Toddlers digging in the sandbox are preparing lunch, while another uses the mounted steering wheel to navigate a boat. Children on swings pretend to fly like superheroes while others *repair* a wagon with toy hammers and screwdrivers. The outdoor play yard is the ideal setting for stimulating cognitive and social development through pretend play.

COMMUNICATION DEVELOPMENT

Pediatricians recommend new parents begin talking to their babies at birth while some obstetricians support the practice of expectant parents talking and singing to their unborn babies still in the womb (Brazelton, 1981). Communicating to babies early in life is supported by brain and linguistic research. Infants' brains are *wired* for learning language for a specific, critical period of time (Reich, 1986; Lenneberg, 1967). Infants need daily, one-on-one verbal interaction with a significant adult for language skills to flourish. It may feel strange to talk to a baby who is incapable of responding, but babies understand the language they hear long before they can speak it. This is called **receptive language** and is evident when a one-year-old is asked, "Where's Mommy?" and he reacts with a smile, by pointing, or running to her. Their repertoire of receptive language gradually increases as infants begin to recognize verbal labels for many familiar objects and actions.

Productive language becomes apparent when babies use some means of vocalization or communication. Some psychologists even consider crying a type of productive language. Infants have different types of cries for different needs. Recognizing differences in their cries and responding accordingly by feeding, changing, burping, singing, holding, playing, or comforting, enhances infants' communication competence.

In 1972, psychologists Bell and Ainsworth made a significant discovery. They learned that when parents respond quickly to the cries of their infants in the *first* year of life, the babies cried significantly less during their *second* year. As they grew, these children were more advanced in their ability to communicate than children whose cries were ignored or parental attention was delayed. A possible explanation for this is parents who respond quickly to their infant's cries are teaching them the power of vocalization and communication which in turn accelerates the beginning of oral language.

Before their first birthday, **babbling** occurs resembling adultlike speech of an unknown language. When babbling occurs in a long string of complex sounds complete with intonation, it is called **expressive jargon** (Mitchell & Kent, 1990). The purpose of expressive jargon is not fully understood, but it is a useful way for babies to make verbal contact with others before they master language. When caregivers hear infant's expressive jargon, they almost instinctively react by carrying on a conversation using elements of real language such as turn-taking and voice inflection.

Babies' first words are generally spoken between eight and eighteen months of age. While there is variation as to which words are spoken first, most infants name significant adults, or refer to animals, games, food, and drink in their first fifty words (Tomasello & Mervis, 1994). Parents and caregivers can reinforce these early attempts to talk by their enthusiastic reactions to first words.

Between eighteen and twenty-four months, toddlers begin putting words together in a unique way. These speech patterns are called **telegraphic speech** because words that are not crucial to the message are omitted, just as they were sending a telegram. Although his vocabulary is limited, it does not prevent the toddler from getting his message across as can be seen by the following examples: "go poo-poo," "clock broke," "uh-oh juice," "bad cat," "me eat," and "go birthday party." A great deal of meaning can accurately be drawn from each of these telegraphic messages. As their vocabulary expands, so does the use of speech patterns. Speaking directly to toddlers and engaging them in conversation is the best way to encourage language learning. Outdoor play experiences are valuable to language development and production during these early years. Children have more freedom to experiment with volume and pitch when not confined indoors. Outdoor activities that coordinate large motor skills and language can be planned, such as games involving music, rhythm, and movement.

SOCIAL-EMOTIONAL DEVELOPMENT

According to Erikson (1963), infants from birth until around eighteen months experience the dichotomy of "Trust vs. Mistrust." When their needs are met within a reasonable period of time, they develop a trust in parents, caregivers, and their world. Requiring infants to wait to be held, changed, fed, or comforted leaves them with a feeling of mistrust that effects future relationships after infancy and into adulthood. It is vital, therefore, that centers caring for young children abide by low adult-child ratios as suggested by professional organizations such as the National Association for the

Education of Young Children (Bredekamp & Copple, 1997). Having an adequate number of adults to care for the endless needs of infants is crucial to promoting a sense of trust.

Within the first six months, infants are capable of recognizing familiar caregivers and of expressing their desire to be with them. **Separation anxiety** (or the fear of being separated from a familiar caregiver) emerges during this period. An infant may, for the first time, become quite upset when important people, such as his mother or father, are not around, especially when he is in need of some type of attention. Infants also develop **stranger anxiety,** a fear of unknown people, around this time. This combination of anxieties makes it difficult to leave infants with substitute caregivers because they will use cries and screams to express their fears.

Infants begin expressing their emotions through facial expressions within a few days of their birth (Izard & Harris, 1995), a testament to how quickly they learn because they could not have observed adult facial expressions in the womb. Parents play a crucial role in teaching emotions as they intuitively use exaggerated expressions such as opening eyes and mouth wide to show surprise and excitement and closing eyes and holding baby close to show contentment. It is important that infants be exposed to happy, calm, positive emotions from adults so they too will learn how to express such feelings.

As infants make the transition to toddlerhood they exhibit a unique cognitive limitation, their inability to understand the perspective of other people. This trait has been labeled **egocentrism** (Piaget, 1952) and means young children are centered on their own needs and feelings and are severely limited in their ability to understand the thoughts and feelings of others. Egocentrism is the primary explanation for why toddlers are so demanding. Two- and three-year-old children are not able to understand why they can't have everything their way.

Egocentrism becomes obvious on the playground. It is extremely difficult to convince a toddler to take turns on the spring riding toy or share a shovel in the sandbox. However, adults will, at times, observe toddlers voluntarily behaving in very social ways such as offering assistance to a child who is hurt. This may be because the toddler is emulating the actions of other adults. The following vignette illustrates this contradiction:

A group of three-year-olds are outdoors enjoying a cool fall day. Barina approaches Sydney who is playing quietly in the sand. She grabs the purple shovel out of Sydney's hand and begins to dig. Sydney spots another shovel and continues scooping sand into a large mound. A few minutes later, Arie runs through the sand box destroying Sydney's sand mountain. She begins to cry and kick her feet. Barina immediately moves next to her, places her arm around Sydney's shoulders, and tries to console her.

When kind, compassionate behavior such as that shown by Barina, is reinforced by adults through praise, the toddler will most likely repeat it again. This discrepancy between egocentrism and occasionally showing empathy and generosity is also explained by the toddler's struggle between wanting their own needs met and their gradually increasing desire to be with peers (Trawick-Smith, 2000).

Another social characteristic of the toddler is her gradual attempt to gain independence from parents and caregivers. This is evident in demands to do many self-help tasks for herself. Even though it is unlikely that a two- or three-year-old will be able to tie her own shoe, she should be given the time and opportunity to try. When her attempts finally leave her with untied shoes, the patient caregiver needs to be available to tie them upon her request. Obviously, some requests to be independent will not be allowed if the child's health or safety is at stake, such as climbing playground equipment designed for older children or walking through a busy parking lot without holding an adult's hand. Toddlers will quickly learn which attempts at independence are acceptable, but at times will still test these limits. When they fail to get beyond set limits, they may become verbally or physically aggressive, expressing their frustration at being told, no! Adults must put in perspective children's need to be assertive, independent, and at times, their need to exhibit negative behaviors.

Learning social behaviors requires a calm and patient adult who understands this difficult age and who has time to give toddlers the support they need. It is important to remember that egocentrism is a cognitive trait and is typical in young children until about age seven. Their limited ability to fully understand the needs of others does not represent a flaw in their character, only a limitation in their intellectual ability (Piaget, 1962). Playing outside boosts toddlers' self-esteem as they sense their growing competency (Dombro, 1995). They are free to move and make noise in ways that are typically not permitted indoors. New opportunities for interacting with peers exist, contributing to toddlers' emerging social skills that are so important now and in later childhood.

PHYSICAL PROGRESSION

The rates at which infants typically learn new motor skills has been thoroughly researched and documented. In 1933, Arnold Gesell, a pioneering researcher who studied child growth and development, published normative charts showing the average ages at which infants exhibit different physical milestones, such as rolling over, crawling, and walking. Today, the Bayley Scales of Infant Development (1969) are used to assess motor development, as well as other areas of growth. These charts are accepted as accurate for assessing physical development. However, when evaluating children's development, adults should keep in mind the wide variation among the physical progression of individual children, even within the range of what is considered typical development. Therefore, the best use of normative charts is to inform parents, caregivers, and medical personnel of the sequence in which infants learn motor skills, and to determine if a child's development is within the norm. See Figure 2–1 for a portion of the Bayley Scales.

Babies continue to develop rapidly in terms of physical growth and development throughout the second year of life. Brown (1998) summarizes milestones in gross motor skills over the first two years as follows:

- By 5 months, infants can roll over, lift their head and chest, and sit with adult support.

Figure 2–1   Milestones of infant motor development.

Motor skill	Average age achieved	Age range in which skill is achieved by most infants
Holds head erect and steady when held upright	7 weeks	3 weeks–4 months
When prone, elevates self by arms	2 months	3 weeks–5 months
Rolls from side to back	2 months	3 weeks–5 months
Rolls from back to side	4.5 months	2–7 months
Grasps cube	3 months 3 weeks	2–7 months
Sits alone, good coordination	7 months	5–9 months
Pulls to stand	8 months	5–12 months
Uses neat pincer grasp	9 months	7–10 months
Plays pat-a-cake	9 months 3 weeks	7–15 months
Stands alone	11 months	9–16 months
Walks alone	11 months 3 weeks	9–17 months

- At about 8 months, they're crawling and walking while holding on to something; between 10 and 16 months, they can walk on their own.
- Between 7 and 12 months, babies can grasp and hold objects.
- By 20 months, toddlers are walking up and down steps, throwing objects, and standing on one foot.
- By the age of 2, they can kick and catch large balls, climb steps, go down low slides, and run without falling.
- Twos are able to jump, climb, roll, and even do somersaults! (p. 34)

Toddlers who have turned two will develop additional gross motor skills over the next twelve months, including kicking a large ball, jumping in place, walking up and down stairs alone, and marching to music (Herr & Libby, 2000). This is quite an impressive list of physical accomplishments for such a short period of time. Never again in a child's lifetime will his growth and development be so rapid.

During their second and third years, toddlers learn many ways to propel themselves from one place to another including running, hopping, jumping, galloping, climbing, and twisting. The combination of having the ability to move quickly from one place to another and feelings of strong independence can be exciting but dangerous for toddlers. The following story illustrates this danger.

A mother and her 30-month-old daughter were playing at a playground adjacent to a lake. When the mother announced it was time to leave, the little girl darted away and began running in the direction of the water. The mother first called out in a strong voice for her to stop, but the girl behaved as if it were a fun and familiar game of chase. The mother took off running and her daughter squealed in delight as she headed toward the water. A few moments later, the mother returned to the playground carrying a kicking, screaming toddler who did not fully understand why the game had ended so badly.

Two other significant motor skill milestones emerge during the toddler years. First, they have mastered the ability to climb and unfortunately, exhibit little fear of reaching new heights to explore. Objects on storage shelves or in cabinets, which were safely out of reach during infancy, are now easily accessible. Toddlers may also attempt climbing up slides and equipment designed for older children. Second, their fine motor abilities are more fully developed. Toddlers have mastered the use of the **pincer grip** (the ability to pick up small objects using the thumb and forefinger) (Trawick-Smith, 2000). With the pincer grip, toddlers practice and learn many important self-help skills such as zipping, buttoning, and securing shoes with Velcro. They also enjoy new types of materials including puzzles, modeling dough, stringing beads, and painting. Outdoors they use small muscles to grip the rails or rungs of a ladder, hold on to a swing in motion, grasp a steering wheel, and release a ball. With each new skill, however, comes additional opportunities for injury. The pincer grip enables toddlers to remove *child-proof* caps from medications and household cleaners and to pick up small objects, such as pebbles and coins, which they often put in their mouths. Injuries from falls, poisoning, and choking are rampant during toddlerhood. Additional childproofing and constant vigilance and supervision are needed to ensure toddlers stay safe indoors and out.

AGE-APPROPRIATE OUTDOOR PLAY EXPERIENCES

Young children from birth through thirty-six months demonstrate a surprising range of abilities, and the experiences provided by caregivers, indoors and out, must reflect the ever-present changes in cognitive, language, social-emotional, and physical skills. Frost (1992) recommends four principles for designing outdoor spaces for infants and toddlers that will allow for such changes.

First, allow a wide range of movement. Infants need a relatively confined space which is "gentle for crawling, kind for falling, and cool for sitting" (p. 260). The play yard supports emerging abilities to sit, crawl, pull-up, stand, walk, and balance. Attaching bars horizontally to fences and buildings at the height of a seated infant encourages them to pull-up and cruise while holding on for balance. Hard surfaces can be covered with outdoor carpeting for added protection and comfort.

Next, stimulate the senses. Look first to nature to provide a variety of experiences to stimulate the senses such as wind blowing music chimes, light filtering through trees, and surfaces of different textures: grass, sand, water, leaves, bark, and rocks. When these elements are not accessible, supplement by playing soft music, erecting an overhead cover from lattice, and creating or purchasing texture panels. These panels consist of objects with various textures and appearance, secured to a smooth backboard made of plastic or wood protected with a weather resistant coating such as lacquer or varnish.

Also, offer novelty, variety, and challenge. Infants and toddlers need to be gradually exposed to novel objects, sights, and sounds, as they become comfortable with old ones. They also need to be introduced to new challenges as old ones are successfully mastered. Keep in mind, novelty experiences introduced too quickly or profusely can overstimulate and have a negative effect. The same is true for promoting challenges that are too difficult. Adapting the play yard to provide novelty, variety, and challenge requires an observant, sensitive, and skillful caregiver.

Finally, address safety and comfort. Safety is the number one concern of adults who have been entrusted with the care of infants and toddlers. (An extensive discussion of playground safety can be found in Chapter 6.) Of particular importance is separating play areas for infants and younger toddlers from older toddlers and preschoolers who have more developed gross motor skills. Infants ranging in ability from lying on their back or tummy to those who are walking and just beginning to climb must have a play area separate from toddlers and older children who have mastered running, jumping, and kicking. A chain-link fence or other see-through barrier is ideal so the two groups can still observe and interact verbally with one another.

Children acquire new skills at different rates and ages depending on a number of factors including genetics, environment, prior experiences, health, and nutrition. Wortham and Wortham (1992) divide the youngest age group into two categories—nonmobile infants and very mobile toddlers. Miller (1989) classifies infants as tummy babies, crawling babies, cruising babies, or climbing babies. The guidelines provided here for infant and toddler outdoor play have been divided to reflect three stages of ability: no mobility, low mobility, and high mobility. No mobility is the designation given young infants who still lack the ability to move from one place to the next unless carried by an adult. Low mobility describes children whose motor skills include rolling, crawling, cruising, walking, and

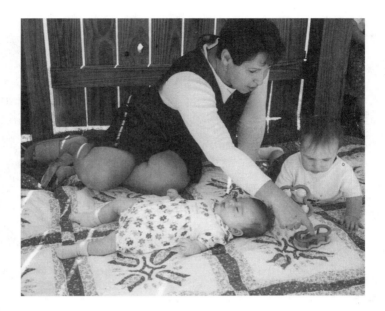

climbing. High mobility toddlers are those who can run, dart, jump, hop, leap, and kick. Because of differences in physical abilities, there will be variations in the outdoor play environment and experiences for no mobility, low mobility, and high mobility children.

No Mobility Children

No mobility describes infants who are not yet capable of propelling or moving themselves from one place to the other. Special preparations must be made for taking no mobility children outdoors. Caregivers must choose an appropriate area to lay or sit infants and identify equipment or materials needed to make them comfortable. Attention must be given to placing children out of direct sunlight, ensuring they will not be bitten by insects, avoiding choking hazards, and steering clear of poisonous materials such as insecticides which have been spread or sprayed, and poisonous plants. Since these children are in the sensorimotor stage of development (Piaget, 1952), they need opportunities to learn about their world by through their senses, primarily, by exploring sounds, sights, and textures.

Listening   Infants are highly sensitive to sound so allow them to enjoy the natural and human-made sounds of an outdoor environment. Outdoor sounds may include birds singing, dogs barking, insects buzzing, and trees rustling, as well as cars, airplanes, and children at play. Hanging wind chimes from a low tree branch introduces another pleasurable sound to infants' ears. Talk to infants about the sounds they hear. Infants in group care are often restricted from making loud, joyful noises indoors so encourage them to make sounds outdoors, as loud as they please. Offer toys and devise other ways to introduce sounds. Rattles, aluminum pie pans, and empty two-liter plastic bottles with bells inside are good noisemakers. Ensure play items are safe before making them available to infants to hit, bat, roll, or mouth.

Looking   Simply moving an infant outdoors gives him a whole new world to explore visually. As his position is alternated between lying on a blanket and sitting upright in a baby seat, his visual perspective of the outdoors changes. There is much for the nonmobile child to see outdoors, including trees blowing, older children running and climbing in an adjacent yard, and his caregiver's face in a natural light. Visually stimulating objects can be introduced as well, such as pinwheels placed firmly in the ground a safe distance away, crepe paper streamers tied to a fence, and brightly colored helium-filled balloons, which have been securely anchored.

Feeling   The sense of touch is strongly stimulated outdoors. Placing infants on a sheet as opposed to a thick blanket allows them contact with the course texture of grass underneath without it directly touching their skin. Infants will experience a number of natural physical sensations outdoors such as gentle or brisk breezes, warmth of the sun, and cool shade. A new dimension is added when typical caregiver behaviors such as stroking, patting, holding, and rocking occur outdoors. Moving infant swings onto a level surface outdoors offers new physical and visual sensations.

Low Mobility Children

Low mobility children include older infants and young toddlers who are gradually gaining balance, strength, and agility. Their play yard should offer experiences relevant to their level of development. Low mobility children are capable of moving their bodies from one place to another by rolling, crawling, or scooting. A clean, empty, plastic swimming pool lined with a quilt or blanket offers a safe area for children to play outdoors because it provides both a physical and visual boundary that makes them feel safe (Wittmer, 1996). Place toys such as small rubber balls, board books, and soft objects in the pool. Two to three small children can comfortably share a large pool. Blankets, sheets, fabric shower curtains, and tablecloths can be used to cover a grassy area where infants can lie, or they may be placed in playpens, strollers, or infant swings that have been brought outdoors.

As they begin climbing out of the pool or crawling off blankets, provide equipment that satisfies their next physical milestones, which include pulling up, creeping (holding onto an object while walking), climbing, and eventually taking those first awkward steps. Frost (1992) recommends installing *cruising bars* to sides of equipment or buildings. These offer low mobility children the challenge of pulling themselves up and holding on as they take steps. Appropriate equipment for low mobility children can be purchased from playground manufacturers, school supply catalogs, and retail businesses. It can also be designed and built to suit a particular play yard. (See Appendix C for a list of manufacturers of playground equipment.)

High Mobility Children

High mobility children are confident in walking and are learning to climb steps, jump from low surfaces, hop, and run. Therefore, they need environments that provide appropriate experiences and accommodate their developing gross motor abilities. Lowman and Ruhmann (1998) make recommendations for arranging indoor environments that are equally suitable when planning outdoor play spaces. Four basic activity areas or zones can accommodate the developmental needs of most toddlers: (1) large motor zone, (2) dramatic play zone, (3) messy zone, and (4) quiet zone.

Large Motor Zone The main focus of the large motor zone is permanent modular structures designed

Figure 2–2 Example of permanent playground equipment for toddlers.

specifically for toddlers. The toddler structure pictured in Figure 2–2 offers challenging steps leading to a small deck and partially covered slide. Also on this playground is a tire climbing unit with a moderate incline. Equipment for toddlers often includes features such as bubble panels, activity panels, and steering wheels. Permanent structures such as these can be utilized by high mobility toddlers as well as risk-taking low mobility toddlers with close adult supervision.

Moveable equipment designed for large motor play should also be available such as Little Tykes® slides, playhouses, and basketball goals. Permanent and moveable equipment is supplemented with toys that require the use of large muscles such as push/pull toys, wagons, hula hoops, balls, and ride-on toys (Cundiff-Stith, 1995). Open spaces encourage running, jumping, and other modes of movement that toddlers enjoy practicing.

Natural elements of the environment can easily be incorporated into this zone. A line of low tree stumps of graduated heights can be used for climbing and jumping or walking across with adult support. A log partially buried to prevent it from rolling can be used as a makeshift balance beam. Pebbles, leaves, pinecones, and other natural objects can be loaded into wagons for hauling and dumping. Discarded materials can be recycled for use outdoors as well. An appliance box from a washer, dryer, or refrigerator with different sizes and shapes cut out offers a new perspective on how objects look when viewing them from inside the box (Wittmer, 1993). Large empty boxes from office supply stores can be taped closed and used like wooden hollow blocks. Objects for throwing and catching can be selected or made from soft materials to minimize children's fear of being hit by a moving object. Nerf® balls, Koosh® balls, and a pair of socks or panty hose rolled into one another are all soft and safe for high mobility toddlers. Imaginative teachers will find opportunities to incorporate other commercial, natural, and recyclable materials that motivate high mobility children to use newly developed large motor skills.

Dramatic Play Zone   Equipment and materials in the dramatic play zone are essential to promoting socialization and language development among toddlers. At this early stage of pretend play, toddlers imitate familiar adults in well-known (typically home-related) situations. Therefore, props, which enable them to reenact everyday situations, are preferable. Playhouses (originally branded as *Wendy* houses from the memorable character in the story of Peter Pan) are ideal for promoting dramatic play. These can be built by a skilled carpenter or purchased commercially. These ready-made structures represent houses in a variety of colors, log cabins, forts, and castles.

Accessory equipment is needed to stimulate toddlers' imaginations and help them carry out their play. In addition to dolls, strollers, and shopping carts which are traditionally used in indoor dramatic play areas, materials such as child-size plastic shovels, rakes, hoes, lawn mowers, buckets, hammers and other tools, wagons, and vehicles they can push along with their feet (e.g., Little Tykes Cozy Coupe®) enable toddlers to imitate familiar actions of others. Remember, toddlers typically do not coordinate play scenarios with peers and they are just learning the difficult task of sharing. Therefore, it is more important to have multiples of the same item, rather than expect toddlers to use a single item cooperatively. Preschoolers will assign or choose different roles and coordinate their actions.

Toddlers, on the other hand, *do not* assign roles such as mother, father, and child. Instead, they acquire ideas for role-playing from one another and several children may choose the same role. If one child simply declares, "I'm daddy" and climbs into the Cozy Coupe® car, several others may wish to do the same. In this case, it is imperative to have several cars available to allow their play to continue and to minimize problems associated with sharing and taking turns.

Messy Zone   An outdoor play yard is the ideal place to establish a zone where children are free to make messes. Water play, sand play, painting, modeling dough, and bubble blowing are activities well suited for the outdoors where minimal clean up is required. Two weather-resistant child-size tables are adequate for the messy zone. Chairs are not necessary because most young children prefer to stand and work at tables. Picnic-style tables with built-in benches interfere with children's need to stand and move. Tables outdoors facilitate water play, sand play, painting, modeling with dough, and quiet activities.

  Water Table   Dishpans or other small tubs are an excellent choice for toddler water play. Children can stand side-by-side, each with his individual tub and toys. This set-up has many advantages over commercial water tables. They are economical, easier to clean, can be transported to a water source, and children are not required to share. As children become more skilled in sharing, slightly larger tubs can be made available for children to work in pairs. Simple equipment such as cups, small buckets, watering cans, sponges, and toys that sink and float encourage discoveries.

  Sand Table or Sandbox   Dishpans and other similar containers can be used for sand play with the same advantages as cited previously for water play. Containers with secure lids prevent rain, leaves, grass, trash, and animals from contaminating the clean sand inside. Two or three covered sandboxes designed for the backyard can be placed in the messy zone for pairs of children to dig, build, and play. A single, large sandbox may be built-in for more children to use at once. Regardless of the container, sand must be replenished regularly to maintain a depth useful for play. In boxes, sand depth should be kept at a minimum of eight inches. The amount of sand needed per square feet of sandbox is:

Area of sand box (square feet)	Number of 50-lb bags of sand needed
6	8
12	16
24	32
27	36
54	72

Sifters, small strainers, and cups with holes pierced through the bottom permit children to manipulate and pour sand along with hand shovels, scoops, and large spoons for digging.

Painting Easels can be set up for outdoor painting but a flat surface offers the advantage of fewer drips and less running, which is more suitable to toddlers who can become frustrated with a lack of control over paints. Recycled yogurt cups that have been secured to a piece of scrap lumber with screws or glue can be used to hold paints. This prevents the containers from tipping over, spilling paints, and upsetting toddlers. Medium weight rocks or stones can be used to hold down corners of papers to prevent them from flying away. Completed paintings can be left on the table to dry or set aside in a designated place to give other children an opportunity to paint.

Table surfaces can also be used for finger painting. Toddlers are intensely more interested in the process of painting than producing a final product. Therefore, children can be donned in smocks and finger paints generously applied to the tabletop. A few materials made available to toddlers who are uncomfortable with the feel and texture of finger paints gives every child a chance to take part. Small brushes, cotton swabs, and sticks can be used to move the paints around. At the end of outdoor playtime, the table can simply be hosed off, doused with a bucket of water, or sprayed with a pump-bottle and wiped away.

Modeling Dough While the texture of modeling dough is much less fluid than water, sand, and paint, it can still be classified as a messy material because small pieces naturally flake off and chunks can slip out of small fingers and fall from the table.

Outdoors there is no worry of dough imbedding in carpets and it can be wiped from the tread of small shoes
before children return indoors. Tabletops can easily be
wiped down with a damp sponge to prepare them for
the next activity.

There are many good recipes available for making
homemade modeling dough. It is often recommended
that food coloring and extracts be added to dough to
enhance the sensory experience. However, when working with toddlers who are prone to tasting materials
that look and smell appealing, it is best not to add
these extra elements until they outgrow this tendency.
Herr and Libby (2000) recommend several modeling
dough recipes including Favorite Playdough (p. 295).

Favorite Playdough

Combine and boil until dissolved:
2 cups water
1/2 cup salt

While hot, mix in:
2 tablespoons cooking oil
2 tablespoons alum
2 cups flour

Knead approximately 5 minutes until smooth.
Store in covered airtight container or individual
zip-lock sandwich bags.

Quiet Zone   The quiet zone is the most overlooked
and underrated area for children's play, especially in
an outdoor environment. Playing outdoors naturally
elevates children's activity level and aggression. As
they exert themselves physically, heart rate and blood
flow increase causing children to take in more oxygen
and expel more carbon dioxide. They are working hard
both physically and mentally to coordinate various
muscle groups and motor activity. Socially, they may
feel overwhelmed by the presence and activity level of
other children in the play yard, much like adults feel
in a large crowd. All of these factors require exertion,
which can leave toddlers feeling overwhelmed and ex-
hausted. A logical and sensitive option is to provide
them with a place to sit, play quietly, and rest. If no
quiet zone is available, children may respond to stress
by overly aggressive behavior (becoming angry, frustrated, or annoyed) or overly passive behavior (crying,

whining, or brooding). This area should be available for children to choose as needed, not imposed on them as a place for punishment such as time-out. The quiet zone should be soft, comfortable, and somewhat private. A large blanket or several individual blankets laid under the shade of a tree are adequate. Pillows, stuffed animals, books, and small manipulatives organized in baskets offer a transitory, quiet alternative to the high activity level of outdoor play.

Music and Movement

Responding to music through movement is a natural response in very young children. From birth, infants are sensitive to sound. Babies can be observed reacting to lively music with kicking legs and flailing arms, as well as responding to soothing, familiar music by relaxing and falling asleep. Toddlers experiment with music through their voices and body movements. They sing, chant, or shout, and inevitably hop, wiggle, or dance to music with an upbeat tempo.

The outdoor environment offers the perfect arena for children's reactions to music. They have the open space needed to move safely to music and teachers have fewer concerns about the noise level. Impromptu as well as planned activities contribute to children's growing awareness of music and movement and should be a standard component of the outdoor play routine. According to Sanders and Yongue (1998):

> A combination of play and planned movement experiences, specifically designed to help children develop physical skills, are the most beneficial in assisting young children in their development. When frequent, regular, appropriate movement experiences are combined with daily indoor and outdoor play, children freely practice and develop their skills (p. 12).

Infants and toddlers follow a developmental sequence for responding to music and movement (Isenberg & Jalongo, 1997). Infants are sensitive to dynamics or the volume of sound. This is obvious by the way in which they startle or jump at loud sounds and are comforted by soothing lullabies, especially when sung by a familiar voice. They move to music using their entire bodies, either bouncing, rocking, or swaying. Young toddlers begin to imitate sounds as they respond to songs that are familiar and they may join in on repetitive phrases. They explore with making sounds using objects by banging toys or household objects. Young toddlers use large muscles (primarily arms and legs) to respond to different tempos. They use small muscles (hands and fingers) as they repeat finger plays and action songs. Around age three, children gain better voice control, rhythmic responses, and memory for songs. Along with singing familiar tunes some can play rhythm instruments with a steady beat and tempo. Older toddlers are capable of more graceful movements and will experiment by walking fast and slow and on tiptoe.

When infants and toddlers respond positively to rhythmic action songs it stimulates the brain and results in the formation of synapses, the vital connections between brain cells. Infants thrive on repetition, so memorizing and reciting regularly three to five different rhymes to an infant contributes to his brain response. Be watchful of infants' reactions and discontinue the recitation and play when they signal they have had enough. Signs of overstimulation include looking away, arching their back, and trying to crawl or move away (Wittmer, 1997a). The following scenario demonstrates the value of reciting rhymes with infants.

Gabrielle, the primary caregiver for a group of three infants, kneels beside the babies lying on their backs on a blanket under a shady tree. She holds and claps four-month-old Jean Paul's hands together as she recites:

> *"Clap your hands, one-two-three,*
> *Play a clapping game with me.*
> *Now your hands have gone away.*
> *Find your hands so we can play."*

Jean Paul squeals with delight and the other infants react with wide-open eyes and flailing arms. Each infant is given a turn as Gabrielle claps their hands and repeats the rhyme.

Older infants and toddlers respond to rhymes and music by imitating sounds with their voices, exploring noises made with objects, and moving their bodies (Isenberg & Jalongo, 1997). Each of these reactions contributes to the rapid brain growth that occurs until around age three. As they sing, pound, and dance, signals are rapidly firing between neurons and they are able to release stress and tension, minimizing the release of cortisol, a hormone that threatens brain development (Shore, 1997). Below is the story of a caregiver who capitalized on a popular finger play.

Raphael teaches a group of toddlers who have adopted "Five Little Monkeys Jumping on the Bed" as their favorite rhyme. Lately, they have begun dramatizing the rhyme as they jump off a row of low tree stumps on the playground. The timing of their jumps does not coordinate with the words and rhythm of the song, but they find the activity enjoyable. One day, Raphael introduces a small exercise trampoline during outdoor playtime. As an assistant teacher supervises toddlers running and climbing on equipment in the play yard, individual children take turns holding Raphael's hands while the rhyme "Five Little Monkeys" is recited as they jump on the trampoline. Most children are busy concentrating on their jumping and the sensation of the new experience and do not say the rhyme. So Raphael, along with other children who are watching and waiting, recite the rhyme aloud.

Rhythmic chants such as those used by Gabrielle and Raphael are ideal for introducing music and movement experiences to very young children. Figure 2–3 is a small selection of the many rhymes suitable for infants and toddlers. Additional rhymes can be collected by looking through published collections, asking veteran preschool teachers, and checking websites on preschool curriculum and activities.

Toddlers between eighteen and thirty-six months are capable of new challenges presented in an organized movement session. Pica (2000) advises teachers to be well aware of what toddlers are capable of in terms of movement activities and suggests the following:

- Remember toddlers have short attention spans so be realistic about how much time they can attend to an organized movement session.
- Give simple one or two part directions. Show rather than tell.
- Plan movement experiences with *and* without music.
- Don't require toddlers to wait for a turn.
- Plan more activities than you anticipate using. This allows you to move quickly from one activity

Figure 2–3 Rhymes for infants and toddlers.

Apple Tree
Way up high in the apple tree
Two little apples smiled at me.
I shook that tree as hard as I could.
Down came the apples.
Mmmm-they were good.

Daisies
One, two, three, four, five
Yellow daisies all alive.
Here they are, all in a row.
The sun and the rain will help them grow.

Here is the Bee Hive
Here is the bee hive. Where are the bees?
They're hiding away so nobody sees.
Soon they're coming creeping out of the hive,
1,2,3,4,5. Buzz-z-z-z-z.

Little Leaves
The little leaves are falling down
Round and round, round and round.
The little leaves are falling down,
Falling to the ground.

Mitten Song
Thumbs in the thumb place, fingers all together.
This is the song we sing in mitten weather.

Pat-a-Cake
Pat-a-cake, pat-a-cake, baker's man.
Bake me a cake as fast as you can!
Roll it
And pat it
And mark it with a "B"
And put it in the oven for baby and me!

Rainy Day Fun
Slip on your rain coat.
Pull up your galoshes.
Wade in puddles,
Make splishes and sploshes.

Rock-a-Bye, Baby,
Rock-a-bye, baby,
On the tree top.
When the wind blows,
The cradle will rock.

Figure 2–3 Continued.

When the bough breaks,
The cradle will fall,
And down will come baby,
Cradle and all.

Row, Row, Row Your Boat
Row, row, row your boat
Gently down the stream.
Merrily, merrily, merrily, merrily
Life is but a dream.

Twinkle Twinkle Little Star
Twinkle, twinkle, little star,
How I wonder what you are.
Up above the world so high,
Like a diamond in the sky.
Twinkle, twinkle little star,
How I wonder what you are.

Source: Herr, J., & Libby, Y. (2000). *Creative Resources for the early childhood classroom* (3d ed.). Albany, NY: Delmar.

---

to the next (to keep toddlers' attention) or to discontinue an activity that does not seem to be working.

- Ideally, movement sessions should be planned for mornings when toddlers are most alert. Avoid planning movement activities immediately after naptime.
- To meet their need for individual attention, the ideal ratio is four toddlers to one adult.
- Rather than trying to gather a group of toddlers together before beginning a movement activity, simply begin the activity and interested toddlers will cheerfully join in (Miller, 1985).
- Familiarize yourself with appropriate expectations for toddler behavior.

Pica (2000) also recommends choosing movement experiences that reflect toddlers' expanding cognitive development such as their ability to use their imagination, recognition of body parts, and rapidly developing sense of self. See Figure 2–4 for a list of movement activities for toddlers.

Figure 2–4 Suggested movement activities for toddlers.

Countdown
In a crouched position with knees bent, count down from ten. Children *launch* themselves by jumping up as the words *Blast Off* are said.

Dancing with Scarves
Toddlers are uninhibited and will begin moving simply because they hear music. Play songs with different tempos and rhythms. Give *each child* a simple prop, such as a scarf for them to incorporate into their movement.

Follow the Leader
Each child is given a turn demonstrating a motor skill or other movement and the rest of the group follows their direction.

Heads, Bellies, and Toes
In this simplified version of "Head, Shoulders, Knees, and Toes" the teacher starts out slowly repeating the name of the body parts in order: head, belly, and toes. The children touch their body on the part named. As the children gain experience, the teacher varies the tempo and order in which body parts are called.

If You're Happy and You Know It
After singing this song through, children can choose other emotions to be inserted and demonstrate how a child might look when experiencing that emotion. Examples of other emotions include sad, grumpy, excited, surprised, tired, scared.

If you're happy and you know it, clap your hands.
If you're happy and you know it, clap your hands.
If you're happy and you know it, then your face will surely show it.
If you're happy and you know it, clap your hands.

Ring Around the Rosie
This traditional song reinforces the spatial concepts of around and down. It is an ideal way to introduce toddlers to small group participation.

Ring around the rosie,
Pocket full of posy,
Ashes, ashes,
We all fall down

Source: Pica, R. (2000). *Experiences in movement with music, activities, and theory* (2d ed.). Albany, NY: Delmar.

Recorded music offers a broader variety of movement experiences for children. When selecting music recordings for young children, preview recordings, when possible, before purchasing in order to determine if (a) singing voices lie within the children's pitch range (neither too high or too low), (b) adults' and children's voices sound natural, (c) music has rich and interesting orchestration, and (d) songs that teach concepts such as colors and shapes are kept to a minimum (Achilles, 1999). During the infant and toddler years the goals are to promote an appreciation and love for music and to encourage children to respond to music in some way. This may include jumping, swaying, dancing, clapping, moving with scarves or streamers, and simply sitting quietly and listening.

As toddlers grow into preschoolers, they can be introduced to simple musical concepts and vocabulary such as tempo, dynamics, and pitch. Their understanding of music is broadened as they are introduced to variety including classical music and rhythms from other cultures. Tapes and compact discs, such as *Ella Jenkins Multi-Cultural Children's Songs,* offer music representing various cultures. Older three-year-olds and young preschoolers also enjoy creating their own music through simple rhythm instruments. Traditional rhythm band sets can be purchased from educational supply catalogs and most offer instruments that represent diverse cultures as well. Unique instruments to add to a rhythm band set include a spin drum, shakeree, gallon drum, bobo balaphon xylopipes, Chilean rainstick, agogo bells, den den drum, maracas, and a guiro.

A generous supply of batteries enables a tape or compact disc (CD) player to be easily moved outside. Remote controlled CD players are practical for selecting a specific track while keeping watch over children (Achilles, 1999) or copies of the previously selected songs from a tape can be made (Isenberg & Jalongo, 1997). Players with multiple headphone jacks enable several children to peacefully enjoy music in the Quiet Zone.

Movement Experiences for Children with Special Needs When adapting movement experiences for young children, it is important to remember that there are more similarities between children with and without disabilities than there are differences (Bayless & Ramsey, 1991). Similarly, we must keep in mind that the degree of each child's disability is unique to that child. In order to find the appropriate modification, teachers should concentrate on what a child *can* do, as opposed to what they cannot do. Pica (2000) makes recommendations for adaptations for children with physical challenges, hearing impairments, visual impairments, limited understanding, and emotional disabilities.

Children with physical challenges need periods of rest to avoid pain or discomfort. Climbing activities are avoided for children who experience seizures. Teachers can give extra assistance for activities involving laterality and directionality (Bayless & Ramsey, 1991). Accommodate by substituting lower body movements with upper body movements such as swaying or head nodding. If a rhythm instrument cannot be held by the child, slip an elastic band with bells attached around the child's wrist. Plan activities with goals directed toward the child's needs; watch a tossed balloon descend to strengthen back of the neck and wave streamers while peers march to strengthen arms (Zinar, 1987).

Children with hearing impairments should be placed closer to the front of the group and the teacher faces the child when speaking. Teachers speak in a low-pitched voice (Zinar, 1987) and use visual signals to get attention such as flickering overhead lights. Communicate instructions through simple signing and encourage children to imitate the actions of peers. Allow children to place their hands on the CD player or instrument to feel vibrations. Eliminate distractions such as background music and people talking.

Children with visual impairments should also be placed near the activity leader and hold hands with an adult. Verbal cues and clear descriptions are needed when giving directions. Brightly colored objects such as balls or mats enable children with visual impairments to track objects (Craft, 1990). Fluorescent tape can be used to mark the edges of mats or boundaries on the floor (Craft, 1990).

Children with limited understanding need activities with repetition such as simple, familiar songs. Expect children to imitate others and offer encouragement when they attempt new responses (Hirst & Michaelis, 1983). Do not expect children to perform two actions at once, such as clapping and stomping. Introduce activities that incorporate stopping after the body is in motion and use movement activities that reinforce academic concepts.

Children with emotional disabilities need activities that emphasize basic movement skills such as balance, locomotor skills (moving the whole body from one place to another), nonlocomotor skills (moving body parts while remaining in one place), and perceptual motor activities (Loovis, 1990). Provide activities in which the child can be successful and verbally praise desired behavior. Reward desired behavior by allowing the child to assist in some way, such as choosing or leading the next activity (Zinar, 1987). Avoid physical contact during activities. Offer songs and activities that allow for self-expression and an outlet for emotions.

In many cases, children under the age of three may not yet be identified as having a special need. The suggestions and adaptations suggested here may be used before a formal identification of a child's special need is made.

TEACHERS' ROLES

Perhaps one of the most difficult roles of the teacher is preparing children to go outdoors. This can be especially problematic in colder climates where several layers of outdoor wear are required to protect children from low temperatures. Plan ahead to make the task of preparing children for outdoor play easier. Enlist the help of another adult to get infants ready for the outdoors. This may include applying sunscreen or bundling them in blankets and hats. This should be done as efficiently as possible so one or two children do not become overheated as they wait for other infants to be dressed for cooler weather. Look for ways to make toddlers more independent in preparing themselves for the outdoors. Hang jackets and scarves on hooks at a height where children can reach them and label each hook with the child's color-coded name or individual symbol, which they can recognize to minimize confusion. It is difficult for many toddlers to zip, button, and snap their own jacket while they are wearing it but somewhat easier to manipulate closures on the jacket worn by another child. Encourage toddlers to help one another as they dress for cool weather. This promotes fine motor development, self-help skills, and socialization with peers. Also, consider taking toddlers outdoors in smaller groups with a second adult supervising the remaining children inside the classroom (Dombro, 1995).

Infants and toddlers are rapidly developing in all areas, so when outdoors, use the opportunity to stimulate cognitive and language growth as well as physical development and social skills. Wittmer (1997b) suggests arousing children's curiosity as a way to stimulate cognitive and language development. The latest brain research leads us to believe that human curiosity begins even before birth. In the womb, fetuses are moving, twisting, touching, and sucking. At birth they continue to investigate their new world gathering information through rudimentary senses. As babies begin feeling safe, loved, and secure, they can use their energy to explore their world rather than for self-preservation. As toddlers, they need caring adults nearby to provide security, support, and to answer relevant questions. According to Wittmer (1997), "Curiosity flourishes when we answer questions patiently. Curiosity is dulled when we scold or say no too often, restrict toddlers to small areas, or herd them around in groups" (p. 53). Instead of dulling curiosity, teachers can cultivate it by modeling curiosity and encouraging discovery, responding positively to children's questions, setting up an environment filled with choices, and nurturing social behavior. The caregiver in the following scenario exhibits each of these methods for promoting curiosity among the young toddlers in her care.

Katrina has worked as a child care provider for three years and greets each school day with fresh enthusiasm. Rather than focusing on having children complete the activities she has planned for the day, she strives to look at the world from the perspective of an eighteen- to twenty-four-month-old. She has learned that for toddlers the outdoor play yard offers new and exciting opportunities for exploration with each visit. An early spring rain from the day before has left the play yard fresh and ready for a group of naturally curious toddlers. As they totter into the play yard, several children notice the small pools of water in fallen, overturned magnolia leaves. The large canoe-shaped leaf holds almost an inch deep of water and the children are fascinated. Katrina asks, "What has happened? How did the water get here?" and then helps the children verbalize their answers. Next, she takes a small twig lying nearby and places it in the water. One child pushes it along with his finger while others collect more twigs, smaller leaves, and pebbles for an impromptu "sink and float" science lesson. As the children rush to drop items in the magnolia leaf, it is overturned and they become angry and frustrated. Katrina reassures them and directs a child to fill a small bucket from the water table. She helps the children as they clumsily refill the leaf and then overfill several others lying nearby. She leaves the children to their experimentation and turns her attention to another group disturbed by the dampness on the slide and the mud puddle at its exit. Katrina is prepared with old towels that the children use to dry the slide and a rubber mat that is placed over the mud at the end of the slide. Three children begin singing "Clean up, clean, everybody everywhere . . . " and use the towels to dry off swings, steps, and railings, with a new interest in wiping equipment dry. Next, her attention is drawn to a pair of children watching in delight as a brave turtle attempts to cross the play yard and return to its home.

Katrina's experience, education, and intuition made this trip to the play yard one filled with exploration and learning. She successfully cultivated the children's curiosity by modeling her own curiosity about the water-filled magnolia leaf and encouraged discovery by placing a twig in the water. She responded to an unfortunate event (the overturned leaf) in a positive way and included the children in the simple solution to the problem. There were different activities available to interest the children (some provided by Mother Nature herself) and opportunities to promote socialization by working and playing cooperatively.

As infants and toddlers explore the outdoor environment, they are exposed to new opportunities to interact with peers. These interactions may be pleasant at times, but inevitably will be a source of aggravation, frustration, and anger because of their limited ability to communicate, cooperate, and negotiate with others. Disputes between very young children are to be expected and are perfectly logical in terms of their cognitive and social-emotional development. Recall, very young children are egocentric in their thinking. Infants and toddlers see the world as revolving around their personal wants and needs and they are incapable of fully understanding the perspective of others. At the same time, they are emotionally demanding as they strive for autonomy and independence. This combination makes toddlers appear difficult and demanding when, in fact, their challenging and often defiant behavior is perfectly normal and predictable.

Although caregivers can expect toddlers to be difficult at times, it is impossible to anticipate every situation that will require adult intervention in order to achieve a peaceful resolution. It is for this reason, and others, that Reynolds (2001) recommends applying *limits* rather than rules to young children's behavior. Reynolds states, "Rules often place artificial, illogical restrictions on the natural and logical behavior of children and rob them of their option to think for themselves" (p. 184). Limits, on the other hand, keep children within boundaries of safety, respect, and responsibility. Rather than quoting arbitrary rules, teachers can discuss with children the reason behind setting a particular limit. Including children in explanations as to why limits are necessary in a given situation is more compatible with toddlers' emerging awareness of the need to get along with others. Explaining authentic limits rather than setting subjective rules helps children learn self-control.

Setting limits can be used with infants and toddlers, as well as older children. The following example is from *Guiding Young Children: A Problem-Solving Approach,* Third Edition by Eleanor Reynolds.

Move!

Trevor and Carrie are among several children on the outdoor climber and slide. Trevor is twenty-one months old, and Carrie is twenty-three months old. Trevor is at the top of the slide, ready to come down. Carrie is sitting at the bottom, swinging her legs. Trevor has waited for several minutes for her to move and finally starts to go down the slide.

TEACHER: *Trevor, looks like Carrie is on the slide, too. I'm afraid someone will get hurt if you go down now.*

Trevor becomes frustrated and begins to kick his feet.

TEACHER: *Looks like you're getting frustrated. Is there something you can say when you want someone to move?*

TREVOR: *Move! Move!*

TEACHER: *Carrie, I hear Trevor saying "move." He's waiting to go down the slide.*

Carrie turns and looks up the slide at Trevor. She wriggles off the slide.

CARRIE: *Come down, Trevor.*

Trevor slides slowly down the slide. At the bottom, both are excited about Trevor coming down.

TEACHER: *I like the way you solved your problem.*

What if Carrie had not moved off the slide? It may have gone like this.

TREVOR: *Move! Move!*

CARRIE: *I sitting here.*

Trevor continues kicking his feet and others are also waiting to come down the slide.

TEACHER: *Carrie, I see Trevor and other kids waiting to come down the slide. I'm afraid someone will get hurt if*

*they slide down on you. Carrie continues to sit at the
bottom of the slide, swinging her legs.*
TEACHER: *Carrie, it's important to listen when someone
asks you to move. You may get hurt if you don't.*
*Kids waiting at the top are getting restless and begin push-
ing. The teacher talks to them about the danger of pushing children on the climber. She returns to Carrie.*
TEACHER: *This is not a safe situation. I'm really afraid
someone will get hurt. I'm going to help you get down.*
The teacher takes Carrie's hand and helps her get down.
TEACHER: *Thank you, Carrie.*

> E. Reynolds, from *Guiding young children: A problem-solving
> approach,* 3d ed. (pp. 153–155). Copyright © 2001 by Mayfield
> Publishing Company. Reprinted with permission of the publisher.

In this scenario, Trevor learned how to express
his needs by saying, "Move, move!" to Carrie who re-
fused to move from the bottom of the slide. Rather
than imposing a rule such as, "You must move off the
slide immediately after going down," the children in
this scenario learned the importance of taking turns,
expressing their needs, listening to others, and not
pushing on the climber. The result was the same—
Carrie moved off the slide, but the approach taught
children several valuable lessons instead of simply
showing them who was in charge.

Additional strategies for negotiating with toddlers
include (Nixon, 1999):

1. Be familiar with each child and her individual
   means of communication. Did Augustus push
   Abigail down on purpose or does he habitually
   forget to look forward while running? Is this the
   first time this has happened or have teachers repeatedly talked with him about knocking other
   children down? Background information is helpful when resolving dilemmas involving toddlers
   who have limited language skills.
2. Keep your emotions in check. Respect children's
   emotions by acknowledging all humans (children
   and adults) have similar feelings. Encourage children to express their emotions, but provide labels
   for those children who are unable to do so, by
   asking questions such as "Are you feeling left

out?" Use a calm voice and reassuring manner when negotiating with an upset child.

3. Address the conduct, not the child, when correcting behavior. If a child grabs a sand shovel away from another child, say "Kaley was using that. Have you asked for a turn?" rather than labeling the child as selfish, thoughtless, or bad. Redirect his behavior by suggesting another toy or making another digging implement available.

4. Allow time for problem solving. Although it may be frustrating to the adult, it is important to allow children the time to work out their own problems. Intercede only when children experience frustration or feelings of helplessness. Self-confidence and self-reliance grow from mastering challenges and solving problems.

5. Acknowledge efforts and successes. Positive reinforcement can be very powerful especially when used to recognize difficult accomplishments such as sharing, turn-taking, or using words to express emotions rather than physically hurting another child.

CONCLUSION

Infancy and toddlerhood is a unique period of childhood and these very young children have unique developmental needs. Children's bodies and brains are growing and developing at a rapid rate, effecting them physically, cognitively, and linguistically. Socially and emotionally they are experimenting and just beginning to learn how they impact their world. The outdoors offers a multitude of new experiences that incite learning in all domains. Teachers can incorporate the natural elements of an outdoor setting and supplement these with materials and experiences to stimulate the senses, the basic mechanism through which young children learn. By understanding their unique needs and demonstrating sensitivity, teachers can provide appropriate limits that keep children safe outdoors, as well as teach self-control and independence.

KEY TERMS

functional play   telegraphic speech
pretend play   separation anxiety
receptive language   stranger anxiety
productive language   egocentrism
babbling   pincer grip
expressive jargon

THEORY INTO PRACTICE

1. Choose either the no mobility or low mobility group and design an age-appropriate play area.
2. Select one of the zones suggested for high mobility toddlers: large motor zone, dramatic play zone, messy zone, or quiet zone. Develop a plan for the zone. Coordinate with others doing this exercise to complete the play yard design.
3. Interact with a group of infants and toddlers with the goal of cultivating their curiosity. Afterward, write a narrative of the experience, highlighting the moments when curiosity flourished.
4. Observe adults supervising children's outdoor play. How were limits used?

RELATED WEB SITE

www.catalog.kaplanco.com
Kaplan's online catalog for purchasing books and educational materials including multicultural music and rhythm instruments.

RELATED RESOURCES

Herr, J., & Swim, T. (2000). *Creative resources for infants and toddlers*. Albany, NY: Delmar.

Pica, R. (2000). *Moving and learning: Toddlers (ages 18 to 36 months)*. Albany, NY: Delmar.

Silberg, J. (1999). *125 brain games for babies*. Beltsville, MD: Gryphon House, Inc.

Silberg, J. (1995). *Games to play with babies*. Beltsville, MD: Gryphon House, Inc.

REFERENCES

Achilles, E. (1999). Creating music environments in early childhood programs. *Young Children, 54*(1) 21–26.

Bayless, L.M., & Ramsey, M.E. (1991). *Music: A way of life for the young child.* New York: Merrill.

Bayley, N. (1969). *Bayley scales of infant development: Birth to two years.* New York: Psychological Corporation.

Bell, S.M., & Ainsworth, M.D. (1972). Infant crying and maternal responsiveness. *Child Development, 43,* 1171–1190.

Bredekamp, S., & Copple, C. (Eds.) (1997). *Developmentally appropriate practice in early childhood programs* (Rev. ed.). Washington, DC: National Association for the Education of Young Children.

Brazelton, T.B. (1981). *On becoming a family: The growth of attachment.* New York, NY: Dell Publishing Company.

Brown, M.B. (1998). Kids in motion. *Scholastic: Early Childhood Today, 12*(7) 34–35.

Craft, D.H. (1990). Sensory impairments. In J.P. Winnick (Ed.), *Adapted Physical education and sport* (pp. 209–28). Champaign, IL: Human Kinetics.

Cundiff-Stith, D. (1995). Backyard basics. *Scholastic: Early Childhood Today, 9*(8) 16.

Dodge, D.T., Dombro, A.L., & Koralek, D.G. (1991). *Caring for infants and toddlers* (Vol. 1). Washington, DC: Teaching Strategies.

Dombro, A.L. (1995). The great outdoors. *Scholastic: Early Childhood Today, 9*(8) 50.

Erikson, E. (1963). *Childhood and society* (2d ed.). New York: Norton.

Frost, J. (1992). *Play and playscapes.* Albany, NY: Delmar.

Gessell, A. (1933). The maturation and patterning of behavior. In C. Murchison (Ed.), *Handbook of child psychology.* Worcester, MA: Clark University Press.

Herr, J., & Libby, Y. (2000). *Creative resources for the early childhood classroom* (3d ed.). Albany, NY: Delmar.

Hirst, C.C. & Michaelis, E. (1983). *Retarded kids need to play.* New York: Leisure Press.

Isenberg, J.P., & Jalongo, M.R. (1997). *Creative expression and play in early childhood.* Upper Saddle River, NJ: Merrill/Prentice Hall.

Izard, C.E., & Harris, P. (1995). In D. Ciccetti & D. J. Cohen (Eds.), *Developmental phychology: (Vol. 1.) Theory and methods* (pp. 467–503). New York: Wiley.

Johnson, J.E., Christie, J.F., & Yawkey, T.D. (1999). *Play and early childhood development* (2d ed.). Glenview, IL: Scott, Foresman.

Lenneberg, E.H., (1967). *Biological foundations of language.* New York: John Wiley & Sons.

Loovis, E.M. (1990). Behavioral disabilities. In J.P. Winnick (Ed.), *Adapted physical education and sport* (pp. 195–207). Champaign, IL: Human Kinetics.

Lowman, L., & Ruhmann, L. (1998). Simply sensational spaces: A multi-"S" approach to toddler environments. *Young Children, 53*(3), 11–17.

McCune, L. (1995). A normative study of representational play at the transition to language stage. *Developmental Psychology, 31,* 198–206.

Miller, K. (1989). Infants and toddlers outside. *Texas Child Care Quarterly, 13,* 20–29.

Miller, K. (1985). *Ages and stages: Developmental descriptions and activities birth through 8 years.* Chelsea, MA: Telshare.

Mitchell, P.R., & Kent, R.D. (1990). Phonetic variation in multi-syllable babbling. *Journal of Child Language, 17,* 247–265.

Nixon, P.D. (1999). Negotiating with toddlers. *Young Children, 54*(3), 60–61.

Piaget, J. (1962). *Play, dreams, and imitation in childhood.* New York: Norton.

Piaget, J. (1952). *The origins of intelligence.* New York: International Universities Press.

Pica, R. (2000). *Experiences in movement with music, activities, and theory* (2d ed.). Albany, NY: Delmar.

Reich, P.A. (1986). *Language development.* Englewood Cliffs, NJ: Prentice-Hall.

Reynolds, E. (2001). *Guiding young children: A problem-solving approach* (3d ed.). Mountain View, CA: Mayfield Publishing Company.

Sanders, S.W., & Yongue, B. (1998). Challenging movement experiences for young children. *Dimensions, 26*(1), 9–17.

Shore, R. (1997). *Rethinking the brain: New insights into early development.* New York: Families and Work Institute.

Tomasello, M., & Mervis, C.B. (1994). Commentary: The instrument is great, but measuring comprehension is still a problem. In L. Fenson, P.S. Dale, J.S. Reznick, E. Bates, D.J. Thal, & S.J. Pethick (Eds.), Variability in early communicative development. *Monographs of the Society for Research in Child Development, 59,* Serial No. 242.

Trawick-Smith, J. (2000). *Early childhood development: A multicultural perspective* (2d ed.). Upper Saddle River, NJ: Merrill.

Vygotsky, L. (1976). Play and its role in the mental development of the child. In J. Bruner, A. Jolly, & K. Sylva (Eds.), *Play: Its role in development and evolution.* New York: Basic Books.

Watson, M.M., & Jackowitz, E.R. (1984). Agents and recipient objects in the development of early symbolic play. *Child Development, 55,* 1091–1097.

Wittmer, D.S. (1997a). Games to grow on. *Scholastic: Early Childhood Today, 11*(7), 37–40.

Wittmer, D.S. (1997b). The learning sparkle. *Scholastic: Early Childhood Today, 11*(8), 53–57.

Wittmer, D.S. (1996). "Sense-able" outdoor play. *Scholastic: Early Childhood Today, 10*(7), 19–21.

Wittmer, D.S. (1993). Sensational play outdoors. *Scholastic Pre-K Today, 7*(8), 34–35.

Wortham, S., & Wortham, M. (1992). Special essay. In J. Frost, *Play and playscapes.* Albany, NY: Delmar.

Zinar, R. (1987). *Music activities for special children.* West Nyack, NY: Parker.

CHAPTER 3

Outdoor Play in the Preschool and Kindergarten Years

Guiding Questions

1. What are the developmental differences between infants and toddlers and children three to six years old in each of the following domains: cognitive, language, social-emotional, and physical development?
2. What are three possible curriculum goals for outdoor play in the preschool or kindergarten?
3. How can an existing play yard be improved or expanded?
4. What is a topic for a developmentally appropriate, integrated unit with an outdoor theme?

INTRODUCTION

The rate of growth and development in the preschool and kindergarten years is slower than that of the infant and toddler, but rapid when compared to older children. Changes are evident in all domains; cognitive, language, social-emotional, and physical. Piaget (1962) emphasized the prevalence of **pretend play** and **constructive play** for children ages three to six. As preschoolers and kindergarteners engage in pretend play, they incorporate objects to represent props needed for the scenario. Examples might include singing into a spoon while pretending it is a microphone, pulling a doll around in a box while pretending it is a wagon, and wearing a sand bucket on their head while pretending it is a helmet. Constructive play entails creating or building through manipulating objects, such as paper crafts, block building, or molding with wet sand. These are only two of the many remarkable characteristics to be observed in the preschool and kindergarten child.

Learning occurs naturally in outdoor settings. However, teachers dedicated to outdoor play will quickly see the many benefits of specifically planning an outdoor environment that optimizes play and learning experiences. Because preschoolers' and kindergarteners' interest in the outdoors is so strong, teachers can also plan for integrated units with an outdoor theme, field trips, nature walks, and other relevant experiences.

COGNITIVE DEVELOPMENT

The intellectual ability of three- to six-year-olds is more sophisticated than the toddler's, yet still quite different from that of adults. According to Piaget (1952), preschoolers and kindergarteners exhibit **preoperational thought,** meaning it is a period before they are capable of using logic to solve problems. This type of thinking and reasoning emerges around age two and continues until about seven years of age. One of the most obvious ways their thought-processes differ from adults is they rely almost completely on their senses which, at times, actually interfere with accurate problem solving. A classic example is a Piagetian task designed to learn more about the way preschooler and kindergarten children reason. In the conservation of number task, the evaluator spreads an equal number of chips in two rows spaced evenly apart. The adult then, in front of the child, spreads one row further apart and leaves the second row in its original position. When asked "Are there still the same number of chips in each row?" the preoperational child will respond with the answer of "No." One typical explanation is that the altered row has *more* chips because it is longer. See Figure 3–1 for an illustration of a conservation of number task.

Figure 3–1   Piagetian task: Conservation of number.

Step 1: Form two identical rows with five chips in each. Ask the child if he/she agrees the rows are the same.

Step 2: Spread the five chips in one row further apart. The second row remains as it was in Step 1. Ask the child if the rows still have the same number of chips or if one row has more.

Step 3: Listen to the child's response. Preoperational thinkers will state that the row of chips that has been spread out has more objects in it (because it visually *appears* longer).

The following story illustrates the difference between the logic of a preschooler who thinks preoperationally and an older child. Two brothers, ages four and eight, were given one candy bar to share. The older brother took on the task of dividing the candy bar in two equal pieces. He broke the candy bar in two, measured the difference by holding the pieces side by side, bit off the longer half, and showed the younger brother that both pieces were now the same size. The younger brother smiled showing he was satisfied that he had received an equal share. His preoperational thinking did not allow him to reason that the older brother got more than his fair share by eating the difference!

Preschoolers and kindergarten children's thinking is limited in some ways, yet their progress since infancy is amazing. This is due primarily to their ability to think symbolically, that is, they now fully understand that abstract symbols can represent something meaningful. This is accomplished after much pretend play in toddlerhood which allows them to practice using symbols. Teachers and parents may have watched a toddler pick up a block, hold it to her ear, and carry on a conversation with "grandma" as if someone was listening and responding. In this scenario, the block was a symbol for a telephone. As a preschooler, her use of symbols is more complex. One major difference is her use of spoken language in place of using objects or actions needed for play. A four-year-old had the following conversation with her peer as they sat in a playhouse: "O.K. You are the dad, and I'm the mom. I've just finished mowing the lawn and want to play with the children, so you make dinner." In this example, language replaced the action of mowing the lawn, which enabled the pair to begin their play in the middle of a scenario.

Young children demonstrate their understanding of symbols when they recognize print around the home and community. Some of the first words they recognize are their name and the names of family members. They may also call out familiar print from their environment such as the sign above a well-known grocery store or a label on their favorite bottle of juice. Their knowledge of print is also evident when they create their own symbols in an attempt to communicate a message in writing. Preschoolers create their own written symbols through scribbling, drawing, and other forms of early writing.

Two other important shifts in thinking that occur during the preoperational stage of cognitive development are **object permanence** and *egocentrism*. Object permanence means a child now has the ability to mentally picture an object even when it is not in sight. Egocentrism describes the young child's inability to understand another's perspective.

Lev Vygotsky (1896–1934), the well-respected Russian psychologist, emphasized the essential role of adults in supporting children's learning throughout the early years. As preschoolers and kindergarten children wrestle with preoperational thought, adults facilitate learning by providing support (Vygotsky, 1978) or *scaffolding*. Scaffolding involves providing hints, clues, or suggestions while still allowing the child to play the major role in solving the problem. Many parents as well as teachers naturally scaffold children's learning without realizing it (Freund, 1989). Consider the following example of a preschooler attempting a new piece of playground equipment.

The children immediately named the curved ladder on the new climbing structure the "half rainbow." The arched supporting frame with crossbars leading to a platform and slide looked just as they described. Teachers closely supervised as children attempted the new challenge of climbing not only up, but also across a ladder. Some did it with ease, and others did not attempt it at all.

Tarah, a rowdy three-year-old wanted desperately to reach the platform via the half rainbow, but was a little unsure how to go about it. Her teacher first suggested she watch two other children climb the ladder until she was ready to try it herself.

When Tarah made her first attempt she quickly ascended the first rungs but, upon reaching the arc of the ladder, was unsure what to do next. The teacher touched her hand and showed her where to place it on the next rung, then her foot and showed her where it should be placed. As Tarah stepped and pulled, the teacher held her waist to prevent her from falling.

On the next attempt, the teacher gave fewer reminders as to which hand or foot went where and with some trial and error, Tarah figured it out. On her third try, the teacher held her hands inches away from Tarah's waist but allowed her to balance her own weight.

By the fourth try, Tarah was climbing the ladder alone, with her teacher physically available if needed. Through gradually allowing Tarah to take more responsibility for climbing, the teacher provided the scaffolding necessary for Tarah's success.

COMMUNICATION DEVELOPMENT

Language skills of the three- to five-year-old are developed well enough to communicate effectively with adults and peers. They are learning skills related to reading and writing in a predictable order much like the progression of motor skills. Preschoolers and kindergarteners pretend to read familiar books (often staying true to the text) even before they have phonetic knowledge of individual letters. They draw pictures and orally tell a story related to their drawing even before they have the skills needed to write words and sentences. It is extremely important that adults recognize these early behaviors as the foundation necessary for later success at traditional reading and writing and respond appropriately.

Preschoolers' ability to think symbolically opens up a new world of make-believe that in turn influences their literacy development. Children three to six years old firmly understand that imaginary objects can take the place of real ones, and scribbles on a page can represent something meaningful to them. While toddlers may be seen talking to (or through) their action figures or stuffed animals, preschoolers and kindergarteners take pretend play further. They often recruit others for their play scenes, act out more sophisticated storylines, and stay in their roles for longer periods of time (Smilansky, 1971). Language plays a very important role in their pretend play. It is used in place of real actions, to identify roles, and to work out differences. Observe young children and the magic of pretend play becomes evident.

The informality of outdoor play periods provides an ideal setting for pretend play scenarios to emerge. The following is an example of two kindergarten students at play with props borrowed from the indoor dramatic play center.

MARIA: *I'm the mom who just came home from shopping and you're my little girl.*

OLIVIA: *I don't want to be the little girl. I'll be your older sister.*

MARIA: *You can be my twin sister if you want.*

OLIVIA: *O.K.!*

MARIA: *Now, I just got home from shopping and you have to help me put the groceries away.*

(The girls step inside the playhouse and act out putting away groceries.)

OLIVIA: *Since you went to the store, I'll make dinner. What do you want?*

MARIA: *Wait! Let's have a tea party instead.*

OLIVIA: *O.K. You sit down while I make the tea.*

(Together the girls sip pretend tea and carry on conversations moving in and out of their roles as twin sisters as they plan their unfolding drama.)

The ability to think symbolically (understand the use of symbols) is crucial to learning to read and write. Adults play an important role in children's development of symbolic thought. Children whose parents read aloud regularly to them and allow experimentation with writing tools are more likely to be successful in reading and writing. This is because the children are allowed to play with and learn about symbols in a meaningful way.

Behaviors such as pretending to read a book or scribbling on a page and "reading" their message aloud are positive signs that these children will have success in the area of literacy (Teale & Sulzby, 1986; Schickedanz, 1999).

Parents and teachers should reinforce these playful, early attempts at reading and writing by showing their enthusiasm, just as they did when their infant first attempted to walk and talk. Literacy experts have identified stages of both reading and writing development. (Refer to *More Than ABC'S: The Early Stages of Reading and Writing* by Judith A. Schickedanz for a complete review of this topic). Being familiar with children's progression in learning to read and write enables teachers to support children through indoor and outdoor activities during this important period of learning.

SOCIAL-EMOTIONAL DEVELOPMENT

Current research on brain development and attachment supports the classic psychological theory of Erik Erikson (1963) who divided the human lifespan into eight distinct stages. In the third stage, children ages three years to six years are in the struggle between "Initiative vs. Guilt." They need to express themselves creatively through drawing, singing, writing, or dancing, and they begin to take on new risks and challenges. Encouraging adults promote confidence by supporting their child, while critical adults trigger negative feelings such as remorse and inadequacy.

Parents are typically concerned with the intellectual and physical changes in their children. However, healthy social-emotional development is crucial to overall happiness and mental health later in life (Hartup & Laursen, 1993; Parker et al., 1995). Therefore, the importance of this area of development should not be underestimated. Parents and teachers play a significant role as a model of socially effective behaviors and in guiding children as they learn to get along with others.

Social-emotional development of children in preschool and kindergarten is a topic of study that has been thoroughly researched, primarily because this area has long been a goal of early childhood education. Typically, researchers look for characteristics of children who are or are not accepted by peers as playmates. A *sociometric interview* is used to study which children are and are not accepted by their peers. This research tool determines each child's position in three separate categories: popular, rejected, and neglected.

Popular children are those who are named often as preferred playmates by their peers. These children exhibit characteristics such as taking initiative and they demonstrate leadership in play situations without bossing or bullying (Crick, Casas, & Mosher, 1997). They can accurately read others' emotions (Dodge & Price, 1994) and this helps them join peers at play successfully (Putallaz & Wasserman, 1989). They are diplomatic in accepting others' suggestions for play or they offer alternatives without aggression (Hartup & Laursen, 1993; Trawick-Smith, 1988).

Rejected children are identified as undesirable playmates. Their peers fervently avoid them, primarily because they exhibit unpredictable, physical aggression. Rejected children are not competent at reading others' emotions or at judging social situations. They typically have a negative, whiny disposition and are therefore unpleasant in the eyes of their peers (Dodge & Price, 1994). Some rejected children choose to play alone and can become aggressive if approached by others (Asher & Dodge, 1985).

Neglected children are those who are not named by their peers in a sociometric interview. These children are typically ignored by peers, and, sadly, by teachers as well. A common characteristic of children in the neglected social-status category is that they prefer to play alone and will withdraw when children approach them (Scarlet, 1983). Peers quickly learn which children will not join in their play and give up extending requests to neglected-rated children. A common characteristic among children rated as neglected by peers is that they are shy (Nelson, Hart, Robinson, Olsen, & Rubin, 1997).

There are many theories attempting to explain differences in personality and behavior that result in a peer-rating of popular, rejected, or neglected. These include temperament of the child, parenting practices, and cultural influences. Whatever the reason, caring adults are the most effective tools for helping preschoolers become accepted into their peer group.

PHYSICAL PROGRESSION

Physical growth and development of small and large muscles and motor skills during this period follows a predictable sequence, just as it did during infancy and toddlerhood. Figure 3–2 reviews developmental benchmarks of fine motor and gross motor skills of children two to six years old. Individual physical progression is determined by several factors including genetics, maturation, diet, and activity level. While the first two factors are beyond the control of teachers (and even parents), the last two can be easily controlled when parents and teachers work together. Most adults are aware that the greatest culprits of unhealthy physical

Figure 3–2 Developmental benchmarks of fine motor and gross motor skills.

Ages	Fine motor skills	Gross motor skills
Two-year-olds	Turns pages in a book singly Imitates drawing a circle, vertical and horizontal lines Fingers work together to scoop up small objects Constructs simple two and three piece puzzles Enjoys short, simple finger play games Strings large beads on shoelace Builds tower of up to eight blocks	Kicks large ball Jumps in place Runs without falling Throws ball without falling Walks up and down stairs alone Marches to music Tends to use legs and arms as pairs Uses whole arm usually to paint or color
Three-year-olds	Cuts paper Builds tower of nine small blocks Pastes using a finger Pours from a pitcher Copies a circle from a drawing Draws a straight line Uses fingers to pick up small objects Draws a person with three parts Strings beads and can arrange by color and shape Uses a knife to spread at meal or snack time	Catches ball with arms extended forward Throws ball underhand Completes forward somersault Walks up stairs with alternating feet Rides a tricycle skillfully Runs, walks, jumps, and gallops to music Throws ball without losing balance Hops on one foot
Four-year-olds	Buttons or unbuttons buttons Cuts on a line with scissors Completes a six- to eight-piece puzzle Copies a "t" Buckles a belt Zips separated fasteners Adds five parts to an incomplete man	Walks up and down stairs one foot per step Skips on one foot Rides a bicycle with training wheels

Figure 3–2 Continued.

Ages	Fine motor skills	Gross motor skills
Five-year-olds	Uses a knife Copies most letters Traces objects Draws crude objects Colors within lines Copies square, triangle, and diamond shapes Models objects from clay Laces shoes	Tries roller and ice skating Catches ball with hands Jumps from heights Jumps rope Walks on stilts Skips Climbs fences
Six-year-olds	Ties bows Hand preference established Reverses letters while printing Paints houses, trees, flowers, and clouds	Plays hopscotch Enjoys ball play Plays simple, organized games such as "hide- and-seek"

Source: Herr, J., & Libby, Y. (2000). *Creative resources for the early childhood classroom*, 3d ed. Albany, NY: Delmar.

development are diets high in fats and sugars, such as junk food, and inactivity due to sedentary activities such as watching television or playing computer games. Information on proper nutrition for children of all ages is readily available. The food pyramid in Appendix D, provides a guideline for a nutritious diet with examples of good foods and appropriate serving sizes. (See the invited essay in Chapter 4, pages 122–126, for suggestions on working with children who are clinically obese.)

Fine Motor and Gross Motor Skills

Fine motor development is increasing rapidly during the preschool and kindergarten years, as children's small muscles of the hand and fingers become more coordinated. This assists children in performing self-help tasks such as zipping, buttoning, and tying shoes. It is also crucial to their drawing and writing development. Fine motor skills are useful in outdoor play as children grip bars and handles, dig and pour sand or dirt, and engage in tumbling and keeping balance.

It is vital that children have opportunities to move physically, contributing to the development of **gross motor skills.** These skills require the use of large muscles such as those in the legs, arms, and trunk, as well as developing strength and stamina. Trawick-Smith (2000) identifies the following as some of the most rapidly developing gross motor skills and related behaviors during the preschool years.

Walking and Running   Different walking styles are learned during the preschool and kindergarten years, such as walking at a slow versus quick pace, tiptoeing, and walking up and down inclines and steps. Opportunities to run typically occur outdoors. Children enjoy participating in rule-free chasing games where they frequently take turns being chased and chasing others.

Climbing and Jumping Down   Climbing and jumping down require strength and coordination as well as overcoming the fear of varying heights. As children climb they must coordinate the hand-over-hand action as well as maintain enough strength to pull themselves up. The ability to jump down develops gradually in stages beginning with stepping down from elevated surfaces, such as a step, to leaping and landing on one foot at a time. Eventually, with regular playful practice, children can jump with a successfully balanced landing.

Throwing and Catching   Young children with emerging motor skills encounter a number of limitations when they attempt to throw a play object such as a ball. Their overhand throws lack control and the object rarely lands near its intended target. They focus on moving only the arm holding the ball rather than their entire body and can't always time the release of the object.

Catching an object presents a different set of difficulties for the young preschooler. Typically they stand with feet planted firmly on the ground and arms outstretched. Unless the object lands directly in their hands, they rarely make the catch because no attempt is made to adjust their position or grasp the object.

As they approach age five or six, children with experience throwing and catching make significant improvement in their skills. They begin using their whole body and their throws become longer and more accurate (Cratty, 1986). When catching, they begin to move their arms toward the oncoming object and grasp or bend arms to catch it.

There is a wide assortment of different objects available for practicing throwing and catching. Balls that are hard and will hurt on impact should be replaced with balls made from foam or other soft, synthetic material. A pair of socks rolled into one another helps children who are afraid of being hit by tossed objects. Beanbags are ideal for young children learning to catch. Kaplan® educational products offers three different sets of beanbags featuring different colors, numerals/number words, and shapes. Each set is labeled in English, Spanish, and French. Beanbags are also simple and inexpensive to make using leftover fabric and a loose filling.

Balancing　Balance is influenced by the center of gravity, which is higher for young children than teens or adults. See Figure 3–3 for a center of gravity comparison by age. The center of gravity for a five-year-old child is in the ribcage area as opposed to the waist where the center of gravity is for adults. This differentiation in center of gravity influences preschoolers' balance as they run, bend, slide, and land.

Size comparison of children

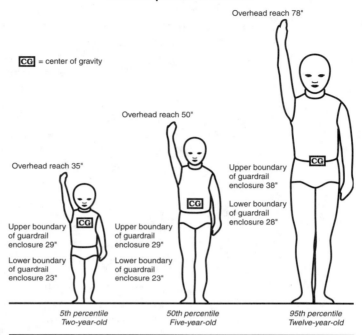

Figure 3–3 Center of gravity comparison chart.

Reprinted with permission National Playground Safety Institute
Certification Curriculum, National Recreation and Park Association,
1999.

Rough-and-Tumble Play Preschoolers and kindergarteners need multiple opportunities throughout the
day to freely walk, run, climb, jump, catch, and throw.
In most cases, children naturally engage in these
movements unless they are restricted. Children in
some group care situations, for instance, are discour-
aged from exhibiting some of these movements out of
fear they will be injured or hurt others. One example is
the rough-and-tumble play many young children
enjoy, which is more pronounced in boys than girls
(Smith, 1997). Many early childhood teachers fear this
type of play will lead to aggression. However, research
shows that the play-fighting, running, and screaming
associated with rough-and-tumble play is beneficial to
motor development and socialization (MacDonald &
Parker, 1986). Sutton-Smith (1988) distinguished be-

tween "real aggression" and "playful aggression" in children's rough-and-tumble play. Ideally, adults should be able to make the fine distinction between the two and permit playful aggression because it does have developmental value (Pellegrini & Perimutter, 1988).

Guidelines for Developmentally Appropriate Preschool Movement Programs

Even though children are naturally engaged in movement experiences as they play in an outdoor setting, experts on physical education and movement emphasize that the development of fundamental motor skills should receive special attention during the preschool years. As a result, the Council on Physical Education for Children (a division of the National Association for Sport and Physical Education) published the document, *Developmentally Appropriate Physical Education Practices for Young Children ages 3–5 (1992)*. The primary focus of this position paper is to emphasize appropriate practices in movement programs for preschoolers enrolled in child care centers, private and public preschools, and kindergartens. According to the National Association for Sport and Physical Education (NASPE) (1990), initiating movement programs for preschoolers is believed to be an important first step toward becoming a *physically educated person* who:

- *has* learned the skills necessary to perform a variety of physical activities.
- *does* participate regularly in physical activity.
- *knows* the implications of and the benefits from involvement in physical activities.
- *values* physical activity and its contributions to a healthful lifestyle.

In other words, participating in and enjoying physical activities has immediate benefits to children as well as contributes to positive, life-long attitudes toward health and fitness.

The preschool and kindergarten years are characterized as the **fundamental movement phase** (Gabbard, 1992; Gallahue, 1989; Wickstrom, 1983), a period when children are learning movement skills that are the foundation for learning more complex skills in later phases of development. The Council on Physical Education for Children (COPEC), 1992, outlined five premises for understanding movement programs for preschoolers who are in the fundamental movement phase:

1. Three-, four-, and five-year-old children are different from elementary school-age children in terms of motor development.
2. Young children learn through interaction with their environment.
3. Teachers of young children are guides or facilitators.
4. Young children learn and develop in an integrated fashion.
5. Planned movement experiences enhance play experiences.

The document, *Developmentally Appropriate Physical Education Practices for Young Children ages 3–5* (COPEC, 1992), is a valuable resource for teachers, parents, directors, school administrators, and policy makers. Twenty-five different components describe the characteristics of appropriate practice in movement programs including: teaching strategies, fine and gross motor activities, cognitive development, affective development, integration with other curriculur areas, frequency, equipment, safety, and assessment. Following the format of an early position paper published by the National Association for the Education of Young Children (Bredekamp, 1987), the guidelines are specific to help the reader identify practices that are in the best interest of children (appropriate) and practices that are counterproductive (inappropriate).

AGE-APPROPRIATE OUTDOOR PLAY EXPERIENCES

Outdoor play offers a wide spectrum of opportunities for promoting growth and development in the cognitive, language, social-emotional, and physical domains of development. As children experiment and interact with different materials they are learning to problem-solve, adding to and strengthening their repertoire of cognitive processes. Language skills multiply, as children must find words to express their unique thoughts and individual needs, with peers as well as with adults. The freedom of playing outdoors presents new challenges for learning to play with peers as well as finding peaceful resolutions to the ever-present conflicts. Children's emotional needs are met as they express themselves in different ways, through shouting, jumping, or simply finding a quiet place to sit and think. And of course, adequate physical development cannot occur without the opportunity to run, jump, climb, and throw—activities that typically occur only outdoors. Fine motor as well as gross motor skills are developed with experiences such as pouring, digging, and gripping.

Because of the many benefits, outdoor play for preschoolers is much more than a time for simply letting off steam. It is a crucial part of the overall preschool experience. In order to emphasize the necessity of outdoor play and its value as part of the overall curriculum, teachers can determine goals for outdoor play and share these with parents. Examples of goals for outdoor play include the following.

Provide children with opportunities to:

- experience new physical challenges.
- develop strength and stamina.
- use large muscles and fine muscles in new ways.
- express themselves verbally with different voice levels.
- engage in problem solving during outdoor play.
- physically interact with peers by chasing, talking, and playing.
- appreciate nature and protect the environment.
- contribute to the improvement of their school, community, and world.

Planning for Complexity and Variety in Outdoor Play

Kritchevsky, Prescott, and Walling (1977) are pioneers in analyzing and planning play spaces for young children, both indoors and out. This well-respected group of researchers suggests, that adults consider the **complexity and variety of play units** when planning physical spaces for children. A play unit is a single, designated area containing objects for play and it may or may not have tangible boundaries. For example, a sandbox, playhouse, and trike path are play units with obvious visible boundaries. The area around a slide and swing set may not have tangible boundaries. Complexity refers to play units and "the extent to which they contain potential for active manipulation and alteration by children" (Kritchevsky, Prescott, & Walling, 1977, p. 11). In other words, the complexity of a play unit dictates the approximate number of children that can be accommodated at one time as well as the potential for keeping children interested for some period of time. Determining the complexity of the various play units available in a play yard is crucial to understanding and designing outdoor spaces for young children.

The three different levels of complexity used to analyze play units are simple, complex, and super. Each type of play unit is defined with supporting examples. A simple unit is a play area with one obvious use and no available loose parts or accessories. Examples of a simple unit are a swing, a tricycle, or a spring riding toy. A complex unit is a play area with two different types of play materials that enable children to improvise. Examples of a complex play unit are a play house with dolls, or a water table with a toy boat. A super play unit is a complex play area with one or more *additional* play materials. Examples of a super play unit are a collection of packing crates with hollow blocks and boards or a log cabin playhouse with a table, chairs, and dishes.

A final example distinguishing among simple, complex, and super play units is a sandbox. When it contains only sand, it is considered a simple play unit. By offering a shovel and pail set, it is now a complex play unit. Adding, a spray bottle filled with water now makes this a super play unit that will accommodate more children and extend the time they remain interested in the sandbox.

In addition to play units, Kritchevsky, Prescott, and Walling (1977) recommend teachers plan for **potential units.** There are empty spaces surrounded by tangible boundaries. Potential units may be arranged by placing a table and chair or blanket in a remote corner of the play yard or they may evolve naturally, such as a shady area under a tree. These poten-

tial units encourage children to use the space in their own unique way (such as dramatic play) or they can be used to introduce materials available for a limited time (such as puzzles or a basket of books).

In order to calculate how many play spaces are needed to accommodate the number of children playing at once, a value system was devised. Simple units are given a value rating of one, complex play units a value rating of four, and super units a value rating of eight. After determining the complexity of the play unit for each available activity, a value can be assigned. The assigned values are totaled and divided by the number of children playing at one time. In order for an environment to offer enough choices to children, there should be a least 2.5 play spaces per child. This process is illustrated by evaluating an existing play yard and calculating its complexity of play units. (See Figure 3–4.)

In addition to the complexity of play spaces, the variety of experiences offered need to be analyzed. Variety in play units is explained as the "particular activity they invite from the children" (Kritchevsky, Prescott, & Walling, 1977, p. 12). A broad variation in the types of activities offered provides more opportunities for play and learning. Variety of play units and complexity of play units should be planned together. Clearly, a play yard that can accommodate preschoolers and kindergarten children in terms of complexity

Figure 3–4 Evaluating and making improvements to an existing preschool playground.

A suburban church preschool recently did a "makeover" of their outdoor play yard. From the parking lot, parents and children view a colorful, fenced play area divided into two sections. The following equipment is on the right side of the dividing fence and intended for preschoolers three to five years. Unit values are presented.

Play unit	Complexity	Value
3 swings	simple	3
1 freestanding slide	simple	1
1 elevated barrel-type tunnel	simple	1
1 playhouse	simple	1
1 combination slide, platform/ lookout	complex	4
TOTAL		10

Even though the play yard is attractive and the equipment is new, the majority of activities offered are simple units thus limiting the number of children that can be accommodated at one time and the potential for keeping children interested. If the 2.5 play spaces per child rule is enforced on the play yard as it currently exists, only 4 children could effectively play outdoors together! When a few minor changes are made, the playground is more appropriate and able to accommodate a realistic number of children. Unit values are given for each.

Play unit	Complexity	Value
small table and 2 chairs placed inside the playhouse along with dishes, tub, and sponge	super complex	8
3 sets of binoculars (with strap removed) placed in plastic basket on the platform/lookout	complex	4
4 railroad ties form a square pit filled with playground sand. 4 buckets, shovels, sieves, rakes, and pump water bottles are available.	super complex	8
child-size table placed in a shady corner with a tub full of modeling dough stored in sandwich bags, cookie cutters, and rolling pins	super complex	8
4 plastic milk crates and two 2"×6"×4' boards	complex	4
2 playground balls	simple	2
TOTAL		34

Figure 3–4 Continued.

While relatively few changes are made to the playground with minimal expense and labor, the complexity and variety of play activities offered to children is increased significantly. When the play units from the updated playground are added to the existing units that were not altered (3 swings, 1 freestanding slide, and 1 elevated barrel-type tunnel), the total is 39 play units. The same play yard can now accommodate 15 children as opposed to the original 4. From this example, it is easy to see how minor modifications can be made to transform an existing play yard.

---

without meeting the need for variety in their play cannot be considered adequate. The categories and examples for variety of play equipment are listed in Figure 3–5. The list contains play equipment and materials typical to many preschool playgrounds but it is not all-inclusive.

When planning age-appropriate playgrounds, equipment should be selected from each category to ensure variety. The preschool playground evaluated in Figure 3–4 offers the following types of variety: slide, swings, playhouse, art activity, crates and boards, digging area and equipment, and playground balls.

OUTDOOR LEARNING CENTERS

A familiar and logical way to add complexity and variety to outdoor play spaces is to introduce materials typically used indoors. Explore the learning centers found in preschool and kindergarten classrooms and replicate these in the play yard using supplies better suited for outdoor play. Introducing materials outdoors sometimes makes them more desirable from a teacher's perspective when it reduces clean-up of the more fluid or messy types of materials, such as paints, sand, and water. Incorporating learning centers such as art, manipulatives, blocks, dramatic play, and woodworking into the play yard gives children more choices, extends the time they will spend in a play area, and contributes to the overall appropriateness of outdoor play. Attention to modifications for children with special needs such as physical challenges, hearing and visual impairments, and limited understanding can make the outdoor play area an ideal learning environment for all children.

Figure 3–5 Planning for variety in outdoor play spaces.

The following categories can assist adults as they plan for a variety of equipment and materials in outdoor play spaces.

1. Arm-hanging units: jungle gym, monkey bars, rings
2. Blocks: large hollow packing crates, boards, sawhorses, pole, milk crates, large cardboard boxes
3. Boats/cars: stripped boat/car, canoe, inflatable raft
4. Climbing units: climbing steps, jungle gym, ramps, tree stump
5. Digging area: built-in sandbox, sand table, designated area with soil
6. Play house: commercial, plastic, homemade, wooden tent, cardboard (appliance box)
7. Slides: sliding "firefighter's" pole, tubular slide, flat sliding board
8. Spring-based toys
9. Swings*: tire (hung horizontally or vertically), traditional swing, bucket swing, porch swing
10. Tunnels: stationary barrel, cardboard
11. Water area: water table, hose and dishpan
12. Wheeled toys: tricycles, pedal cars, wheelbarrow, wagons

Text above reprinted with permission from the National Association for the Education of Young Children.

Author's note: For children ages 0–4, swings have the highest injury incident rates according to the NPPS. If swings are included in the play yard, they must be placed away from other areas where children play. In addition to injuries sustained by children on swings, the height and speed achieved can bring harm to other children in the vicinity. Young children typically focus on a desired activity and become unaware of what is occurring around them. This leads to injuries as children walk directly in front of or behind swings in motion on their way to another area in the play yard. Replacing heavy swing seats with lightweight materials such as canvas or rubber belts can reduce injuries. Another way to reduce chances of injury is to set individual swings far enough apart to avoid collisions. Frost (1992) suggests 24″ between swings and 36″ between swings and support posts with an appropriate height based on the age and size of the child using equipment. Another option is to replace traditional strap swings with tire swings hung horizontally. Tire swings accommodate more than one child and naturally promote socialization and cooperation. However, they also require a great deal of space. CPSC Guidelines require 30″ to 36″ of clearance between extended swing arc and support post (Frost, 1992). An additional danger associated with swing sets occurs when children use the horizontal bar designed to support swings for swinging, sitting, and standing. These bars are a dangerous height for children and often have no safe surfacing underneath to cushion falls. In order to omit the many types of injuries associated with swings, Theemes (1999) recommends excluding swings from preschool play yards, especially where space is limited and when children have opportunities to swing at home or on public playgrounds with vigilant parental supervision.

Outdoor Art Center

Art experiences appeal to children's need for constructive play (Piaget, 1962) and practice using symbols (Vygotsky, 1962). One way to expand children's opportunities to express themselves through art is to incorporate experiences into outdoor play. This may be done simply by adding folding tables where children can stand and have access to simple art supplies such as paper, crayons, scissors, and glue (Frost, 1992). Old sheets or butcher paper can be attached to a fence with tape or clothes pins and colored with markers, paints, or pump spray bottles filled with diluted tempera paints. Easels can be dismantled and attached side-by-side to a wall or fence to encourage conversation and socialization as children paint.

The outdoors is a perfect place to introduce *messier* materials such as talc-free moist clay, a material used by potters. This material offers many advantages over other modeling materials and has been reintroduced to the early childhood community as a result of observations made at the Reggio Emilio preschool programs in Italy. (Koster, 1999). Sun Clay is another good option because it can be hardened in the sun but

won't crumble like dried Play-Doh™ (Scholastic Early Childhood Today, 1995, p. 57).

Sun Clay Recipe

Materials needed:	Ingredients:
• measuring cup	2/3 cup water
• cooking pot	2 cups salt
• large spoon	1/2 cup water
• mixing bowl	1 cup cornstarch
• plastic bag (w/seal)	food coloring (optional)
• smocks	
• plastic trays	

Directions: Combine salt and 2/3 cup of water in the pot. Stir over medium heat for 4–5 minutes, until the salt is dissolved. Remove from heat. In a separate bowl, gradually mix 1/2 cup of water with the cornstarch. Stir until smooth and add to the salt mixture. Return the pot to the heat and cook over low heat, stirring until smooth. Add food coloring to the mixture if desired. Store the clay in a sealed bag.

Children can easily create collages from objects they find in the play yard. In addition to gluing items on paper, children can make nature bracelets by sticking small objects such as acorns and leaves to a strip of wide electrical tape which has been wrapped adhesive-side-up on their wrists (Elmore, July 2000). Creating art outdoors offers new challenges and opportunities for problem solving as well as a natural setting for working with organic materials.

Kieff and Casbergue (2000) suggest helpful adaptations for the traditional indoor art center that apply to the outdoor play area as well. Children with physical challenges respond well to modeling dough. The density of the dough can be varied to match the strength and fine motor skills of the child. A child can simply poke, pat, and roll the dough or use basic tools and utensils as they play with it. Paper can be secured to the table or easel with light-tack tape to prevent it from slipping when children with physical limitations are coloring, painting, or drawing. Select scissors from the different types available to best fit the needs of individual children.

Outdoor Manipulative Center

Manipulatives are made available to children outdoors on tables or on separate trays in shady, quiet areas. Puzzles of differing degrees of difficulty offer opportunities for feelings of success and challenge. Pairs of children can work together to complete puzzles with more pieces and fewer visual clues. Floor size puzzles can be put together on concrete or other hard play surfaces.

There is a wide variety of manipulative materials available. These may include objects collected from around the home or manipulatives purchased from a commercial vendor or school supply store. Buttons, keys, marbles, golf tees, and milk caps can be sorted and stored separately offering opportunities to explore, observe, discuss, and classify. Commercial manipulatives include pattern blocks, counting bears, attribute blocks, stringing beads, pegboards, and puzzles. Offering these materials in an outdoor setting provides children with a quiet activity to balance out more physical actions.

Kieff and Casbergue (2000) emphasize the connection between manipulating objects and developing physical and logico-mathematical knowledge in children with special needs. Their suggestions for the classroom manipulative center are relevant to an outdoor version as well. Making materials accessible to children with physical challenges is a priority regardless of adaptive devices such as wheelchairs and walkers. Attaching handles or knobs to manipulatives such as puzzle pieces and pattern blocks makes it easier for children with limited fine motor skills to handle objects. Children who are hearing impaired benefit from learning new signs to reflect concepts being learned such as shapes, colors, and sizes. Include materials for children with visual disabilities that can be sorted by touch such as manipulatives that vary in size or texture. Children with limited understanding may need more time and opportunities to interact with materials, grasp concepts, and explain their observations and discoveries.

Outdoor Block Center   Hollow blocks, designed by Caroline Pratt early in the twentieth century, were once considered essential equipment for the preschool play yard. Originally, the blocks were completely enclosed, but manufacturers today leave them open on one side for easier gripping and handling. Unlike smaller blocks, hollow blocks can be used to build child-size buildings, which are later utilized for dramatic play. Because of their size (the double square measures 5 1/2″ × 11″ × 22″), hollow blocks require group effort to lift, carry, stack, and arrange. Hollow blocks can be stored in an outdoor shed or closet, or carried indoors in a wagon so children can also play with them in the classroom.

If hollow blocks are not an option, other types of bulky building materials can be substituted such as cardboard boxes with flaps closed and taped down or milk crates in conjunction with long, wide boards at least 3/4″ thick. These substitute materials cannot replace the value of playing with wooden hollow blocks, but provide key building and play experiences.

Children with a range of abilities will benefit from a variety of different types of building materials as well as modifications made to blocks (Wellhousen & Kieff, 2001). Children with physical challenges may prefer lighter or soft, grippable blocks. Smooth blocks can be adapted by wrapping a section with a nonslip surface such as several wide rubber bands. Blocks are a highly visible material; therefore, children with hearing impairments can communicate to peers by demonstrating building strategies. Adults can enrich the experience through signing with the child and translating to the play group. A child who is visually impaired may be most comfortable with blocks that interlock or snack together such as Waffle Blocks®, Snap Blocks®, or Legos®. Children with limited understanding need to be given additional time to explore and experiment with the material, especially if they show and express interest in remaining in the block area for an extended period of time.

Outdoor Dramatic Play Center

Pretending dominates play in preschool and kindergarten so making props available outdoors facilitates their understanding of symbols and symbolic play. Many preschool playgrounds offer a playhouse but

often it is a site of aggression and conflict. This generally occurs because there are no materials to keep the role-playing going once it is initiated. Therefore, a small group of children may decide to be the members of one family with assigned roles but lack objects that support their role-play. By simply adding a few items such as a broom and dustpan, dishes and dish tub, and table and chairs, the children have the props necessary to engage in valuable pretend play.

Materials to motivate role-play can be added to other parts of the play yard, such as placing binoculars (with strap removed) on platforms, dress-up clothes representing community helpers near the trike path, and baby dolls in the water table. Large appliance boxes can be temporarily introduced as play houses. Many dramatic play materials used in the classroom can be brought outdoors for dramatic play.

Dramatic play boosts confidence as well as reinforces concepts through pleasurable activity, which makes it an ideal learning center for children with disabilities. Include all children in dramatic play outdoors by considering the following modifications (Kieff & Casbergue, 2000). Children with physical disabilities are limited in their ability to act out ideas so adults should be prepared to physically move props or act out ideas themselves. Children who are hearing impaired benefit from visual clues used in play such as realistic props. Introduce visually impaired children to props by allowing them to hold and explore them, thereby picking up on tactile clues. Those with limited understanding benefit from the extra opportunities to explore basic concepts in a meaningful context. More realistic props are needed until they develop the ability to substitute objects for props.

Outdoor Woodworking Center

Children need experiences with different creative materials including those that come from nature (Sosna, 2000) and there are many rewards for children and teachers in a woodworking center. Some adults, however, disregard this form of constructive play (Frost, 1992) and others have specific reasons for their hesitation regarding woodworking experiences. Huber (1999) offers typical reasons for concern along with explanations for overcoming hesitation. A common concern about working with tools in a woodworking center is the safety of the children. Working with real materials does alert us to the fact that injuries could occur. Proper safety measures, however, will considerably reduce risks, just as they do in other aspects of children's play. Huber (1999) suggests the following rules for a woodworking center.

1. Safety goggles must be worn at all times.
2. An adult must be present when tools are in use.
3. Use tools only as they were intended.
4. Return all tools and materials to their proper place.

A second common concern is the expense of setting up and maintaining a woodworking center (Sosna, 2000). Good tools can be expensive but a one-time investment will last for years. Teachers can also request donations from parents and the community. When finances are extremely limited, start with only a few basic tools and add to them gradually. It is important to invest in quality, authentic woodworking tools as opposed to those made for children. Large pieces of pine or poplar can be purchased from a lumber yard and cut into sizes more manageable for children. This is preferable to using donated wood that may be treated with toxic chemicals or have nails, staples, and splinters. Teachers do not necessarily have to be woodworders but they should be thoroughly familiar with tools and materials. Adults can occasionally encourage children's creativity in the woodworking center, but also need to encourage them to work as real builders, by following a design, pattern, set of instructions, or model. Figure 3–6 offers a list of suggested basic equipment needed to set up a woodworking area.

The woodworking center should be closely supervised and safety precautions such as wearing goggles should always be taken. Outdoor woodworking has many advantages such as less concern over noise levels and debris; however, special care and storage of materials must be taken into consideration. The woodworking center may be placed in a private corner of the playground or in a separate outdoor location.

Figure 3–6 Basic equipment for woodworking center.

hammers
hand saws: crosscut, coping, keyhole, or compass
pliers
metal clamps
drills: hand drill, brace and bit
rulers/tape measures
pencils
scissors
sandpaper
nails
screwdrivers: standard and Phillips
screws
vise grips
planes
levels
glue
safety goggles
files
crowbars

Reprinted with permission from the National Association for the Education of Young Children.

PLANNING THE PHYSICAL ARRANGEMENT OF THE PLAYGROUND

Equally important as the complexity and variety in play units is the physical arrangement of the outdoor play area. The arrangement of fixed and portable playground equipment influences children's play choices, the amount of time spent in an area, and social behavior. Permanent equipment on playgrounds typically consist of modular components combining steps, decks, slides, bridges, ramps, climbers, horizontal ladders, sliding poles, and other manufactured or constructed play equipment. Combinations of equipment can be linked together to increase the overall size of the structure, as well as provide variety and increase the number of children that can be accommodated. These *superstructures* begin with a basic 4 × 4 foot or 6 × 6 foot deck with an activity component attached to each of the four sides (Frost, 1992). Sizes of superstructures increase as decks are linked together with additional activity components such as a bridge. Manufacturers offer many options when selecting a superstructure and most equipment can easily be customized to suit a school's particular needs.

Dramatic play often emerges as children climb, slide, and move around superstructures. Play scenarios can be enhanced by placing additional dramatic play equipment, such as play houses, forts, and castles nearby. Spring-mounted action vehicles that accommodate two to twelve children will naturally be integrated into dramatic play. PlayDesigns® offers the "Rockin' Rides" line that includes a pickup truck, school bus, fire truck, sailboat, and helicopter. This company's "Themed Play" activity centers are also designed to promote imaginative play and include a bulldozer, schooner, train, and spaceship.

The second type of permanently fixed structure common to most playgrounds is the swing set. Ideally, it will be placed in a remote area of the play yard, out of direct traffic (Frost, 1992). Regardless of whether single-axis swings (conventional swings with strap seat), multi-axis swings (tires mounted horizontally to accommodate two or three children at once), toddler swings, or wheelchair platform swings are used, they can all be a hazard to preschoolers who are not aware of the ever-present danger. (See Figure 3–5 for a detailed discussion of the danger of swings.)

An area for riding and parking wheeled vehicles is an essential component of the play yard. Toys that children can ride in under their own power offer opportunities for children to feel autonomous, develop gross motor skills, learn to follow rules, and role-play. Ideally, the play yard will have a wheeled vehicle track where children can ride tricycles, pedal, and push cars. The surface must be hard and smooth enough for children to ride on and should lead riders through visually interesting parts of the play yard. A traffic pattern needs to be planned in advance to minimize accidents and prevent interruption of other children's play. At minimum, a concrete slab with a pathway identified by paint or chalk provides a place where children can ride.

Ancillary play areas, such as learning centers, activity areas, or zones, can be placed along the perimeter of the play yard. These areas should be highly visible yet set apart from areas that promote more physically active play. Accommodations also need to be made for quiet, restful areas. These may be situated by placing a bench or blanket under a tree that provides natural shade or a table and chairs under a canopy, awning, or porch overhang.

Space that is not occupied with play equipment or learning centers can be used for play with loose parts. Children enjoy finding and claiming an unused area to set up an obstacle course, play jump rope, or build a hut with crates, boards, and blankets.

Children appreciate play areas that are aesthetically pleasing rather than sterile. Ensuring that natural, green spaces are retained provides places for children to run, chase, and play games. Small gardens at the edge of the play yard offer meaningful opportunities to dig, sow, water, observe, and harvest plants. An undisturbed, natural area adjacent to the play yard can be established as an animal habitat.

Provisions for storage must also be considered when designing a play yard. A waterproof, locked storage area ensures that wheeled vehicles, materials for learning centers, loose parts, and gardening supplies will be protected.

An additional feature of a good play setting for children under the age of six is a covered patio or enclosed porch. This area offers opportunities for gross motor play even in extreme weather conditions. Covered play areas are essential in extremely hot or wet climates. Even when weather conditions would otherwise prevent it, children can move to a protected area where they are less restricted in movement and making noise. Confinement to the indoors can be stressful, so providing an alternate, protected area for children to play is essential to helping them release excess energy (Wolfgang & Wolfgang, 1992).

An ideal outdoor play design provided by Grounds for Play® is presented in Figure 3–7. Notable features of this artist's rendering include the following:

- The toddlers' play space is separate from older children's but both groups of children can see and communicate with one another.

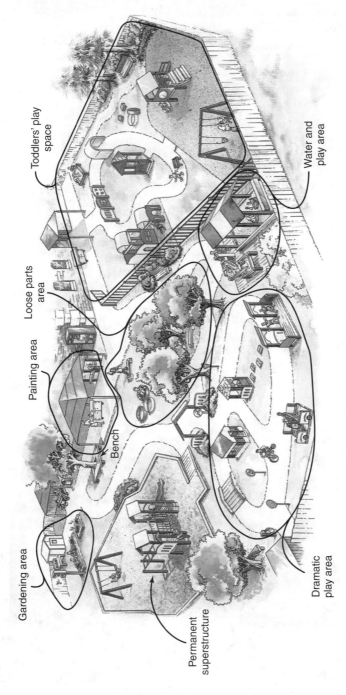

Figure 3–7 Artist's rendering of playground (labeling by author).

Reprinted with permission from Grounds for Play, Inc., Mansfield, Texas.

- Permanent superstructures are in a prominent area and offer multiple opportunities for gross motor play.
- There are several structures that can be used for dramatic play, and these are clustered together.
- Swing sets are not attached to the superstructures and are placed away from high traffic areas.
- The wheeled vehicle track is an interesting formation and leads to the large storage area. Traffic signs help minimize accidents and contribute to children's growing awareness of symbols.
- Activity areas such as a paint easel, water play center, and sand box are placed around the perimeter of the play yard.
- Accommodations for rest and quiet time have been made by placing benches under and around shade trees and by adding a table under a canopy.
- Space for play with loose parts is available.
- Green spaces have been retained along with trees and bushes that contribute to the aesthetic quality of the play yard.
- A small gardening area is designated by deep borders and placed close to the storage shed. An adjacent bird feeder attracts wildlife.
- Several storage facilities are available throughout the play yard. Two of the smaller storage units are on wheels so they can easily be relocated as needed.

- Fall zones have adequate surfacing and the play yard is wheelchair accessible.

Designing Pathways

A crucial feature of smooth-functioning play yards is the designation of clear paths. Kritchevsky, Prescott, and Walling (1977) define paths as "the empty space on the floor or ground through which people move in getting from one place to another; it need be no different in composition from the rest of the surface. A clear path is broad, elongated and easily visible. Paths are very difficult to describe in words, but when they are well defined they are easily seen" (p. 16).

Paths should be clear, lead to play units (not a dead end), and be easily visible to the child. Too much large equipment placed closely together in a small play yard makes it difficult to establish and see paths. The opposite scenario can create the same problem. When a large amount of empty space (dead space) is prevalent, it is difficult for children to logically follow paths. Instead, they are drawn to the dead space, which offers little to do, and they inevitably engage in potentially dangerous, aggressive play. Dead space can be eliminated by placing an activity in the area (such as hollow blocks, crates, and boards) or by creating an obvious boundary so it becomes a potential unit. When planning pathways, adults should kneel down to a child's eye level to determine how a preschooler would view the area and where they may go based on the choice of paths visible.

Adding Immediate Interest to Outdoor Play

Many ideas have been presented to encourage teachers to add complexity, variety, and interest to outdoor play yards as well as plan for appropriate physical arrangement and paths. A list of fifty additional ideas for spicing up children's outside play is presented in Figure 3–8. Introduce only one or two new ideas at a time to minimize confusion and overstimulation. Most of these activities require little expense or labor so when children become bored or show a lack of interest, materials can simply be removed from the play yard. Activities that have the most success in involving children in play and learning can be retained for a longer period of time or reintroduced periodically.

Figure 3–8 Adding immediate interest to preschool playgrounds.

1. Dig and collect rocks from the play yard. Wash with detergent, water, and scrub brushes. Note differences when wet and dry.
2. Classify rocks according to different criteria selected by the children, big, bumpy, reddish, heavy.
3. Color pavement with sidewalk chalk. Explore changes when sprayed with a pump water bottle.
4. Paint with water using different size brushes and rollers.
5. Introduce a large, empty appliance box. It can become a house, bus, boat, barrel, or puppet theatre. Paint with tempera.
6. Bury small items in the sandbox. Make rebus cards to represent each item. Children take turns finding the item on their card.
7. Create tool kits for excavating with a trowel, magnifying glass, sieve, and brush.
8. Attach crepe paper to dowels, and make flags and pinwheels available for windy days.
9. Mix 12 cups water, 4 tablespoons glycerin (from pharmacy) and 1 cup dishwashing liquid to make a bubble solution. Make wands from pipe cleaners and plastic 6-pack drink holders.
10. Make sun clay.
11. Make sun tea.
12. Pack up items used in the classroom in old suitcases to be carried outdoors, such as books, magnetic board and magnets, portable chalkboard and blanket, or beach towel.
13. Empty and wash clean dishwashing soap bottles. Fill bottles over a bucket with a funnel and cup. Squirt at a designated target or water plants.
14. Attach wipe-off boards to chain link fence with velcro. Make available suitable markers and eraser.
15. Bring in bales of pine straw for climbing. Clip wires and straw can be pulled apart and scattered under trees or used to create a "farm" scene.
16. Plant seeds in small containers placed outdoors. Water and observe. As they grow, transplant to larger containers such as barrels.
17. Lay down an old conveyor belt to be used as a trike path.
18. Hang wind chimes in trees or from roof.
19. Play rhythm band instruments in an outdoor circle time.
20. Supply children with a toy microphone for giving weather reports and news reports of outdoor events.
21. Wash dolls and their clothing. Hang on a fence with clothespins.
22. Hold a car wash to clean trikes, wagons, and other wheeled toys. Wear smocks and rubber gloves. Use pump spray bottles and sponges.
23. Fill pump spray bottle with water and a few drops of food color. Spray on old sheet or mural paper taped to wire fence or spray on snowdrifts.
24. During warm weather add ice cubes and larger blocks of ice (frozen in reusable plastic containers or plastic sandwich bags) to water table.
25. Add food color and craft sticks to ice cube trays filled with water. When frozen, paint with melting ice.

Figure 3–8   Continued.

26. Draw around shadows using sidewalk chalk and trace footprints. Return to same spot at different times of the day and compare shadow sizes and placement.
27. Bring cassette player outside and play music, which inspires dance and movement.
28. Fill the bottom of 1-liter soda bottles with sand and set up as bowling pins.
29. Provide light hand weights for children to lift.
30. Offer plastic milk-type crates and wide boards for constructing.
31. A plastic wading pool can be a boat for two children or a quiet place to read or color alone.
32. Weave crepe paper through a chain link fence. Create a pattern.
33. Add scented bubble bath to the water table.
34. Unhinge a two-sided easel and attach to fence where children can paint side-by-side.
35. Measure and record rainfall using a clear container with 1/2" markings.
36. Offer beanbag type animals for dramatic play, tossing, catching, sliding, and balancing.
37. Give children balloons to throw and catch. They give children more time to move in position and hit.
38. Make ice cream with a crank ice cream maker.
39. Make body paints by mixing Ivory Snow Flakes™ with water until a paste consistency forms. Then add a few drops of food color. Use brushes to paint legs, arms, or trunk when children are wearing swimsuits. Rinse off in hose or sprinkler.
40. Sprinkle brightly colored fish aquarium gravel in sandbox and provide cups for children to collect their found "treasure."
41. Tie bells to top of swings.
42. Use old watercolor markers to draw in snow.
43. Add plastic flowers, plastic pots, hand shovels, and pump spray bottles to the sandbox for planting and arranging.
44. Attach one end of a dryer vent hose to fence within children's reach. Drop tennis balls through top. Later add containers such as buckets to be used as targets. Children can hold opposite end of hose to hit the mark.
45. Place a blanket and basket of books in a shady area.
46. When weather permits, nap outdoors in tents.
47. Cut plastic gutters in 3' pieces and snap on end caps to protect children from sharp edges. They can be used for pouring water or racing small cars.
48. Spray paint pebbles or rocks gold and bury in sand.
49. Use an old sheet for parachute activities.
50. From a tree, hang an object 6"–12" above children's heads so they can attempt to jump and reach it.

✿INTEGRATED UNIT

There are many opportunities for play and learning outdoors beyond the play yard. One way to offer new experiences is through units that integrate curricula and are planned around or include elements of the outdoors. Teachers may choose to watch for topics that emerge from children's play and implement a project approach to learning as suggested by Katz & Chard (1989). For the purposes of this chapter, an integrated unit has been designed for a preschool classroom in order to illustrate how they can be centered around an environmental topic.

Integrated Unit: Establishing and Maintaining a Wildlife Habitat

The purpose of the Wildlife Habitat thematic unit is for children to understand the needs of living creatures and contribute to the survival of different species in the region. Through the guidance of a knowledgeable teacher, they will learn about wildlife, conservation, and the environment as well as important literacy and numeric skills. Concepts to be learned through this unit include:

- All living things needs food, water, shelter, and a place to raise their young.
- People can help animals by providing the things they need (creating a wildlife habitat).
- Wildlife habitats help butterflies, birds, frogs, turtles, and other animals, depending on where it is created.
- Each species in a wildlife habitat needs different types of food, shelter, and places to raise their young. They all need water.
- There are many different varieties of butterflies, birds, frogs, and turtles. You can learn about different kinds from books, videos, and experts.
- Birds and turtles hatch from eggs.
- Butterflies begin life as a caterpillar and later spin a chrysalis and emerge with wings. This process is called *metamorphosis.*
- Frogs begin life as tadpoles. They also go through a metamorphosis as they develop into frogs.

Throughout the unit, additional concepts may naturally surface.

Information for the Teacher

Establishing a wildlife habitat can be as simple as placing a birdfeeder and birdbath near a large tree, but most young children's interest and curiosity will take the theme much further. A wildlife habitat requires that four elements be present: food, water, shelter, and a place to raise young. The variety and species of animals attracted to the habitat will depend on the geographic location, climate, season, species indigenous to the area, and the types of food and shelter provided. Most wildlife habitats can easily support butterflies and birds. Some habitats will also attract frogs and turtles, depending on the factors listed above.

Butterflies Butterflies can be drawn to a wildlife habitat by creating a *butterfly garden* that has all the things they need to live, grow, and reproduce. Find an area that is accessible to the children but away from noisy, high-traffic areas such as a playground. There should be no insecticides used near the butterfly garden since they are insects and the chemicals will kill them. It is advisable to plant the butterfly garden in an area sheltered from wind and in a sunny location. This prevents them from getting too cold from breezes and having to use extra energy to fight wind currents when feeding. Butterflies can fly well only when their body temperature is between 85 and 100 degrees Fahrenheit. When air temperature is cooler, they bask themselves in the sun.

The main food source for butterflies is nectar from flowers that they are attracted to by color. Plant clusters of flowers with red, orange, and bright pink blooms. (Check with local nurseries to identify the best variety for your area.) Also provide food for caterpillars, which include a different variety of plants such as dill, parsley, and sunflowers. A birdbath serves as a fresh water source and it should frequently be replenished during dry weather.

Birds Although the variety of birds attracted to the wildlife habitat will depend on a number of geographical factors, most varieties will thrive on the birdseed mixes that can be purchased in bulk. Birdfeeders can be placed in trees or on poles designed to hold them. If feeders are out of children's reach, move them so children can refill them as needed. Feeder poles can be greased to prevent squirrels from devouring the food meant for birds. Birdbaths must be refilled daily and cleaned as needed.

Birds find their shelter in trees but children can assist with nest building by making nesting balls. Place bits of string, yarn, fabric, and cotton in mesh bags (the type bunches of grapes are packaged in). Tie the bags closed and hang them in trees. Birds can pull out needed materials to use in building their nests. Children can later observe nests built in the habitat and surrounding area and perhaps discover items from the nesting balls. Do not include materials that can be harmful to birds and their young such as lint from clothes dryers and materials containing plastics.

Hummingbirds are a challenge to attract but placing a special feeder for them in the butterfly garden will encourage them to visit. They are attracted to red, so purchased feeders with red casings are preferable. Or tie something red to an existing feeder. (It is not recommended that red food color be added to the nectar solution because the effects of red dye on hummingbirds are not known.) Nectar solution can be purchased but it is more meaningful for children to mix it themselves. Simply mix one part granulated sugar with four parts warm water. *Note:* Do not use sugar substitutes as they have no nutritional value and *never* use honey, because hummingbirds cannot digest it and will die.

The hummingbird feeder must be kept clean by pouring out unused solution at least once a week (more often if solution becomes cloudy) and cleaning with vinegar and hot water. Never use a dishwashing detergent. If ants take over the feeder, coat the string used to hang the feeder with vegetable oil to prevent them from climbing on it. Leave the feeder up as long as hummingbirds are returning to it because they naturally migrate to their winter homes.

Turtles   Land turtles will be attracted to some wildlife habitats. They live in fields or woods near water and cannot stand long exposure to heat or cold. Land turtles like to emerge themselves in water and crawl on rocks or a log to sun themselves. They have no teeth but sharp jaws for cutting and biting food (or enemies). Many land turtles eat earthworms, crickets, grasshoppers, slugs, mice, tomatoes, strawberries, dandelions, and other green, leafy plants. To attract turtles to the wildlife habitat, provide fresh water, large flat rocks in sunlight, and a brush or log pile for hiding, sleeping, and hibernating.

Frogs   Frogs are amphibians with moist smooth skin (as opposed to toads that have dry bumpy skin). Unlike toads, frogs need to be near water at all times. Since they lay their eggs in water to keep them moist, frogs prefer calm, shallow water such as a pond, marsh, swamp, or even a large puddle. To attract frogs, the National Wildlife Federation recommends creating a home for them with a medium-size clay pot and saucer. The pot is turned upside down and propped up on a rock so frogs can hide underneath it. Another method is to turn the pot on its side and bury 1/3 of it into the ground. The saucer is used to provide water next to the shelter. Frogs eat pesky insects in their environment.

Frog eggs are laid in groups or clumps. Each egg is a tiny dark spot surrounded by a thick, clear, jelly-like substance that protects the egg. The tiny tadpole inside grows longer and curls into a comma shape. In order to attract egg-laying frogs that can be observed as they grow and develop into tadpoles, build a simple pond such as the one described in Figure 3–9.

Introducing the Integrated Unit

Help children hang a birdfeeder from a tree visible through a classroom window but away from high-traffic and noisy areas. Place a birdbath or other water source nearby. Replenish with birdseed and fresh water regularly. Provide binoculars and informational books on birds with color pictures. Model interest in looking at birds and trying to identify their species. Keep a log-book where the different types of birds and behaviors are recorded. (The exact species does not have to be used to record observations. For example, children may illustrate and dictate, "Black bird with red throat chases blue jay away from feeder.") Also, taking children on a

Figure 3–9 Directions for building a pond.

A backyard pond can be just about as simple or complex as you want it to be. In fact, you can start out with a simple design, which I recommend, and then gradually make it as complex as you want. If you're just getting started, don't let the diagrams you've seen . . . kidney-shaped ponds lined with fancy rock, a fountain in the center, bi-level, etc., get the best of you. Just go out and dig a hole in the ground, pad it with sand (old carpet works very well too) to even out the rough spots and protect the liner, and then install the liner. When you've filled the liner with water, add a few plants from a local nursery and you're done. Oh yes, one more important thing, you'll have to spend lots of time watching all the critters.

If you want something a little more complex, that's quite easy too. Make the difficult job of digging the hole easier by spreading it out over a few weeks. If your soil is clayey like mine, spraying the excavation edges with water after each digging session will loosen it up for the next time. If you're using a preformed liner, place it on the ground first to mark the shape you'll dig. With a PVC or rubber fabric liner, be sure not to dig the hole so large that there isn't enough liner to cover the hole and some distance back from the edge. It's a good idea to have flat areas—both on the bottom and on shelves that flank the sides. A good flat bottom area will offer you secure footing as you finish shaping and digging your pond. Dig your pond at least one foot and preferably 2–3 feet deep. Use the dirt you removed to contour and cover the edges of the liner. If your pond site yields lots of roots and rocks, digging will be harder and you'll need to make an extra effort in protecting that liner. Old carpet is ideal for covering jagged edges and poking root stubs. After you're sure your liner covers that hole well, the fun part begins. Turn on the hose, grab a soda and watch it fill.

If you're like me, you want to attract frogs. The best way, the experts say, is to leave fish out of your pond. They'll eat most of the frog eggs and tadpoles. But, I like fish! Besides, you can have fish and some frogs, too, by creating lots of hiding and feeding cover for the frogs. I put some leaves and branches in my ponds. These provide cover as well as added nutrients and structure for small tadpole and frog foods to prosper. Piles of rocks, emerging as islands, and healthy emergent vegetation are also important as they provide emerging and perching places for frogs and for other pond life like dragonfiles. Don't make the sides too steep as it will be very difficult for the frogs and other animals that may venture into the pond to escape. With many nooks and crannies, like in a natural pond, the frogs will have a chance.

You can jumpstart your pond with frogs, if you'll pardon the pun. Contact a local nature center or resource agency and find out about tadpole relocation efforts that may already be underway. Ask if you can obtain some tadpoles for your pond. If you don't want to go to all that trouble, worry not as chances are the frogs will find their own way to your pond. As you can see, making a frog pond is simple. Yes, it takes some effort and time, but I found just creating it to be almost as much fun as enjoying it afterwards.

Good luck.

Doug Inkley's backyard is certified as a part of NWF's Backyard Wildlife Habitat program. Dr. Inkley is NWF Senior Scientist and Special Assistant to the President of the National Wildlife Federation. Reprinted with permission from the National Wildlife Federation. Copyright © 1998, 2001, Dr. Doug Inkley. For more information on backyard habitats, go to the National Wildlife Federation's Web site at www.nwf.org.

walk with the specific purpose of observing their natural surroundings will stimulate conversation and ideas.

These simple activities will be enough to promote interest in wildlife and the role people play in establishing habitats for animals. From here, the teacher can create a *wildlife habitat web* with children and make plans for expanding the existing habitat. There are many variations on creating webs and they will vary based on age of the children, interest, and background knowledge. The web in Figure 3–10 is just one example of the ideas that may emerge.

Concrete and Indirect Activities

Activities associated with the theme are divided into two categories: concrete activities and indirect activities. Concrete activities include those in which the children are personally engaged, such as designing, setting up, observing, and maintaining the wildlife habitat. Indirect activities take place in the classroom, on a field trip, or somewhere else other than the habitat itself. A few sample activities in each category are presented to guide teachers as the theme develops.

Concrete Activities

1. The National Wildlife Federation (NWF) suggests the following steps for starting a Backyard Wildlife Habitat: (a) assess your space; (b) provide food, water, cover, and places to raise young; (c) conserve natural resources (such as collecting rainwater); and (d) certify your habitat with the NWF program. Once the area has been selected, begin doing research and establishing the wildlife habitat. (See the NFW Web site at www.nwf.org.)
2. Provide food to birds with homemade bird feeders. Keep commercially purchased feeders filled with birdseed and make additional birdfeeders. Here are two suggestions. (1) Smear peanut butter in between spaces of a pinecone and sprinkle with birdseed. (2) Purchase suet from a meat department and roll it in birdseed. Wrap in a 12″ × 12″ piece of netting, tie four corners together, and hang in tree (Herr & Larson, 2000).
3. Mix hummingbird nectar (syrup) and hang in shade.

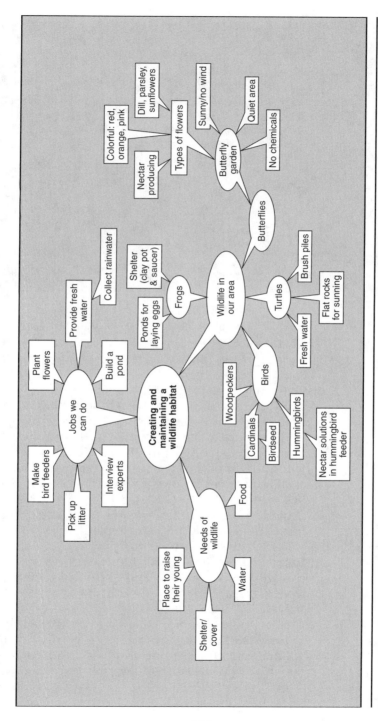

Figure 3–10 Sample web for integrated unit: Establishing and maintaining a wildlife habitat.

4. Create a shelter for frogs.
5. Provide brush, piles of leaves, or log pile so turtles can hide and hibernate.
6. Plant appropriate flowers and plants for the region to attract different species. Butterflies are attracted to dense clusters of red, yellow, orange, pink, or purple blossoms, and eat flowers such as zinnias, marigolds, buddleia, and milkweeds. Hummingbirds need plants that provide nectar such as trumpet honeysuckle, scarlet petunia, and bee balm.
7. Provide places for fresh water to pool, such as birdbaths and saucers, and replenish with fresh water when there is no natural supply.
8. Pick up litter from the habitat. Rather than throwing it away, keep and chronicle each item and make a plan for eliminating trash in the habitat.
9. Create a worm farm for children to observe (Herr & Larson, 2000). Later transfer the worms to the wildlife habitat. Place gravel and soil in a large clear jar with a wide mouth. Add worms. Place food (let-

tuce, cornmeal, cereals) on top of the dirt and keep soil slightly moist. Tape black construction paper around the outside of the jar and slide it off to observe the worms and tunnels.

10. The National Wildlife Federation suggests building a pond as a water source and to attract egg-laying frogs. (See Figure 3–9.)

Indirect Activities

1. Take a field trip to a bird sanctuary or nature center.
2. Invite wildlife management personnel, ornithologist, butterfly hobbyist, or other experts to visit the classroom.
3. Make rubbings or modeling clay impressions of objects in the wildlife habitat. Rubbings are made by holding a piece of paper against an object and rubbing with the side of a dark crayon. Rubbings can be mounted and displayed on construction paper. Press clay against an object, such as bark, leaves, or seeds, and carefully remove to see the impression. Display rubbings and impressions so children can try to guess the item used to create the image.
4. Choose children's books pertaining to the wildlife habitat. Include them in the class library and/or set up a special display. Read books on children's listening level. More difficult books can be shared by pointing out specific pictures and orally sharing pertinent information. See Figure 3–11 for a list of suggested books.
5. Explore the Internet for ideas related to the wildlife habitat. Two Web sites to explore are:

   - Ranger Rick's Kid Zone: www.nwf.org/nwf/kids
   - NWF Backyard Habitats: www.nwf.org/habitats/backyard

6. Make wildlife-related magazines available including *Ranger Rick, Your Big Backyard,* and *Wild Animal Babies.*
7. Join the NWF Backyard Wildlife Habitat listserve to learn and share information on habitats.

Figure 3–11   Suggested books for integrated unit: Establishing and maintaining a wildlife habitat.

Arnosky, J. (2000). *All about turtles.* New York: Scholastic.
Arnosky, J. (2000). *Crinkleroot's guide to knowing animal habitats.* New York: Simon & Schuster.
Arnosky, J. (1999). *All night near the water.* New York: Penguin Putnam Books for Young Readers.
Arnosky, J. (1997). *Crinkleroot's guide to knowing the birds.* New York: Simon & Schuster.
Cassie, B., Pallotta, J., & Astrella, M. (1995). *The butterfly alphabet book.* Watertown, MA: Charlesbridge Publishing.
Cole, J., & Degan, B. (1995). *The magic school bus hops home: A book about animal habitats (Magic School Bus Series).* New York: Scholastic.
Colombo, L., & Hernday, S. (1998). *Hummingbirds: A book and build-your-own feeder kit.* Kansas City, MO: Andrews & McMeel.
Hewitt, S. (1999). *All kinds of habitats.* Children's Press.
Marks, M., Baron, J.A., & Rader, L. (1998). *Exploring habitats resource guide: Look once, look again!* Huntington Beach, CA: Creative Teaching Press.
Neye, E., O'Connor, J., & Broda, R. (2000). *Butterflies.* New York: Penguin Putnam Books for Young Readers.
Pfeffer, W., & Keller, H. (1994). *From tadpole to frog.* New York: HarperCollins.
Wallace, K. (1998). *Eyewitness readers: Tale of a tadpole.* New York: DK Readers (Dorling Kindersley Publishing).
Widman, C.B., & Ransome, J.E. (1993). *The hummingbird garden.* New York: Simon & Schuster.

CONCLUSION

There is much to consider when establishing outdoor play and learning environments for preschool and kindergarten children. First and foremost, safety issues must be taken into account. This can best be accomplished by obtaining a copy and following the detailed guidelines in the Handbook for Public Playground Safety (U.S. Comsumer Product Safety Commission, 1997). Regular inspections of the play yard and appropriate supervision will also help reduce the number of injuries incurred outdoors.

The preschool and kindergarten playground needs to offer complexity and variety in the activities offered. This can be determined by following a formula to ensure that children have enough choices that will hold their attention for a reasonable length of time. New interest can be added by bringing traditional indoor learning centers outdoors. Thematic units based on outdoor experiences add another new twist to outdoor learning and exploration. When attention is given to these different elements of outdoor play, the results are happier children and teachers with fewer injuries and conflicts.

KEY TERMS

pretend play	gross motor skills
constructive play	fundamental movement phase
preoperational thought	complexity and variety
object permanence	of play units
egocentrism	potential units

THEORY INTO PRACTICE

1. Analyze an existing playground and calculate the number of simple, complex, and super complex play units available. Check to see if a variety of play equipment is represented. Make recommendations for adding complexity and variety to the playgrounds.
2. Plan and set up an outdoor learning center. Observe children at play to evaluate its effectiveness.
3. Select a relevant topic and plan an integrated unit with an outdoor theme.
4. Review Figure 3–8 (adding interest to preschool playgrounds). Select and implement one idea.

RELATED WEB SITES

www.perpetualpreschool.com
This Web site was established to provide a forum for sharing ideas with other preschool teachers. Activities are organized by themes and learning centers. Teaching tips and professional development opportunities are also available.
www.nwf.org
National Wildlife Federation
For more information on backyard habitats, go to the National Wildlife Foundation's Web site.

RELATED RESOURCES

Beaty, J. (1995). *Converting conflicts in preschool.* Albany, NY: Delmar.

Cohen, R. & Tunick, B.P. (1997). *Snail trails and tadpole tails: Nature education for young children.* St. Paul, MN: Redleaf Press.

Granovetter, R. & James, J. (1990). *Sift and shout: Sand play activities for children ages 1 to 6.* Mt. Ranier, MD: Gryphon House.

Hill, D.M. (1977). *Mud, sand, and water.* Washington, DC: National Association for the Education of Young Children.

Thompson, M.K. (1992). *Jump for joy! Over 375 creative movement activities for young children.* Englewood Cliffs, NJ: Prentice Hall.

REFERENCES

Asher, S.G., & Dodge, K.A. (1985). Identifying children who are rejected by their peers. *Developmental Psychology, 22,* 444–449.

Bredekamp, S. (1987). *Developmentally appropriate practice in early childhood programs serving children from birth through age 8.* Washington, DC: National Association for the Education of Young Children.

Council on Physical Education for Children. (COPEC). (1992). *Developmentally appropriate practice in movement programs for young children ages 3–5.* Reston, VA: Association of Health, Physical Education, Recreation, and Dance.

Cratty, B.J. (1986). *Perceptual and motor development in infants and children.* Upper Saddle River, NJ: Merrill/Prentice Hall.

Crick, N.R., Casas, J.F., & Mosher, M. (1997). Relational and overt aggression in preschool. *Developmental Psychology, 33,* 579–588.

Dodge, K.A., & Price, J.M. (1994). On the relation between social information processing and socially competent behavior in early school-aged children. *Child Development, 65,* 1385–1398.

Elmore, P. (July 2000) Personal communication.

Erikson, E.H. (1963). *Childhood and society* (2d ed.). New York: Norton.

Freund, L.S. (1989). Maternal regulation of children's problem solving behavior and its impact on children's performance. *Child Development, 61,* 113–126.

Frost, J. (1992). *Play and playscapes.* Albany, NY: Delmar.

Gabbard, C.P. (1992). *Lifelong motor development.* Dubuque, IA: Wm. C. Brown.

Gallahue, D.L. (1989). *Understanding motor development in children* (2d ed). Indianapolis, IN: Benchmark Press.

Hartup, W.W. & Laursen, B. (1993). Conflict and context in peer relations. In C.H. Hart (Ed.). *Children on playgrounds: Research perspectives and applications* (pp. 44–84). Albany: SUNY Press.

Herr, J. & Larson, Y. (2000). *Creative resources: For the early childhood classroom* (3d ed.). Albany, NY: Delmar.

Huber, L.K. (1999). Woodworking with young children: You can do it! *Young Children, 54(6),* 32–34.

Inkley, D. (1998) Directions for building a pond. [Online] National Wildlife Federation. Available: www.nwf.org/habitats/backyard/beyond basics/hints/frogpond.cfm (on 7/20/00).

Katz, L.G., & Chard, S. (1989). *Engaging children's minds: The project approach.* Norwood, NJ: Ablex.

Kieff, J. & Casbergue, R. (2000). *Playful learning and teaching: Integrating play into preschool and primary programs.* Boston, MA: Allyn & Bacon.

Koster, J.B. (1999). Clay for little fingers. *Young Children, 54(2)* 18–22.

Kritchevsky, S., Prescott, E., & Walling, L. (1977). *Planning environments for young children: Physical space.* Washington, DC: National Association for the Education of Young Children.

MacDonald, K., & Parker, R.D. (1986). Parent-child physical play: The effect of sex and age of children and parents. *Sex Roles, 15,* 367–378.

National Association for Sport and Physical Education (NASPE). (1990). *Developmentally appropriate physical education practices for children. A position statement of the Council on Physical Education for Children of NASPE.* Reston, VA: Association of Health, Physical Education, Recreation, and Dance.

Nelson, L.J., Hart, C.H., Robinson, C.C., Olsen, S.F., & Rubin, K. (1997, April). *Relations between sociometric status and three subtypes of withdrawn behavior in preschool children: A multi-method perspective.* Paper presented at the Biennial Meeting of the Society for Research in Child Development, Washington, DC.

Parker, J.G., Rubin, K.H., Price, J.M., & DeRosier, M.E. (1995). Peer relationships, child development, and adjustment. In D. Cicchetti & D.J. Cohen (Eds.), *Developmental psychopathology: Vol. 2. Risk, disorder, and adaptation* (pp. 96–161). New York: Wiley.

Pellegrini, A.D., & Perlmutter, J.C. (1988). Rough-and-tumble play on the elementary school yard. *Young Children, 43(2),* 14–17.

Piaget, J. (1952). *The origins of intelligence in children.* New York: International University Press.

Piaget, J. (1962). *Play, dreams, and imitation in childhood.* New York: Norton.

Putallaz, M., & Wasserman, A. (1989). Children's naturalistic entry behavior and sociometric status: A developmental perspective. *Developmental Psychology, 25,* 297–305.

Scarlett, W.G. (1983). Social isolation from agemates among nursery school children. In M. Donaldson, R. Grieve, & C. Pratt (Eds.), *Early Childhood development and education.* New York: Guilford.

Schickendanz, J. (1999). *More than ABCs: The early stages of reading and writing* (2d ed.). Washington, DC: National Association for the Education of Young Children.

Scholastic Early Childhood Today. (1995). *Activity plan.* Scholastic Early Childhood Today, *9*(8) 61.

Smilanksy, S. (1971). Can adults facilitate play in Children? Theoretical and practical considerations. In G. Engstrom (Ed.), *Play: The child strives toward self-realization,* (pp. 39–50). Washington, DC: National Association for the Education of Young Children.

Smith, P.K. (1997). *Play fighting and fighting: How do they relate?* Lisbon: ICCP.

Sosna, D. (2000). More about woodworking with young children. *Young Children, 55*(2), 38–39.

Sutton-Smith, B. (1988). The struggle between sacred play and festive play. In D. Bergen (Ed.), *Play as a medium for learning and development* (pp. 158–184). Portsmouth NH: Heinemann.

Teale, W.H., & Sulzby, E. (Eds.). (1986). *Emergent literacy: Writing and reading.* Norwood, NJ: Ablex.

Theemes, T. (1999). *Let's play outside! Designing the early childhood playground.* Ypsilanti, MI: High/Scope Press.

Trawick-Smith, J. (1988). Let's say you're the baby, OK?: Play leadership and following behavior in young children. *Young Children, 43*(5), 51–59.

Trawick-Smith, J. (2000). *Early childhood development: A multicultural perspective.* Upper Saddle River, NJ: Merrill/ Prentice Hall.

Vygotsky, L. (1962). *Thought and language.* Cambridge, MA: MIT Press.

Vygotsky, L. (1978). *Mind in society: Development of higher psychological processes.* Cambridge, MA: Harvard University Press.

Wellhousen, K.R., & Kieff, J. (2001). *A constructivist approach to block play in early childhood.* Albany, NY: Delmar.

Wolfgang, C.H., & Wolfgang, M.E. (1992). *School for young children: Developmentally appropriate practices.* Boston: Allyn & Bacon.

Wickstrom, R.L. (1983). *Fundamental motor patterns* (3d ed). Philadelphia: Lea and Febiger.

U.S. Consumer Product Safety Commission. (1997). *Handbook for public playground safety* (No. 325). Washington, DC: U.S. Government Printing Office.

CHAPTER 4

Outdoor Play in the Primary Grades

Guiding Questions

1. Why is there a marked increase in interest in cooperation and games with rules in the primary grades?
2. How does outdoor play enhance development in the cognitive, language/literacy, social-emotional, and physical domains?
3. What are "loose parts"? Give three examples.
4. What is the difference between competitive and cooperative games and what are the benefits of each?
5. Where might primary grade students visit on a field trip? Provide two related, follow-up activities.

INTRODUCTION

Following preschool and Kindergarten, children enter the primary grades and begin what is considered, "formal schooling." Primary grade education begins in the first grade and continues through the third grade, spanning approximately the ages between six and nine years. The emphasis during the primary grades shifts from learning through play to an emphasis on academics and student achievement, often determined by imposed benchmarks and mandated standardized tests. Even though our expectations of children shift dramatically during the primary grades, their inherent need to move and play is just as strong as it was in the preschool years. However, these needs are being overlooked and disregarded, as made evident through the gradually diminishing time allotted for outdoor play and physical education classes. Some districts eliminate outdoor activities completely in order to preserve more *instructional time* deemed necessary to improve test scores (National Association for Elementary School Principals, 1999; Svenson, 1999; Cromwell, 1998; Ross & Pate, 1987). The problems associated with limiting opportunities for active movement in school is exacerbated by the fact that children are also becoming more sedentary in their leisure time activities. Children average thirty-five hours a week of *screen time*, either watching television or playing video games. By the time they enter Kindergarten, children are likely to have spent 4,000 hours in front of a television (Levin, 1998). A generation ago, children spent their free time playing outdoors with peers who lived nearby. Today, the majority of their time and attention is devoted to television, video games, and computers. Solitary play is becoming so prevalent that traditional childhood games such as jacks, marbles, and dominos are becoming extinct (Casbergue & Kieff, 1998). This is troubling for three distinct reasons. First, because children are not playing traditional games, the rules and enthusiasm for the games will not be passed on to future generations. Second, present and future generations will miss out on practicing a sophisticated form of social negotiation. Finally, children will not experience the appreciation for shared outdoor play experiences. The result of these circumstances is a threat to children's health, self-esteem, and social competence.

Piaget (1962) characterized the primary years as a time for **cooperation** among peers with a predominance of playing **games with rules.** Cooperation occurs as children interact socially within a small group, typically to organize an activity. Often, the activity is not carried out to completion, but the planning stage itself is emotionally and socially fulfilling. For example, a group of four children decide to set up a lemonade stand. They spend days planning, collecting materials, erecting the stand, and discussing how the money will be spent, but actually spend less than an hour selling lemonade. To adults, it can be frustrating to observe children devoting their time and energy to an activity without a productive conclusion. But to primary grade children, the pleasure comes from conversing, arguing, resolving conflicts, and being a part of a group, rather than completing a planned project.

Games with rules become a major focus of organized as well as spontaneous play. During the preschool years, children are too egocentric in their thinking to fully understand the basic turn-taking and abstract rules required to play formal games. By the primary school years, however, children crave the order that comes from rules and naturally choose games, both organized and spontaneous. A popular children's movie illustrates the organized play of primary grade children. A group of seven neighborhood boys share a passion for baseball. Every spare moment, they escape to a deserted sandlot to play. There are not enough players for two competing teams so the rules are adjusted and the game is organized so that they can play baseball. Their goal is not to win, but to continue the game at all costs.

A second example involves four children, ages six to eight years, living in the same neighborhood. One summer day, they begin a game of Monopoly®. When they are called home for dinner, the children decide to leave the board in place and continue the game the next day. They repeated this routine for a week until the game was finally finished.

Spontaneous games are also prevalent at this stage of development. These may include a game of kick ball, relay races, or personal challenges, such as a foot race or jumping contest. Some spontaneous games will have a greater emphasis on competition than others. This varies according to the game and the players.

The cognitive, linguistic, social-emotional, and physical domains of development in the primary grades are interrelated and interdependent. As children in this age group play they are problem-solving, using language to express viewpoints, experiencing a wide range of emotions relating to competition and personal ability, and using gross motor skills in physical games, and fine motor skills to manipulate small game pieces. Although these events occur instantaneously in their mind and movements, each is discussed separately to highlight the unique characteristics of the primary grade child.

COGNITIVE DEVELOPMENT

Beginning around age seven, children enter Piaget's (1962) stage of **concrete operational thought.** Children at this stage of reasoning are capable of more sophisticated thinking processes than preschoolers, but still think differently from adults. Concrete operational thinkers have a growing understanding of language, number, time, and space. Perhaps this is why formal schooling typically begins during this period in cultures around the world (Trawick-Smith, 2000). One characteristic of the concrete operational stage is a more accurate understanding of **causality,** grasping the concept of cause and effect. Children begin to see and predict connections between an action and consequence. Understanding causality helps children be aware of hazards. Recall preschoolers' inability to judge the danger of a swing in motion and their tendency to run in front of one, resulting in injury. By around age six or seven years, children can cognitively predict and visualize the consequence of being in the path of a moving object, such as a swing. Injuries still occur during the primary grades but now children understand that, when they take a physical risk, injuries can occur.

There are many opportunities in the school day for primary grade children to utilize causality and other types of reasoning that are possible for the concrete operational thinker. Their cognitive reasoning helps them better understand concepts of time (a great limitation in the preoperational thinker). They now understand that time is continuous and moves from the past to present to future (Seefeldt, 1998). This enables children to more fully understand historical events in context as well as practical situations regarding time, such as, it is too soon to pack in March for a vacation in June. However, they are still limited in their understanding of historical time intervals and distinctions between them.

Concrete operational thinkers respond to the Piagetian task presented in Chapter 3 differently from preoperational thinkers (see Figure 3–1). They understand that simply spreading out one row of chips makes the row *appear* longer but does not increase the number of chips. It becomes obvious that both rows contain the same number of chips regardless of the length. Primary grade students are also capable of performing operations on numbers, but only in certain contexts. According to Kamii (1982), children may accurately complete worksheets requiring an understanding of counting and other number concepts but fail to implement these strategies when solving authentic problems. Therefore, she recommends children be given real-life situations that require mathematical processes, such as voting, taking attendance, keeping up with classroom materials, and playing games, such as Battle, Dominoes, and Hi-Ho Cherry-O (Kamii, 1985). These experiences require children to use number skills as they reason and problem-solve under real circumstances thereby contributing to their true understanding of mathematical concepts as opposed to simply solving an equation correctly.

In the subject area of science, concrete operational children are capable of logical thinking regarding natural occurrences such as wind, rain, and snow. Before this period, preoperational children believed that humans played a role in natural causes (such as, Daddy needed the grass to grow so he made it rain). As a result, many science-related topics can be introduced to primary grade children that could not have been comprehended only one or two years earlier.

Multiple Intelligences

The existence of individual differences among primary grade children and their distinct cognitive abilities are becoming widely recognized by psychologists, educators, and parents. Howard Gardner (1993) categorized eight distinct intellectual capabilities used to solve problems: linguistic, logico-mathematical, musical, spatial, bodily-kinesthetic, interpersonal, intrapersonal, and naturalistic.

Gardner theorizes that everyone has the capacity to develop each of these **multiple intelligences,** but to varying degrees of ability due to variables such as temperament and personality. For example, a child with linguistic intelligence will excel at reading and writing. These strengths surface effortlessly and the child receives pleasure from engaging in activities related to a particular *intelligence.* A child with bodily-kinesthetic intelligence uses his body to express ideas, problem-solve, or produce objects. This child's strengths are more obvious on the playground or woodworking center than in a reading group.

Children with **naturalistic intelligence** have a greater sensitivity to the natural world and appreciate learning about living things. These children thrive on outdoor learning experiences as they mentally catalog differences between various plant and animal life. Features of the natural world, such as weather or geology, stimulate their interest (Driscoll & Nagel, 1999). Time must be spent exploring the outdoors so children can use their sense of touch, vision, and smell to broaden their naturalistic intelligence.

Gardner's theory (1993) has much to offer teachers who work with groups of children with different strengths and abilities. By understanding the eight different intelligences, teachers can hone in on the experiences individual children need in order to learn and feel successful.

COMMUNICATION DEVELOPMENT

The social nature of primary grade children motivates them to speak and use language in order to communicate, share ideas, and enjoy the company of peers.

They select words, structure sentences, and use inflections to express their ideas clearly and convincingly. Different situations require different types of communication, known as **pragmatics.** For example, convincing a peer that it is not her turn to jump rope requires persuasion and logic, while pleading with a parent to reduce a punishment requires politeness and humility. Primary grade children are able to adjust their speech patterns accordingly.

Reading and writing now take on a new importance because children are attempting to effectively communicate with their peers and adults in various settings. As their ability to read independently increases, so does their interest in books and other reading materials. In the later primary grades, children are in the *transitional stage* of writing development and their spelling becomes highly conventional. With the exception of a few invented spellings, most words are spelled correctly, and written messages are readable to others. This is important as reading and writing becomes integrated into children's play. In the previous example in which children set up a lemonade stand, they used literacy skills to follow a recipe, make a list of materials needed, assign tasks (in writing) to each child in the group, and create a sign. Primary grade children need many opportunities to use written language through authentic learning experiences rather than isolated, unrelated assignments.

SOCIAL-EMOTIONAL DEVELOPMENT

The primary grades can be a tumultuous time for children. They are forming opinions of themselves as well as of their peers and are constantly comparing their ability to another's. Erikson (1963) labeled this struggle "industry versus inferiority" and describes it as children struggling for success and competence while avoiding feelings of failure and ineptitude. For example, a five-year-old will attribute losing a race as a matter of luck and be agreeable to try it again. But, the primary grade child credits the winner of a race as being a faster runner or better athlete than himself and may refuse a second race to avoid a greater sense of failure. Children are highly susceptible to forming a poor impression of themselves and developing low self-esteem at this age. Adults must be sensitive to this problem and provide every child with an opportunity to be competent in some area.

Friends become particularly important during the primary school years, and children who have friends are more likely to enjoy school and academic success (Schneider, Wiener, & Murphy, 1994). Many children belong to multiple peer groups, often dictated by activity preferences. For example, a child may belong to three peer groups: a group of friends at school who play together at recess, neighborhood children who ride bicycles together, and teammates from a local swim team. Within each group, the child plays different roles—that of leader or follower, and accepted, rejected, or neglected peer. (See Chapter 3 for a complete discussion of these classifications.) In addition to peer groups, children also pair themselves into mutually exclusive friendships (Trawick-Smith, 2000). They tend to select peers who have characteristics they admire or who are like them in some respect (Haselager, Hartup, van Lieshout, & Risen-Walraven, 1998).

PHYSICAL PROGRESSION AND MOTOR SKILL DEVELOPMENT

Primary grade children are refining the gross motor skills acquired during the preschool years. Walking, running, climbing, jumping, throwing, catching, and balancing are coordinated into a smooth series of movements allowing children to participate in physical games and sports. Fine motor skills are more finely coordinated at this age, enabling children to successfully complete self-help skills such as zipping, buttoning, and tying. Their ability to draw, color, write, and cut improve significantly, allowing children to express themselves through artistic mediums.

Advancement in the motor domain affects learning and development in the whole child. The **dynamic systems theory** explains the connection between movement and learning. Trawick-Smith

(2000) explains Sporns and Edelman's (1993) interpretation of the dynamic systems theory this way:

> A child climbs on a climber on the playground. As she does this, she activates and coordinates certain neurons—brain cells—which are needed for this action. If she climbs often, these cells will become organized into a *neural cluster*—a collection of connected brain cells which handle climbing. As the child plays, she combines her climbing with other skills—swinging, jumping, and screaming out to her friends. Each of these actions leads eventually to the formation of new neural clusters. Over time, these clusters connect with one another and become an even larger network of cells, called a *neural map*. A neural map is a complex web of cells which connects a whole region of the brain. From this view, the practice and refinement of specific motor abilities leads to brain organization (p. 336).

The dynamic systems theory has major implications for providing opportunities for outdoor play on a daily basis because of the connection made between movement and other types of learning.

Overall health is another justification for outdoor play in the primary grades. As stated earlier, children are leading sedentary lifestyles due to a number of factors including greater access to television, video games, and computers, a decrease in adult supervision during the after-school hours, and an increase in diets high in fat and sugar. This combination of factors has resulted in a significant increase in the number of obese children in the primary grades. In addition to health issues, these children are at greater risk of being teased, ridiculed, and bullied, which can lead to problems in the social-emotional domain. Overweight children in the primary grades may shy away from outdoor activity due to physical discomforts and feelings of self-consciousness. So classroom teachers must be prepared to encourage hesitant children to participate and be active while approaching overweight students with understanding and sensitivity. The following invited essay by Melinda Sothern, Ph.D., explains problems associated with obesity and provides suggestions for classroom teachers.

Encouraging Outdoor Physical Activity in Overweight Elementary School Children

by Melinda Sothern, Ph.D.

The prevalence of obesity in children and adolescents is higher than 20 years ago in all ethnic, age, and gender groups (Falkner & Michel, 1999; Hill & Throwbridge, 1998; Rippe & Hess, 1998). Currently over 10 million children in the U.S. are overweight. Over 11 percent of these children are considered clinically obese, defined as greater than the 95th percentile for age and height (U.S. Centers for Disease Control Body Mass Index Percentiles), and children are becoming obese at younger ages. Evidence continues to support reduced physical activity and sedentary behaviors, such as television viewing, as primary causes of the current worldwide obesity epidemic (Bouchard, 1997; Epstein & Goldfield, 1999; Epstein, Paluch, Gordy, et al., 2000). It is possible that for many children increasing physical activity may be adequate to prevent the onset of childhood obesity (Epstein & Goldfield, 1999; Goran, Reynolds, & Lindquist, 1999; Moore, Nguyen, Rothman, et al., 1995; Robinson, 1999; Sothern Loftin, Suskind, et al., 1999). In addition, educational studies indicate that physical fitness improves students' self-image and promotes a positive school environment (Hennessey, 1988). Students who are physically fit are shown to be absent less often and illustrate higher academic achievement than non-fit students (Hennessey, 1988). Children's feelings of self-worth or self-esteem begin developing in the early elementary years (O'Brien, 1989). Regular physical activity may promote the attainment of self-esteem during the elementary years which may transfer to improve self-worth in the later, more difficult, pubertal and post-pubertal years.

Because young animals, including humans, are inherently physically active, young children will be physically active if given encouragement and opportunity (DiNubile, 1993; Sothern & Gordon, in review). Childhood physical activity is often intermittent and sporadic in nature (Bailey, Olson, Pepper, et al., 1994); thus, children will not likely participate in prolonged exercise without rest periods. However, if given the opportunity, young children will perform relatively large volumes of intermittent non-structured physical activity (Bailey, Olson, Pepper, et al., 1994, Sothern & Gordon, in review, DiNubile, 1993). Generous periods of free play are highly recommended, along with frequent periods of adult-initiated moderate to vigorous activities including the participation of parents and teachers (Goran, Reynolds, & Lindquist, 1999; Javernik, 1988; Sothern & Gordon, in review). Providing safe environments for young children to actively play outdoors is essential to increasing the physical activity patterns of overweight children and those normal weight children who may be at risk for obesity (Goran, Reynolds, & Lindquist, 1999).

Motivating young, normal weight and physically active children to maintain activity patterns may be less challenging than increasing patterns in already overweight older children. Javernick (1988) suggests that just monitoring children during free play does not encourage the participation of heavier children. Heavier children are often ignored, ridiculed (Adams, Hichen, & Salehi, 1988) and often choose indoor, sedentary activities to escape negative activity situations (Javernik, 1988). Therefore, encouraging the sedentary, overweight child to participate in physical activity is difficult. In addition, even mildly overweight children have a decreased tolerance to exercise; movement may be uncomfortable and, in some cases, painful (Sothern, Hunter, Suskind, et al., 1999; Sothern, Loftin, Oescher, et al., in review; Sothern, Loftin, & Blecker, 1999). Prior failure to motivate and maintain increased physical activity in overweight children may be attributed to inappropriate physical activities (Sothern, Hunter, Suskind, et al., 1999; Sothern, Loftin, Ewing, et al., 1999; Sothern, Loftin, Udall, et al., 2000) and a lack of physical opportunities for overweight children in the traditional school environment (Javernik, 1988). In addition, emotional problems may further inhibit successful motivation of sedentary overweight children (Adams, Hichen, & Salehi, 1988; Hill & Throwbridge, 1998; Sothern, Hunter, Suskind, et al., 1999). Researchers suggest that a task-orientation approach to physical activity and sport that includes individual goal setting may be advantageous for overweight children (Kylo and Landers, 1995). Outcome goals such as winning or scoring are thus replaced with individual self-referenced criteria and mastery of individual skills. Teachers are encouraged to focus the student's attention toward achieving personal goals as opposed to competitive goals. Daily physical activities should alternate between team sports and individual activities to ensure equal opportunity for all children regardless of size or ability (Table 1).

Some researchers suggest that forcing children to participate in structured exercise may actually negatively impact physical activity patterns later in life (Taylor, Blair, Cummings, et al., 1999). This is especially true in overweight children who may already feel inadequate due to a lower tolerance to exercise. All young children, regardless of body

Table 1   Alternative individual goal based activities for elementary school children.

Traditional physical education and sports	Individual goal-based alternatives
ice, field or roller hockey	figure skating, inline or roller skates, cross country skiing
cheerleading, dance team	aerobic dancing or strength circuit training. modified Yoga
football, soccer or basketball	martial arts, kickboxing, Tai Bo
track and field	outdoor cycling, scooters, fun walk/runs or nature hikes, Tai Chi
baseball, softball or volleyball	archery, golf, croquet or horseback riding
water polo	swimming/diving skills
swim team relays	snorkeling

size, are easily distracted and incapable of focused activity for long periods of time (Bailey, Olson, Pepper, et al., 1994; Sothern & Gordon, in review; DiNubile, 1993). This contributes to the sporadic nature of their physical activity. Adults can engage in long duration exercise easily because of their enhanced ability to concentrate and participate without much mental effort. Therefore, physical activities targeting young children in general, and overweight children specifically, should be intermittent consisting of short time frames of vigorous activity alternating with longer periods of low intensity activity (Table 2).

Overweight children will engage in activities they believe they can accomplish and master. Conversely, they will avoid activities that draw attention to their disabilities. Expose overweight children to as many

Table 2 Top ten tips to increase outdoor physical activity in overweight children.

1. Consider organizing activities that alternate students from sitting to standing positions to give overweight children a chance to "catch their breath" and rest their ankles and knees.
2. Limit vigorous activities to 5–10 minutes, alternating these with easier, less intense activities of longer duration.
3. Pick teams this fast and efficient way: Tell the children to make a single file line behind you. Give them alternating colors to designate their team affiliation, such as red, blue, red, blue, and so on. Never pick captains and then allow them to pick the team members.
4. Set up a musical aerobic circuit. Children move from one station to another and perform aerobic dance moves for 1–2 minutes. For example: Station 1: Twist; Station 2: March in place; Station 3: Skip rope; Station 4: Modified jumping jacks (side-jacks).
5. Set up stations for strength and flexibility training or mark out a fitness trail that includes stops for stretching or doing strength exercises. Make sure the exercises are appropriate for the child's physical development and body size.
6. Limit the frequency and duration of high impact activity such as jumping or running up hill. Even normal weight children can experience joint overuse injuries; overweight children are especially at risk.
7. Spend time teaching the students about their different muscle groups while they learn appropriate exercise technique. This provides important physiologic feedback that helps motivate them to repeat the activity and understand what is safe and effective exercise.
8. Spend a class teaching the students about posture, balance, and body alignment while they perform stretching exercises. This will help overweight children choose appropriate movement activities.
9. Use an outdoor activity to teach the students about their body's metabolism. Explain how their bodies can go slowly for long periods of time but that if they go very fast they will run out of "gas" quickly. This will help overweight children understand their limitations.
10. Never allow overweight children to be verbally abused by other children. Provide appropriate consequences to bullies and, if necessary, consult the child's parents or school principal.

different types of movement activities as possible in a non-intimidating and nurturing environment. Lastly, explain to the parents of both normal and overweight students that all types of physical activity improves fitness and burns calories. If children self-select activities they enjoy they are more likely to perform those activities more often and for longer periods of time. Provide opportunities for children to play outdoors as often as possible. Better yet, encourage parents to play outside with their children—the family that plays together stays healthy together.

References

Adams, G., Hicken, M., & Salehi, M. (1988). Socialization of the physical attractiveness stereotype: Parental expectations and verbal behaviors. *International Journal of Psychology, 23,* 137–149.

Bailey, R., Olson, J., Pepper, S., et al. (1994). The level and tempo of children's physical activities: an observational study. *Medicine and Science in Sports and Exercise, 27*(7), 1033–1041.

Bouchard, C. (1997). Obesity in Adulthood—The importance of childhood and parental obesity. *The New England Journal of Medicine, 337*(13), 926–927.

DiNubile, M. D. (1993). Youth Fitness—problems and solutions. *Preventive Medicine, 22,* 589–594.

Epstein, L., & Goldfield, G. (1999). Physical activity in the treatment of childhood overweight and obesity: current evidence and research issues. *Medicine and Science in Sports and Exercise, 31*(11), S553–559.

Epstein, L., Paluch, R., Gordy, C., et al. (2000). Decreasing sedentary behaviors in treating pediatric obesity. *Archives of Pediatric and Adolescent Medicine, 154*(3), 220–226.

Falkner, B., & Michel, S. (1999). Obesity and other risk factors in children. *Ethnicity and Disease, 9,* 284–289.

French S., Story M., & Perry C. (1995). Self-esteem and obesity in children and adolescents: A literature review. *Obesity Research, 3*(5), 479–490.

Goran, M., Reynolds, K., & Lindquist, C. (1999). Role of physical activity in the prevention of obesity in children. *International Journal of Obesity and Related Metabolic Disorders, 23*(3), S18–33.

Hennessy, B. (1988). Administrative exercises to shape up a school fitness program. *Thrust, 18*(1), 8–11.

Hill, J., & Throwbridge, F. (1998). The causes and health consequences of obesity in children and adolescents, *Pediatrics, 101, 3,* 497–575.

Javernik, E. (1988). Johnny's not jumping: Can we help obese children? *Young Children,* Jan., 18–23.

Kylo, B., & Landers, D. (1995). Goal setting in sport and exercise: a research synthesis to resolve the controversy. *Journal of Sport and Exercise Psychology, 17,* 117–137.

Moore L., Nguyen U., Rothman K., Cupples, & Ellison, R. (1995). Preschool physical activity level and change in body fatness in young children: The Framingham children's study. *American Journal of Epidemiology, 142*(9), 982–988.

O'Brien, S. J. (1989). How can I help my preadolescent? *Childhood Education, 66*(1), 35–39.

Rippe, J., & Hess, S. (1998). The role of physical activity in the prevention and management of obesity. *Journal of the American Dietetic Association, 98* (suppl. 2), S31–S38.

Robinson T. (1999). Reducing children's television viewing to prevent obesity: a randomized controlled trial. *Journal of the American Medical Association, 282*(16), 1561–1567.

Sothern, M., & Gordon, S. (in review). Prevention of obesity in young children.

Sothern, M., Hunter, S., Suskind, R., et al. (1999). Motivating the obese child to move: The role of structured exercise in pediatric weight management. *Southern Medical Journal, 92* (6), 577–584.

Sothern, M., Loftin, J., Ewing, T., et al. (1999). The inclusion of resistance exercise in a multi-disciplinary obesity treatment program for preadolescent children. *Southern Medical Journal, 92* (6), 585–592.

Sothern, M., Loftin, J. M., Oescher, J., et al. (in review). Physiologic and metabolic response to weight-bearing exercise in children and adolescents with increasing levels of obesity.

Sothern, M., Loftin, M., Suskind, R., et al. (1999). The health benefits of physical activity in children and adolescents: Implications for chronic disease prevention. *European Journal of Pediatrics, 158,* 271–274.

Sothern, M., Loftin, M., Blecker, M., et al. (1999). Physiologic function and childhood obesity. *International Journal of Pediatrics, 14*(3), 135–139.

Sothern, M., Loftin, M., Udall, J., et al. (2000). Safety, feasibility, and efficacy of a resistance training program in preadolescent obese children. *American Journal of the Medical Sciences, 319,* 370–375.

Taylor, W., Blair, S., Cummings, S., et al. (1999). Childhood and adolescent physical activity patterns and adult physical activity. *Medicine and Science in Sports and Exercise, 31*(1), 118–123.

U.S. Centers of Disease Control. *Body Mass Index Percentiles for U.S. Children,* cdc.org.

An invited essay by Melinda Sothern, Ph.D., Director, Prevention of Childhood Obesity Laboratory, Division of Health and Performance Enhancement, Pennington Biomedical Research Center, Louisiana State University.

For more tips: *Trim Kids: A Parent's Guide to Healthier and Happier Children* by Melinda Sothern, PhD., Heidi Schumacher, R.D., & T. Kristian von Almen, Ph.D., HarperCollins Press, 2001, New York, NY.

OUTDOOR PLAY EXPERIENCES

Outdoor play is an essential part of the overall primary grade curriculum. Play and outdoor learning activities contribute to the development of primary grade children in a number of ways (Brewer, 1998). Cognitive development is enhanced as children create games, negotiate differences, and find solutions to physical challenges. Children gain language proficiency as they confer and collaborate with peers and linguistic skills as they incorporate reading and writing as a part of their cooperative group play. Socially and emotionally, children are learning to interact with peers as they participate in games and sports, and self-esteem is enhanced as they gradually become more physically skillful. Finally, many large motor skills such as running, jumping, climbing, throwing, and hitting are best practiced in an outdoor setting.

In this era of accountability, standardized testing, and insensitivity toward the physical needs of primary grade students, teachers must become advocates for outdoor play and learning. Developing curriculum goals to be achieved through outdoor play is a good beginning for educating administrators, colleagues, and parents. Brewer (1998) recommends the following as goals for physical development programs.

1. Children participate in a variety of activities that foster motor development.
2. Children use gross motor skills, as well as fine motor skills.
3. Children develop a positive attitude toward active movement experiences.

School-agers can be involved in outdoor experiences and meet physical development goals in a number of ways including free play on age-appropriate playground equipment, impromptu and organized games, sports, and field trips. Each of these categories are discussed in greater detail.

Age-Appropriate Playground Design

The U.S. Consumer Product Safety Commission (CPSC), 1997, recommends playground equipment be devised for either the two- to five-year-old age group or the five- to twelve-year-old age group. Most manufacturers of playground equipment are sensitive to this recommendation and design playground components accordingly. Because primary grade students are larger, stronger and possess more defined physical skills than preschoolers, they need playground equipment that suits their specific needs. Recommended features exclusive to equipment for school-age children include

(CPSC, 1997): chain or cable walks, free-standing arch climbers, fulcrum seesaws, long spiral slides with more than one turn, overhead rings, parallel bars, and vertical sliding poles. An example of permanent playground equipment designed for primary school-age children is pictured in Figure 4–1. This modular component offers a variety of safe and accessible playground experiences.

In addition to appropriate playground equipment, children need an adequate amount of time dedicated to outdoor play. Formal physical education classes contribute to children's overall attitudes toward physical recreation and health; however, children also need time every day for free play on outdoor play yards.

Loose Parts   Primary grade students enjoy many types of games, sports, and individual challenges. Their need to create, select, and carry out these activities is facilitated by providing them with various types of equipment and materials to be used outdoors. Transitional, accessory-type materials used expressly for out-

Figure 4–1   Playground equipment designed for primary grade students.

Photo provided by PlayDesigns®. Reprinted with permission from PlayDesigns® (2000). *Early childhood catalog.* Lewisburg, PA: PlayDesigns®.

door play are labeled **loose parts** (Nicholson, 1973). Having these materials readily available supports school-agers' need for imaginative group play. Providing loose parts is also a way to *temporarily* compensate for a lack of adequate age-appropriate playground equipment, a common problem in elementary school settings. Schools lacking safe, age-appropriate equipment can embark on a playground renovation. See Chapter 7, Figure 7–7, for a case study of such a renovation.

An obvious problem associated with loose parts is storage. A weatherproof storage facility with a lock located near the outdoor play area can be used to store most loose parts. Wagons can be used to move loose parts from the storage facility to other areas of the play yard. Children assigned to help with moving and storing loose parts can be given time to bring out materials and return them at the end of outdoor play periods. For example, children building with large hollow blocks need to be alerted ten minutes prior to the end of the outdoor play period so they can dismantle structures and help return blocks to the storage area. Putting away loose parts can be the shared responsibility of children assigned specific *helper* duties, children using the materials, and supervising adults.

The organization and extra time required to incorporate loose parts into children's outdoor play pays off in terms of enjoyment, skill-building, and social development. The following vignette illustrates how loose parts facilitate play:

Mrs. Salinas watches as her class of second-graders quickly disperses on the school playground. Their daily opportunity for outdoor free play is one of their favorite activities and each child appears to know exactly what he or she wants to do as soon as they reach the playground. A group of six children is actively playing on a permanent, modular playground system that includes a slide, overhead ladder, and rock climbing wall. In an adjacent field, ten boys and girls quickly set up traffic cones to represent goals, choose teams, and begin a modified game of soccer. Four other children open a locked storage cabinet and remove several tires and planks. Busily, they place pairs of tires in a row with one plank leading up to the tire run and another plank leading away. The children take turns walking down the plank, stepping through the tires, and exiting down the second plank while using a stopwatch to compare the time it takes each child to complete the course. On an adjacent black top, four students shoot baskets while two others toss a Frisbee to each other.

This fairly modest collection of loose parts allows children to make choices about what they will play and puts them in control of making their own decisions during the recess period. This is especially critical for students who are restricted in their movement and choices of activity for the majority of their day.

Three examples of loose parts that are familiar to most teachers are jump ropes, sports equipment, and obstacle courses. These are described in detail with suggestions for incorporating them into outdoor play. See Figure 4–2 for a complete list of loose parts and their benefits.

Jump ropes Jump ropes are easily accessible, inexpensive, and provide many benefits to children such as cardiovascular exercise, rhythm, timing, and opportunities for socialization. Because jump ropes can be a strangulation hazard if used improperly, it is strongly suggested that a specific area of the outdoor play area be designated for jump rope activities. An area away from permanent playground equipment (so ropes cannot be hung over bars or platforms) and pathways (to prevent children from running into others playing jump rope) is preferable. A flat surface free of debris such as rubber tiles, grass, or concrete is needed. A variety of jump ropes can be offered including those for individual play, longer ropes that require two children to turn the rope as others jump, and long covered, elastic bands (typically labeled *Chinese jump rope*). Jumping rope requires coordination, timing, skill, and patience, making it an ideal activity for primary grade students. An unfortunate trait of jump roping is that it holds a gender stereotype that favors girls and therefore discourages boys from participating. Primary grade boys who choose this activity may be ostracized for joining a traditional girls' game. As a result, boys are missing out on an opportunity to develop new skills. Teachers sensitive to gender stereotypes can try a number of ways to promote jump roping among boys as well as girls. These strategies can be altered to suit other situations where stereotypes become a factor in outdoor play activities.

Figure 4–2 Loose parts and their benefits.

Categories of loose parts

Type	Examples	Comments
playground equipment	pulleys, teeter-totters, merry-go-rounds	first items to break
large, movable, nonobjective pieces	huge blocks, foam chunks, tires	encouraging cooperation and creative enclosures
sand	sand pit or box	needing items for digging, molding, etc.
water	flowing streams being better than standing water	possibly needing pump arrangement
building materials	boards, blankets, cardboard boxes	turning into huts, cages, caves, rocket ships
tools	hammers, saws, nails, screws, vises	requiring instruction and supervision
containers	buckets, cups, pots, pans, watering cans, strainers, etc.	leading to sand and water play and watering of plants
wheel toys	bikes, trikes, wagons, carts	needing pathway systems
toys	balls, games, jump ropes, dolls	subject to new cultural input—TV shows, movies, etc.
natural items	sticks, leaves, rocks, moss, grasses, flowers, insects, pinecones, seeds, pods, berries	the original loose parts

Reprinted by permission from Shaw, L. G. (1987). Designing playgrounds for able and disabled children. *Spaces for children: The built environment and child development,* Weinstein, C. S. & David, T. G. (Eds.). New York: Kluwer Academic/Plenum Publishers.

Although it is rare to recommend that activities be separated by gender, this extreme measure may be required to interest boys in jumping rope among groups where it is heavily stereotyped as a female activity. This temporary solution will introduce boys to jump roping and allow them to work out their own rules for play. Two jump roping areas can be established until boys become comfortable with jumping rope. As soon as plausible, the "boys only" jump roping rule should be lifted and the two groups encouraged to play together as they do in other parts of the outdoor play area.

Engage children in a discussion on how gender stereotypes are unfair. This may occur naturally if a child is experiencing discrimination from a class mate or the teacher may initiate the discussion through a **persona doll story.** These types of stories use a doll, puppet, or stuffed animal as the target of a problem such as gender discrimination. It is easier for children to find solutions for an inanimate object than for themselves or their own peers (Derman-Sparks, 1989). See Figure 4–3 for an example of a persona doll story that may be used in this situation.

Jump roping rhymes have a long and interesting history. These rhymes help children learn rhythm, counting, and other skills. Many jump rope rhymes contain female stereotyped phrasing. Counteract stereotypes by introducing jump rope rhymes that can

---

Figure 4–3   Persona doll story: Jeremy wants to jump rope.

(Teachers may use a boy doll or puppet as they tell the following story to the class.)

Boys and girls, this is Jeremy (show doll or puppet) and he has a problem that maybe you can help solve. Jeremy has two older sisters named Elisa and Rosa and they all play together. One of their favorite activities is jumping rope. At first, Jeremy's sisters included him so that he could hold one end of the jump rope while they took turns jumping. One day, Jeremy asked to have a turn and quickly discovered he was very good at jumping rope! He especially liked to jump fast when his sisters called out "Red hot peppers!" Soon, it became one of his favorite outdoor activities.

But when Jeremy started school something happened that made him very sad. At recess there were many different activities to choose. Jeremy looked around and noticed a group of girls playing jump rope. He ran over but when he tried to join them, one girl said, "No boys allowed!" Jeremy tried to explain that he knew how to jump rope but the girls only ignored him and continued playing.

Then Jeremy noticed a long jump rope the girls were not using. He picked it up and walked over to two boys waiting to slide. "Hey!" Jeremy called excitedly, "Do you guys want to jump rope with me?" The two boys doubled over laughing and said, "Are you kidding? Jump ropes are for girls!" Sadly, Jeremy dropped the jump rope and walked away.

(The teacher then initiates a discussion using some of the following warm-up questions.)

How do you think Jeremy feels?
Why did the girls say, "No boys allowed"?
Why did the boys say, "Jump ropes are for girls"?
What should Jeremy do next?
How would you act if Jeremy asked you to jump rope with him?

comfortably be used by boys as well as girls and encourage children to create their own jump rope rhymes. See Figure 4–4 for examples of well-known jump rope rhymes that are appropriate for boys as well as girls.

Sports equipment   Primary grade children are developing a keen understanding of rules that enables them to participate in organized sports. Space, equipment, and adult supervision may be too limited for children to engage in a formal game, but they can practice skills associated with many team sports. For example, basketball goals can be erected for practicing different shots, ball gloves and softballs can be made available for catching and throwing, and foam rubber footballs (such as Nurf® footballs) can be provided for passing and receiving. These activities emphasize skill practice while de-emphasizing the competitive nature of sports. Encourage children to view this as a cooperative opportunity to improve their own skills while assisting a peer to improve his ability as well.

Children must be given clear guidelines for how sports equipment can and cannot be used. Mandating a "no physical contact" rule, will discourage children from emulating professional players (such as tackling while playing football) and minimize injury and elevated levels of aggression. Girls, as well as boys, need equal access to sports equipment. Even though girls are much more involved in team sports today than ever before, there are still gender stereotypes associated with female participation. Teachers must be conscience of this to ensure that all children have equal opportunities to play with all loose parts available on the playground.

Obstacle courses   Obstacle courses are a planned combination of many loose parts. Moving around, over, under, and through an obstacle course promotes motor planning abilities, physical skills, and movement concepts (Theemes, 1999). Obstacle courses provide a way to extend the activities available outdoors by changing and revising the environment (Griffin & Rinn, 1998). School-age children can design their own obstacle courses with some adult assistance, thus contributing to their desire for cooperative play in a peer group. Griffin and Rinn (1998) advise, however, that teachers should first be thoroughly familiar with

Figure 4–4   Jump rope rhymes for boys and girls.

A My Name Is Alice/Adam
(This familiar rhyme can be changed to include male names.)
A my name is ADAM, my wife's name is ALICE. We live in Alabama and we bring back apples.
B my name is BETTY, my husband's name is BEN. We live in Bermuda and we bring back bugs.
C my name is CURTIS, my wife's name is CAROL. We live in Colorado and we bring back crabs.

(The rhyme continues through the alphabet with a different child jumping on each letter called.)

Apples, Peaches, Pears, and Plums
Apples, peaches, pears, and plums
Tell me when your birthday comes.

(Jumper skips "hot peppers" or very fast skipping while children say the months of the year. Jumper tries to continue skipping until he or she reaches the month of his or her own birthday).

Blue Bell, Cockle Shells
(This rhyme is for beginners who cannot jump into a turning rope. The first two lines may be used with any jump rope rhyme including the one which follows here. To begin, swing the rope back and forth next to the jumper, but not over.)

Blue bells, cockle shells
Easy ivy over

(Swing rope over jumpers head on the word "over" and continue turning rope.)

Oh no, here comes Miss Blackwell
with her big black stick.
Now it's time for arithmetic.
One plus one is?
(Jumper answers) "Two"
Two plus two is?
(Jumper answers) "Four"
Four plus four is?
(Jumper answers) "Eight"
Eight plus eight is?
(Jumper answers) "Sixteen"
Now it's time for spelling.
Spell cat.
(Jumper answers) "C-A-T"
Spell dog.
(Jumper answers) "D-O-G"
Spell hot.
(Jumper answers) "H-O-T"

(When the jumper finishes spelling "hot" turn the rope fast until he or she trips the rope.)

Figure 4–4 Continued.

Coffee and Tea
I like coffee,
I like tea,
I'd like (name of next person in line)
to come in with me.

(The two children now jump together and the second person to come in says the rhyme. When the rhyme is done, the first jumper runs out, and the new jumper runs in, jumps with the second child while reciting the rhyme, and so on.)

Down by the River
Down by the river, down by the sea,
Johnny broke a bottle and blamed it on me.
I told ma, ma told pa,
Johnny got a spanking so ha, ha, ha.
How many spankings did Johnny get?
1,2,3 . . .

(Keep counting until the jumper trips the rope.)

HELP
H-E-L-P (Help is spelled over and over as the rope is turned faster and faster. When the jumper trips the rope, he or she must do what is required of the last letter called.)

H= High waters. The turning rope doesn't touch the ground.
E= Easy over. The rope is turned slower than usual.
L= Leapfrog. The jumper must crouch like a frog while jumping.
P= Peppers. (The rope is turned quickly).

(Players jump until they miss and the next jumper in line starts from the beginning.)

Red Hot Pepper
Red hot pepper
in the pot.
Got to get over
what the leaders got.

(Rope turners speed up while children count by tens . . .) 10-20-30-40-50-
(Continue until jumper trips the rope. Keep track of scores to determine which child had the highest.)

School, School, the Golden Rule
School, school, the golden rule,
Spell your name and go to school.

(Each jumper takes a turn jumping into the turning rope, spelling their name, and jumping out of the turning rope. The next jumper does the same and so on.)

(continued)

Figure 4–4 Continued.

(The game continues with . . .)
School, school, the golden rule,
Tell your grade and go to school.

(The initial grade called out is "kindergarten" and the next person in line must run through the turning rope without jumping. The next child runs in and jumps once while saying "first grade" and runs out. This continues until the twelfth grade is called out and the jumper skips rope twelve times. Children are eliminated from the game when they trip on the rope, and the game continues until one jumper is left *or* when jumpers reach the "twelfth grade.")

Courtesy of www.gameskidsplay.net

---

materials and experienced in building obstacle courses before enlisting the assistance of primary grade children. (Preschool children should not be expected to safely design their own obstacle courses.) It is to be anticipated that children will want to begin playing on an obstacle course as each element is completed. However, they should be encouraged to complete the planned course and may need adult assistance to keep them on task. Parts of the obstacle course that are weatherproof can be left in place until children become bored with them and are ready to design a new challenge, while other materials can be stored away between play periods. Two pictorial examples of obstacle courses designed by Griffin and Rinn (1998) can be found in Figure 4–5.

Obstacle courses can be designed from recycled materials or commercially designed equipment. Griffin and Rinn (1998) suggest the following recycled materials for building obstacle courses:

- appliance boxes
- cable spools available from cable television companies (typically 4 1/2′ in diameter)
- carpet remnants
- milk crates (crates donated by milk distributors are sturdier than those purchased at stores)
- planks and balance beam
- plastic two-liter drink bottles, empty and clean
- plastic hoola-hoops
- plastic swimming pool filled with balls, carpet samples, pillows, bean bag chairs, or bean bags

Low Crawl   The low crawl utilizes plastic hoops, crates, carpets, mats, wedge, plastic sheeting, and tent stakes. This course begins with the plastic hoops as an agility drill leading up to the wedge, which then eases the child into a low crawl. Carpet remnants are placed on the ground with milk crates (set on end) on both sides. Mats cover the crates. The plastic sheeting at the exit provides a slide-across for the belly. Use tent stakes to secure the plastic near the milk crates, then tires to anchor the other ends. The low crawl offers some real spatial concepts for children and their bodies.

Spools and Tires and Planks, Oh My!   This obstacle course also uses spools. Planks and tires lead up to a crate that goes over the first spool. The planks need to be secured between tires. The spools are again covered with carpet remnants, making it easier for children to get traction when going over the spools and decreasing the possibility of splinters. Place a mat between the two spools and a plank over the top of the two. The plank should have a lip (a small board nailed on to each end) to secure it to the spool. The last spool delivers the child onto the wedge. Remember, all obstacle courses should be monitored to ensure safety.

Figure 4–5   Obstacle courses.

Source: Griffin, C., & Rinn, B. (1998). Enhancing outdoor play with an obstacle course. *Young Children, 53*(3), 18–23. Reprinted with permission from Christina Griffin and Brad Rinn.

- tunnels made from plastic trash cans with bottoms removed
- rubber balls of all sizes, including those that do not stay fully inflated
- flat and wedge shape safety mats used for tumbling
- small equipment items such as duct tape, plastic rope, thick plastic sheeting, and shower curtain rings
- small trampoline designed for individual exercise

Grounds for Play®, a playground equipment manufacturer, offers similar loose manipulatives that can be used to design obstacle courses. These include a "Post and Panel System" in which children create structures by sliding colorful, lightweight panels into grooved posts; "Inter+blocks and Inter+playnks," an interlocking system of large blocks and planks made of durable plastic; "Kid Stackers", an interlocking system of ramps, arches, towers, and tires; and "Ring-A-Rounds" circular enclosures that can hold two seated children or be rolled when turned on one side. Of course, each obstacle course does not require all of these materials, either recycled or manufactured, so teachers can begin collecting a few items and gradually add to the stock of supplies. Children will also come up with their own ideas for objects that can be included.

GAMES

Organized and impromptu games are of major interest to children ages six to nine years. These games can be classified as competitive or cooperative. Competitive games conclude with a distinction between *winners* and *losers*. Competition that is too intense for a child can result in stress and ultimately a lack of interest in sports and games (Elkind, 1981). Cooperative games are devised for the purpose of encouraging children to work together. Both types of games contribute to children's growing understanding of sportsmanship. Figure 4–6 offers examples of each.

Figure 4–6 Games for primary grade students.

Alphabet Letters
The object of the game is to get into groups of four players and form the alphabet letters called out by the leader.

Back to Back Tag
Two players start the game as "it" holding hands and chasing other players which they can tag only with their free hands. When a free player is tagged, he/she must join the tag team. Only the end players can tag free players and the tag team must hold hands as they chase. Free players can form a safety area by standing back to back with their hands to their sides with another free player. But they may remain in this position for a maximum of ten seconds. They can then stand back to back with another free player for ten seconds. The game ends when everyone is tagged and therefore joins the tag team.

Batting
Equipment: Lightweight ball, two rackets made by bending a clothes hanger in the shape of a diamond with the hook bent closed to form a handle. The leg of a panty hose is pulled over the diamond shape to create a racquet.

Use racquets to volley a lightweight ball back and forth.

Bed Sheet Ping Pong
Two teams stand at opposite ends of a bed sheet and pull it taut. A ping pong ball is dropped on the sheet and the teams raise and lower the sheet trying to get the ping pong to drop off the opposing team's side of the sheet.

Crocodile Race
Two teams of five to ten players are formed. Each team stands in a straight line behind the leader. Each player puts their hands on the shoulders of the person in front of them and bends their knees to a crouching position. Each "crocodile" races against the other. Note: If the leader goes too fast, the team behind will break up.

Ducks and Cows
This game is used to divide a group into two teams. Players close their eyes while the adult taps each on the shoulder and designate them as "duck" or "cow". On the signal, players must make their animal sounds to gather into their two teams.

Evaporating Tic Tac Toe
Draw a large tic-tac-toe grid on concrete with chalk.

Children use paintbrushes dipped in buckets of water to mark their spot either with an "x" or "o." Continue playing as usual until one child gets "tic-tac-toe three in a row." However, if the water evaporates from a space before the game is over, the space is then available for marking again.

(continued)

Figure 4–6 Continued.

Freeze Tag
"It" tags free players who then must freeze in their places. Frozen players may be unfrozen if a free player touches them.

Hospital Tag
"It" tags runners as in the traditional game. However, the person tagged must hold the place on their body where they were tagged with one hand. This person is now "it" and must chase down the next runner always holding the place they were tagged.

Obstacle Course
Set up traffic cones or other markers (such as gallon milk jugs weighted with sand) in a line spaced far enough apart to move through. Children will move through the cones by running, skipping, hopping, jumping rope, walking backwards, kicking a playground ball, or with a partner. Two courses can be set up to make the game competitive.

Points
"It" is the designated thrower and the remaining players stand within catching distance. The ball is thrown towards the group. The child catching the ball receives a designated number of points according to how the ball is caught. For example: fly ball = 100 points, after first bounce = 75 points, after second bounce = 50 points, after third bounce = 25 points. The first person to reach a predetermined number points becomes "it" for the second round.

Courtesy of www.gameskidsplay.net

FIELD TRIPS

Experiences beyond the classroom walls contribute significantly to children's growing understanding of their world. Field trips are extremely beneficial to primary grade students as they strive to develop a sense of competence in their interactions with people in their community. Children's natural curiosity about their world enables them to learn from all facets of their environment, and their increased understanding, in turn, influences how they behave (Bronfenbrenner, 1979). Consider the following example of a field trip to a fruit stand.

A group of first graders take a walking trip to a corner market that sells fresh fruits and vegetables. They observe customers shopping and interacting with employees. As a group, they weigh and purchase one pound of satsumas (a seedless, easy-to-peel fruit, similar to oranges). Upon returning to the classroom, groups of children react differently to the experience. One group of children anxiously tries the satsuma for the first time. They watch with interest as the teacher peels the fruit and distributes slices to each awaiting child. A second small group goes directly to the dramatic play area, sets up a fruit stand, and begins reenacting the behaviors they observed there. Another group asks to collect seeds from the satsuma to plant during outdoor play. A simple visit to the fruit stand effected the children in different ways.

Primary grade students possess a growing competence in their use of language, literacy, and numeracy enabling them to recall, reenact, and record significant aspects of the field trip. Teachers can plan field trips that will motivate children to use numeracy and language in authentic ways by planning activities for before and after the field trip.

Before the field trip teachers can share relevant books and videos. Read quality children's books that directly and indirectly explore the topic related to the field trip. Before the trip to the fruit stand, for example, a teacher may read *Oliver's Fruit Stand* (French & Bartllett, 1998), *Growing Vegetables* (Ehlert, 1987), and *To Market, To Market* (Miranda & Stevens, 1997). Some children's videos may also explore topics relevant to the field trip. For example, before a trip to a construction site children can view *I Dig Dirt* (Harris, 1995) and *There Goes a Truck* (Kid Vision, 1994) to learn about the names and functions of the machinery they will see.

A week or so before the field trip, introduce relevant activities. Before visiting a pizzeria, bring in pizza dough for children to knead, cheese to grate, and ingredients to try such as pepperoni, mushrooms, and green peppers. (As always, check for food allergies before offering items to children.) Becoming familiar with what will be seen on the field trip reinforces concepts learned.

Before leaving the classroom, create a list or web of everything children already know about the place or people to be visited. Some children will have previous experiences they can share with the class. Then make a list of questions the children have. Don't make the field trip a fact-finding experience in which all questions must be answered. Instead, use the list of questions to narrow down children's interests.

After the field trip, children can absorb what they learned through a number of follow-up activities such as discussing the experience during group time (Leipzig, 1993). If samples were collected, show these to remind children of what they saw and did. Make a display and label each item.

Provide relevant materials for dramatic play. Help children remember equipment, materials, and the roles of people observed. Allow them to gather props from around the classroom and create new ones to use in their play. Reenacting the roles of people strengthens and broadens their understanding of the experience.

Language experience charts integrate literacy into the field trip experience. This activity may be approached in a number of ways. Children may write their own version of the experience using invented spellings and illustrations, or teachers can assist children in writing a story of the experience as a class with individual students contributing ideas and the teacher providing guidance for sequencing and grammar. Teachers may also pose a simple question and record children's responses, such as, "What tools did you see in the hardware store?" This documentation of the children's responses are then dated and reviewed later to help children recall the experience. Another language experience activity involves writing a thank-you note to the people who shared their time and expertise with the children. This can be written as a whole group or children can draw pictures and dictate a message in small groups or individually.

Field trips do not have to be extravagant, time-consuming, or expensive in order to be effective. In fact, the younger the child, the less *exotic* field trips should be. Children learn best by extending and expanding their understanding of people and places that are already familiar in some way. Therefore, trips in and around the local community are more than sufficient. Ideally, local businesses will be within a reasonable walking distance to eliminate the need for transportation. Even though some walking field trips will be impromptu, those involving people at work and businesses need to be politely notified in advance and given a specific date and time of the groups arrival. Some community field trip sites to consider include post office, hardware store, trophy shop, dry cleaners, fruit stand, construction site, pet shop, discount store, drug store, cafe, dentist, optometrist, barber, video store, doctors office, copy shop, restaurant, car wash, car care center, nursery, library, music store, park, bank, and veterinarian's office.

Older school-age students and those with a wealth of experiences in their own community may benefit from field trips that introduce them to people and places they have only read and heard about. These formal field trips require a great deal of preparation including obtaining approval at the district level, organizing transportation, collecting written permission slips, and making arrangements at the field trip site. Figure 4–7 offers tips on organizing a field trip. More time will be needed to prepare children before the field trip using the activities previously suggested. After the trip, be prepared for a range of reactions and suggestions for follow-up information and experiences in the days that follow. Suggestions for prearranged, formal field trips include airport, fire station, outdoor festivals, farm, zoo, nature preserve, aquarium, hot-air balloon race, boat dock, commercial plant nursery, farmer's market, parks, lakes, wooded areas, and fields.

Incorporating Photography

Approaching field trips from a creative angle can launch new interest in familiar surroundings. Savage and Holcomb (1999) introduced cameras to second-graders and developed a complete project around the idea. They learned that children are highly motivated to thoroughly study topics when they use photography as the basis for their investigation. Children can use photography to capture familiar sites and objects around their school and later select, organize, and use photos to communicate ideas, information and feelings to others. Savage and Holcomb (1999) make the following recommendations for using cameras with school-age children.

1. Purchase one inexpensive 35-mm camera with built-in flash for every five children in the class and one roll of 12-exposure, 35-mm film per child. Solicit donations from local businesses and

Figure 4–7 Tips for organizing field trips.

There are seven basic steps to planning and executing a successful field trip experience:

1. Select a location. Choose field trip sites that reflect children's interests, misconception, and classroom themes.
2. Visit the site. Investigate the field trip site without children first to identify appropriate concepts for focus. Be on the lookout for unsafe areas, restrooms, and physical barriers for children with adaptive equipment. Collect tangible materials to be shared with children before the field trip such as brochures, menus, fliers. Take several photos to show in advance.
3. Plan the trip. Identify a contact person at the field trip site who will assist with planning the trip and who will be there to greet children. Choose to visit on a date and time when there are fewer crowds. Mornings are best for children. Field trips scheduled earlier in the week allow for more time to extend the experience.
4. Prepare parents. Send home information, invitation, and permission slips to parents. Assign chaperoning parents specific children for whom they are responsible. Give each group simple tasks to be completed or information to learn. (Ask parents to sign a "walking trip" permission slip at the beginning of the year so the class can take spontaneous walking field trips near the school.)
5. Prepare children. Spend a few days discussing the field trip and what children may see and learn. Read related books, sing songs, add props to dramatic play, and share the tangible items collected when previously visiting the site. Bring in objects related to the site and ask children to do the same. Develop a list of questions children have about the field trip site. (Remember, all of these may not get answered during the visit.)
6. Take the trip. Review safety rules with children. These may include: buckle seat belts, stay seated on bus or in cars, stay with your group and adult leader, walk, and use quiet voices. Provide each child with a tag indicating their name and the name and phone number of the school. Conduct head counts between the school and field trip site. Point out things you see which relate to previous classroom discussions. Take photos to use in later discussions and to document findings.
7. Extend the experience. Upon returning to the classroom, encourage children to talk, draw, and write about what they saw. Capitalize on their enthusiasm with other activities planned throughout the week.

Adapted and reprinted with permission from: Steps to a successful trip. *Scholastic Early Childhood, 12*(6), 38 (1998).

inquire about discounts from neighborhood stores with photo processing services. Display students' photographs at participating businesses.

2. Brainstorm with children possible subjects for photographs. If appropriate, photos could reflect an integrated unit. Students write notes keyed to

the exposure number immediately after taking each picture to help them remember the subject. For example, "Exposure #5—Lizard climbing up brick wall."

3. Take the time to explain and demonstrate the mechanics of the camera; loading film, advancing the picture, activating the flash, and rewinding film. Allow children to practice first without film. Invite parents and other adult volunteers to assist children when they begin taking photographs.

4. When every child has had a turn with the camera, have film developed as one large order. Code each roll so that developed film can easily be returned to the right student. After photographs are returned to students, allow time for them to share pictures with each other.

5. Children organize, write about, and display individual photographs or groups of pictures with a similar theme. Displays are made available for students, teachers, and parents to enjoy in a highly visible area of the school, local business, or library.

Field trips are an ideal way for children to learn about their community and themselves. Both impromptu and previously planned field trips offer creative ways to integrate classroom learning with experiences beyond classroom walls. Introducing a novel element, such as photography, helps children look at familiar surroundings in a new way.

DEALING WITH CONFLICT

The increased time spent in group activities in the primary grades, especially those involving competition, naturally leads to an increase in conflicts among children. Rather than viewing conflict as misbehavior, it should be considered a means for teaching social skills, problem-solving, and conflict resolution; essential skills to be used throughout one's life. Before dealing with specific conflicts during outdoor time, be sure that the playground itself is not the cause of conflicts between children. Check to see if: (1) equipment is age appropriate, (2) the playground is properly designed, (3) there is a variety of loose parts available to suit children's needs, and (4) there are enough activities and space to accommodate the number of children present.

Once it has been determined that the playground is appropriate, teachers can prepare to deal with conflicts that naturally occur among children. A common method used to deal with problems on the playground is to banish one or more children from play for a period of time. Typically the child or children must sit in isolation along the parameters of the play yard until an adult allows them to resume their play. This well-known strategy for dealing with inappropriate behavior is labeled *time-out* when used with preschool children. Although it may be effective in stopping the behavior for the moment, requiring children to sit in isolation is considered a short-term solution and an undesirable practice by many early childhood educators. There are several reasons for this (Schreiber, 1999). First, time-out is an imposed method of controlling behavior that does not allow a child the opportunity to resolve conflicts independently. Adult-imposed isolation makes a child feel powerless and ineffectual. Second, repeated use of time-out negatively effects a child's self-esteem and may lead to negative labeling by peers. Lastly, time-out offers no opportunities for valuable learning experiences regarding appropriate behavior and dealing with conflict. Children become dependent on adults to impose their often illogical consequences.

Rather than imposing time-out for misguided behavior after it happens, McDermott (1999) recommends heading off conflicts by teaching important prosocial skills before problems occur. Teaching prosocial skills broadens children's repertoire for resolving conflict (Carlsson-Paige & Levin, 1992) and decreases aggression by increasing children's understanding of one another (Wittmer & Honig, 1994). Simply teaching rules is not enough to diminish conflict. Children need adult support to avert conflicts before they occur and to guide them when a situation gets out of control. In essence, teachers must be prepared to de-escalate conflict and "scaffold" children as they learn to resolve situations which are beyond their problem-solving ability (McDermott, 1999).

When a conflict cannot be avoided, Jacobs (1997) recommends teachers first observe and monitor how children are dealing with the problem on their own. According to Jacobs (1997), "If they never confront problems, they'll never learn to solve them" (p. 53). If, however, it becomes obvious that adult intervention is needed, Jacobs recommends teachers use one of three different models of conflict-resolution: perspective-taking, self-regulation, or negotiation.

Perspective-taking requires children to express their own thoughts as well as hear the other child's point of view. School-agers are less egocentric in their thinking than preschoolers and are more capable of understanding another's perspective. By keeping the situation calm and encouraging each child to have a turn expressing their view of the situation, teachers are demonstrating resolving conflicts through reasoning. The adult can begin assisting with dialogue by rephrasing a child's anger and asking for clarification: "Sandra thinks you threw the ball to intentionally hit her. Benjamin, can you explain to her what happened?"

Self-regulation is required when children respond to conflict with physical or violent retaliation. Rather than escalating the situation with an alarmed voice and more physical contact, teachers step in and model a calm tone and demeanor. Once the situation is under control, the teacher emphasizes the importance of using words to express feelings rather than violence.

Negotiation is necessary when children lack the maturity to resolve conflict over an object or area of the playground. Emphasize the importance of finding a solution that satisfies both children, and provide them with time to generate ideas. If both children stand their ground unwilling to change their position, the teacher may have to recommend a solution. This should be done compassionately, recognizing the children's displeasure with the outcome. Remind them they have the option of finding a better solution.

Helping children resolve conflicts is one of the most challenging aspects of teaching. Due to high activity levels, group play, and competitive games, there are even greater opportunities for conflicts to arise during outdoor play. It should be remembered, however, that learning to peacefully handle conflicts is one of the most critical skills children can learn.

CONCLUSION

Ironically, school mandates are decreasing the amount of time primary grade children spend outdoors at a crucial period in their development. School-age children need numerous and varied opportunities to use large and small muscles, interact cooperatively with peers, and develop an appreciation for their community. Through experiences on age-appropriate playground equipment supplemented with loose parts, primary grade children can successfully meet fitness goals. Involvement in games teaches good sportsmanship, competitive values, cooperation, and important social skills. Field trips into the community introduce children to another layer of their world and become the foundation for later learning within the classroom. Outdoor play and learning experiences also offer new opportunities for learning to deal with conflict and peacefully resolve problems. Classroom teachers must become advocates for primary grade students and their need for outdoor play and learning experiences.

KEY TERMS

cooperation   dynamic systems theory
games with rules   loose parts
concrete operational thought   persona doll story
causality   perspective-taking
multiple intelligences   self-regulation
naturalistic intelligence   negotiation
pragmatics

THEORY INTO PRACTICE

1. Interview an adult who was in the primary grades during the decades of 1950 or 1960 and ask about their memories of outdoor play or "recess." Ask teachers in your community about the amount of time allotted for free play outdoors for primary grade students. Compare the two and offer reasons why there is a change if a difference exists.

2. Introduce two different varieties of loose parts to school-age children and observe their behavior. How did they use the materials?

3. Teach a group of school-age children a game from those listed in Figure 4–7. Explain why you selected the game you did and how the children reacted to it.
4. Think of a suitable location for a field trip. Select and list three children's books relevant to the field trip experience.

RELATED WEB SITES

www.gamekids.com
Web site for children to exchange ideas for non-computer games and activities. A wide variety of games are listed in separate categories such as tag games, holiday games, water games, and sleepover games.
www.gameskidsplay.com
Extensive list of games including jump-rope rhymes, playground games, circle games, and traditional games. Several choices are available for game searches.

RELATED RESOURCES

Entz, S., & Galarza, S.L. (1999). *Picture this: Digital and instant photography activities for early childhood learning.* Thousand Oaks, CA: Corwin Press.

Erlbach, A. (1997). *Sidewalk games around the world.* Brookfield, CT: Millbrook Press.

Glock, J., Wertz, S. & Meyer, M. (1998). *Discovering the naturalist intelligence: Science in the schoolyard.* Tuscon, AZ: Zephyr Press.

Herd, M. (1997). *Learn and play in the garden: Games, crafts, and activities for children.* Hauppauge, NY: Barron's Educational Series.

Redleaf, R. (1997). *Open the door, let's explore more! Field trips of discovery for young children.* St. Paul, MN: Redleaf Press.

REFERENCES

Brewer, J.A. (1998). *Introduction to early childhood education: Preschool through primary grades.* Boston: Allyn & Bacon.

Bronfenbrenner, U. (1979). *The ecology of human development.* Cambridge, MA: Harvard University Press.

Carlsson-Paige, N., & Levin, D. (1992). Making peace in violent times: A constructivist approach to conflict resolution. *Young Children, 48*(1), 4–13.

Casbergue, R., & Kieff, J. (1998). Marbles, anyone? Traditional games in the classroom. *Childhood Education, 74*(3), 143–147.

Cromwell, S. (1998). Should schools take a break from recess? *Education World*. www.educationworld.com.

Derman-Sparks, L. (1989). *Anti-bias curriculum: Tools for empowering young children*. Washington, DC: National Association for the Education of Young Children.

Driscoll, A., & Nagel, N.G. (1999). *Early childhood education, Birth-8*. Boston, MA: Allyn & Bacon.

Ehlert, L. (1987). *Growing vegetable soup*. New York: Scholastic.

Elkind, D. (1981). *The hurried child*. Reading, MA: Addison-Wesley.

Erikson, E.H. (1963). *Childhood and society* (2d ed.). New York: Norton.

French, V., & Bartlett, A. (1998). *Oliver's Fruit Stand*. Danbury, CT: Orchard Books.

Gardner, H. (1993). *Multiple intelligences: The theory in practice*. New York: Basic Books.

Griffin, C., & Rinn, B. (1998). Enhancing outdoor play with an obstacle course. *Young Children, 53*(3), 18–23.

Harris, S. (1995). *I dig dirt*. Rochester, NY: Dreams Come True Productions.

Haselager, G.J.T., Hartup, W.W., van Lieshout, C.F.M., & Risen-Walraven, J.M.A. (1998). Similarities between friends and nonfriends in middle childhood. *Child Development, 69*, 1198–1208.

Jacobs, P.J. (1997). How to head off conflicts. *Scholastic: Early Childhood Today, 11*(7), 52–54.

Kamii, C. (1982). *Number in preschool and kindergarten: Implications of Piaget's theory*. Washington, DC: National Association for the Education of Young Children.

Kamii, C. (1985). *Young children reinvent arithmetic*. New York: Teachers College Press.

Kid Vision. (1994). *There goes a truck*. New York: A Vision Entertainment and Power to Create.

Leipzig, J. (1993). Community field trips. *Scholastic Pre-K Today, 7*(8), 44–51.

Levin, D.E. (1998). *Remote control childhood? Combating the hazards of media culture*. Washington, DC: National Association for the Education of Young Children.

McDermott, K. (1999). Helping primary school children work things out during recess. *Young Children, 54*(4), 82–84.

Miranda, A., & Stevens, J. (1997). *To market, to market*. San Diego, CA: Harcourt Brace & Company.

National Association for Elementary School Principals. (1999). All work and no play. *Communicator, 22*(5), 1.

Nicholson, S. (1973). The theory of loose parts. *Man/Society/Technology—A Journal of Industrial Art Education, 32*(4), 172–175.

Piaget, J. (1962). *Play, dreams, and imitation in childhood*. New York: Norton.

Ross, J.G., & Pate, R.R. (1987). The national children and youth fitness study: II. A summary of findings. *Journal of Physical Education, Recreation, and Dance, 58*, 51–56.

Savage, M., & Holcomb, D. (1999). Children, cameras, and challenging projects. *Young Children, 54*(2). 27–29.

Schneider, B.H., Wiener, J., & Murphy, K. (1994). Children's friendships: The giant step beyond peer relations. *Journal of Social and Personal Relationships, 11,* 323–340.

Schreiber, M.E. (1999). Time-outs for toddlers: Is our goal punishment or education? *Young Children, 54*(4), 22–25.

Seefeldt, C. (1998). Social studies in the integrated curriculum. In C.H. Hart, D.C., Burts, & R. Charlesworth (Eds.), *Integrated curriculum and developmentally appropriate practice.* Albany: SUNY Press.

Sporns, O., & Edelman, G.M. (1993). Solving Bernstein's problem: A proposal for the development of coordinated movement by selection. *Child Development, 64,* 960–981.

Svenson, A. (1999). A recess for recess? *Family Education Network.* www.familyeducation.com.

Theemes, T. (1999). *Let's go outside! Designing the early childhood playground.* Ypsilanti, MI: High Scope Press.

Trawick-Smith, J. (2000). *Early childhood development: A multicultural perspective.* Upper Saddle River, NJ: Merrill/ Prentice Hall.

U.S. Consumer Product Safety Commission. (1997). *Handbook for public playground safety* (No. 325). Washington DC: U.S. Government Printing Office.

Wittmer, D.S., & Honig, A.S. (1994). Encouraging positive social development in young children. *Young Children, 49*(5), 4–12.

CHAPTER 5

Observing and Assessing Children's Outdoor Play

Guiding Questions

1. *What are three reasons to assess children in an outdoor setting?*
2. *What are the components of the Assessment of Learning Cycle and what does each mean?*
3. *What is the purpose of IEPs and IFSPs?*
4. *How do systematic record keeping, product collection, and standardized tests contribute to the overall assessment of children?*

INTRODUCTION

Henniger (1993/1994) argues that educators and administrators find classrooms and indoor activities much more important than the experiences that come from an outdoor play environment. He bases this argument on three separate findings. First, significantly less attention is given to the subject of planning outdoor play spaces as opposed to preparing indoor spaces in introductory early childhood textbooks. Second, the National Association for the Education of Young Children devotes only a fraction of attention to the importance of outdoor play as compared to other types of play in their guidelines for developmentally appropriate practice (Bredekamp, 1987; Bredekamp & Copple, 1997). Third, teachers spend considerably less planning time organizing and procuring materials for outdoors as compared to time spent planning indoor activities. To summarize, Henniger (1993/1994) states, "Teachers and administrators and others generally consider playgrounds and the activities that occur there less important than indoor spaces in the lives of young children" (p. 87).

Based on these findings, it is a fair assumption that educators also give less time and attention to assessing play and learning outdoors as compared to evaluating children's indoor activities. There are a number of possible reasons for this deficit in assessing outdoor activities, including: an attitude that outdoor activity is only recreational and therefore assessment is not necessary; an overriding emphasis on achievement tests, class work, and teaching skills; or simply a lack of knowledge about how to assess outdoor play. Whatever the reason, failing to assess children during outdoor play results in a unbalanced evaluation of what children can and cannot do. In order to accurately assess the whole child, their skills and abilities should be observed and documented under multiple conditions. Reasons *to* assess outdoor play include:

1. It provides an opportunity to observe gross motor skills and other movements such as running, jumping, and climbing that are typically not allowed indoors.

2. Observing outdoor play contributes to the assessment of the whole child. Individuals may exhibit greater strengths or new weaknesses in an outdoor setting.
3. Valuable data can be collected for making referrals or in designing IFSPs or IEPs.
4. Assessing outdoor play demonstrates to parents, colleagues, administrators, and others its inherent value.
5. It offers a new arena for becoming aware of children's individual interests.
6. Children are observed performing motor skills and other movements in an authentic context rather than in isolation.
7. Outdoor assessment contributes to planning instruction for all developmental domains.

Outdoor play contributes to a child's learning and overall development; therefore, assessment under these conditions is crucial to understanding and planning subsequent experiences for every child.

THE ASSESSMENT PROCESS

The word assessment is a broad term that brings to mind different meanings for different people. To one teacher it may mean a simple checklist that is completed and later reviewed during a conference with the parents of a child. To another it may imply a single standardized test score. And to yet another teacher it may bring to mind periodic grading on a report card. Checklists, tests, and report cards are all considered types of assessment, yet the meaning of the term goes far beyond these examples.

Assessment is defined by Nilsen (2001) as "the process of observing, recording, and documenting a child's actions, skills, and behaviors" (Nilsen, 2001, p. 419). According to the National Association for Sport and Physical Education (1992), systematic assessment is "based on knowledge of developmental characteristics and ongoing observations of children as they participate in activities. This information is used to individualize instruction, plan objective-oriented lessons, identify children with special needs, communicate with parents, and evaluate the program's effectiveness" (p. 10). A third definition of assessment is "any method of collecting information about the current status of an individual child, a group or sample of children, a program or a professional" (Grace & Shores, 1998, p. 142). Collectively, these three definitions provide a complete picture of what is involved in the assessment process.

The Southern Early Childhood Association (Grace & Shores, 1998) identified the following five criteria as a foundation for assessing young children:

1. Assessment must be valid. It must be accurate and supply data which reflects established goals or objectives.
2. Assessment must encompass the whole child. Documentation should reflect information from each developmental domain including physical, cognitive, social, emotional, and language.
3. Assessment must involve repeated observations. Accurate analysis of a child can only be achieved through repeated observations. Hasty decisions based on a few isolated observations lead to inaccurate and unfair assessment.
4. Assessment must be continuous. Benchmarks and developmental profiles are helpful in determining how a child's abilities compare with a norm. However, each child should be compared to himself or herself over time to fairly assess growth and development over time.
5. Assessment must use a variety of methods. Information should be collected in varied ways using different methods to give a clear, accurate picture of a child's abilities.

There are two separate phases to assessment. The first involves the act of collecting information about the child or group of children. This includes observing, recording, and documenting behaviors or abilities. The second part of the assessment process involves interpreting the information and deciding how it will be used. Assessment data can be used for future lesson planning, to report to others such as parents or specialists, and sometimes to evaluate a particular teaching technique or curriculum. Deciding how data collected will be used is a crucial aspect of assessment.

For example, a teacher who invests time and effort in collecting anecdotal records of her students as they play in learning centers is wasting her energy if the notes are simply filed into a child's personal record. In order to be useful, the anecdotal records must be reviewed over time in conjunction with records made using other methods and an evaluation made as to how the child is progressing. Then a specific plan of action for remediation or enrichment can be made so the child can continue his progress. This continuous process is illustrated in Figure 5–1. The assessment of learning cycle represents the ongoing nature of assessment. The major components of assessment—observe, document, assess, report/confer, and plan—continuously flow into one another. "There is virtually no beginning or end to evaluating children's learning, and each phase is dependent on those that come before and after" (Wellhousen & Kieff, 2001, p. 184).

This cyclical approach to assessing children's learning is efficiently organized by means of a **portfolio system.** Portfolios allow teachers to plan their assessment strategy in advance, organize observations from a myriad of techniques, evaluate and report on a child's

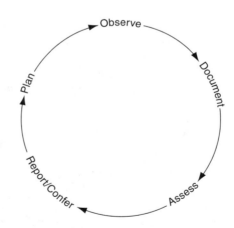

Figure 5–1   The assessment of learning cycle.

Reprinted with permission from Wellhousen, K., & Kieff, J. (2001). *A constructivist approach to block play in early childhood.* Albany, NY: Delmar.

progress, and subsequently make plans for future teaching strategies. Simply defined, a portfolio is "a systematic collection of documentation about the child's development" (Nilsen, 2001, p. 421). There are unlimited ways to implement and organize a portfolio assessment system and fortunately, a wide variety of resources that provide guidelines for initiating this process. (See Related Resources at the end of this chapter.) The Southern Early Childhood Association (Grace & Shores, 1998) recommends organizing portfolios around developmental domains including fine motor development, gross motor development, concept development, language and literacy, and personal and social development. This particular organizational process is well-suited for documenting and evaluating children's development as it relates to outdoor play and learning.

The National Association for the Education of Young Children (NAEYC) and the National Association of Early Childhood Specialists in State Departments of Education (NAECS/SDE) jointly developed eighteen guidelines for appropriate assessment in programs serving children ages three to eight years (NAEYC, 1991). As assessment strategies are developed, such as designing a portfolio system, these guidelines should be considered. Examples of these essential guidelines include:

- Are the results of assessment used to benefit children, i.e., to plan for individual children, improve instruction, identify children's interest and needs, and individualize instruction, rather than label, track, or fail children?
- Does the assessment procedure address all domains of learning and development—social, emotional, physical, and cognitive—as well as children's feelings and dispositions toward learning?
- Does the assessment procedure rely on teachers' regular and periodic observations and record keeping of children's everyday activities and performance so that results reflect children's behavior over time?
- Does the assessment examine children's strengths and capabilities rather than just their weaknesses or what they do not know?

- Is there a systematic procedure for collecting assessment data that facilitates its use in planning instruction and communicating with parents?

This sampling of guidelines reflects the stated need for assessment systems that are useful, fair, and straightforward enough to communicate findings to others.

ASSESSING CHILDREN WITH SPECIAL NEEDS

The field of Early Childhood Special Education (ECSE) provides detailed explanations for assessment and recommended follow-up services for young children with special needs. Integral to this process are the **individualized family service plan (IFSP)** and the **individualized education program (IEP).** Access to early intervention programs and preschool special education are mandated under the Individuals with Disabilities Act (IDEA), a federal program created in 1986.

The individualized family service plan (IFSP) is a written document that outlines the early intervention services to be received by an infant or toddler (birth to the third birthday) with a disability and may also include the family. The IFSP includes the infant's or toddler's special needs based on an evaluation of five domains: physical development, cognitive development, communication development, social/emotional development, and adaptive development. Services to be received are described, such as: physical, occupational, or speech and language therapy; psychological services; and special instructions for the infant or toddler along with a statement and timeline of major outcomes expected. Additional family services can also be offered. The IFSP is reviewed at least every six months and evaluated every year.

The individualized education program (IEP) contains the terms of the special education and related services a child with a disability will receive. It may be written for children as young as two years of age who are turning three years old during an academic year. IEPs are written for students through the twelfth grade. The complete contents of the IEP include: (1) present levels of educational performance and special needs;

(2) annual goals for meeting the needs of the child; (3) services to be provided; (4) extent to which the child will participate with typically developing children; (5) beginning date and duration of services; and (6) process for informing parents of child's progress (IDEA section 602). Parents of children with special needs must not only be apprised of their child's progress as outlined on the IEP but also be asked to make a judgment concerning their child's improvement or lack of improvement. Both IFSPs and IEPs are confidential.

The Individuals with Disabilities Act mandates that children with disabilities be placed in the *least restrictive environment (LRE)*. This means that special education students should, when possible, be placed in educational settings used by nondisabled children. These inclusive practices are believed to benefit children receiving special services as well as children who have no disabilities (Bowe, 2000).

"Increasingly the early childhood teacher is faced with the inclusion of young children with special needs and challenges in the classroom or child care facility" (Klein, Cook, & Richardson-Gibbs, 2001, p. 4). Because continuous assessment is integral to evaluating and planning for young children with special needs, teachers in regular education classrooms need to be aware of the following (Klein, Cook, & Richardson-Gibbs, 2001):

- IFSPs and IEPs are legal documents specifying goals, outcomes, and priorities.
- The teacher *must* have a copy of the document and be aware of its contents.
- The teacher should help plan how the goals will be addressed in the classroom.
- The teacher will be at least partially responsible for monitoring and documenting progress.
- Progress must be monitored regularly.

Opportunities for outdoor play are equally (in some cases more) necessary for children with special needs. Playing outdoors offers a change from the classroom environment and additional opportunities to develop gross motor, self-help, and social skills (Klein, Cook, & Richardson-Gibbs, 2001). Teachers can include evaluations of children's accomplishments outdoors as part of the continuous monitoring necessary for IEPs.

To assist with planning adaptations for children with special needs in an inclusive setting, Klein, Cook, and Richardson-Gibbs (2001) suggest teachers use the Inclusion Adaptations Checklist (see Figure 5–2). The checklist indicates the type of adaptation needed in the following areas: personnel, physical assistance, curriculum, pacing and amount of time per activities, hierarchy of prompts, environment, and behavior. A separate Inclusion Adaptations Checklist should be prepared for outdoor play because outdoor activities will usually require different adaptations from those in a classroom setting. For example, a child seated in a wheelchair may need little or no physical help in the classroom but partial or full physical help in order to participate in outdoor activities. The checklist will aid teachers and other support personnel plan for individual children's needs outdoors as well as indoors.

DESIGNING A PLAN FOR ASSESSMENT

Designing a plan for assessing young children involves making decisions about what aspect of their play and learning will be observed, documented, and interpreted. This requires a thorough understanding of basic child growth and development principles. Teachers must also decide what types of assessment techniques will be utilized and how the information will be shared with others.

One of the primary areas teachers will be assessing in the outdoor play environment is gross motor skills and related movements. Even though the best measure of progress comes from comparing a child to his prior capabilities or limitations, teachers need to be aware of developmental milestones for typically developing children. This information contributes to assessment by determining whether a child falls within or outside a range of what is considered *typical* development. For example, most three-year-olds climb stairs alternating feet and using the hand rail for balance. If a four-year-old is consistently observed climbing stairs by placing both feet on a step before ascending to the next one, the teacher will want to watch his climbing

Figure 5–2 Inclusion Adaptations Checklist.

Child's Name _____ Date _____

**Inclusion Adaptations Checklist
Check adaptations anticipated for this child.**

Personnel

_____ No extra support necessary
_____ Part-time extra support (specific parts of day)
_____ Full-time extra support (1:1 aide)

Physical Assistance

_____ No physical help necessary
_____ Physical help as needed
_____ Partial physical help
_____ Full physical help

Curriculum

_____ Adapt for lower cognitive level
_____ Adapt for vision impairments
_____ Adapt for hearing impairments
_____ Adapt for physical handicaps

Pacing and amount of time per activities

_____ Same pace and time as all other children
_____ Less time than other children (e.g., less attention)
_____ More time than other children (e.g., goes slower)
_____ Slower pacing necessary for understanding (e.g., more wait time
for comprehension and/or action)

Hierarchy of prompts

_____ Full physical help to complete activities
_____ Partial physical help to compete activities
_____ Direct verbal reminders to complete activities (e.g., "Sit down")
_____ Indirect verbal reminders to complete activities (e.g., "What do you
need to do?")
_____ Gestures to complete activities (e.g., pointing)

Environment

_____ Seating adaptations (e.g., chairs too high, child does better sitting
next to specific peers, etc.)
_____ Reduce/minimize distractions or stimulation
_____ Define limits (e.g., physical and/or behavioral)

(continued)

Figure 5–2 Continued.

Behavior

_____ Define limits (e.g., physical and/or behavioral)
_____ Use positive reinforcement
_____ Determine behavior plans through use of ABC (antecedent,
_____ behavior, consequences)

Reprinted with permission. Klein, M.D., Cook, R.E., & Richardson-Gibbs, A.M.
(2001). *Strategies for including children with special needs in early childhood
settings.* Albany, NY: Delmar.

progress carefully and, if needed, implement a screening test that assesses motor development. The Bayley Scales (Bayley, 1969) show motor milestones in infancy and can be found in Chapter 2, Figure 2–1. Benchmarks of fine motor and gross motor skills are reprinted in Chapter 3, Figure 3–2 (Herr & Larson, 2000). The National Association of Sports and Physical Education (NASPE, 1990) developed a set of benchmarks that reflect skill and knowledge outcomes expected of children participating in a quality physical education program. Benchmarks for kindergarten physical education include:

- demonstrates competency in many movement forms and proficiency in a few movement forms
- applies movement concepts and principles to the learning and development of motor skills
- exhibits a physically active lifestyle
- achieves and maintains a health-enhanced level of physical fitness
- demonstrates responsible personal and social behavior in physical activity setting
- demonstrates understanding and respect for differences among people in physical activity setting
- understands that physical activity provides the opportunity for enjoyment, challenge, self-expression and social interaction

These benchmarks can be used for assessment purposes to determine if a child's physical skills fall within a range of development that can be considered *typical.*

(See Figure 5–4 for a checklist designed for assessing children based on the NASPE benchmarks.)

Even though physical skills are an obvious area to assess outdoors, observations should extend to other developmental domains as well. Children free to use louder, "outside voices" may express themselves better using a greater range of dynamics and larger vocabulary. A child who does not excel in academic areas can have the opportunity to be a leader and role model outdoors as he exhibits the ability to run faster than other peers. With fewer restrictions on how and where to move, and more opportunities for free play, children may show fewer signs of stress and be more cooperative as they interact with playmates. Outdoor play offers many valuable opportunities to observe children in authentic play situations.

Methods for documenting children's learning in outdoor play settings have been divided into three categories: **systematic record keeping, product collection,** and **standardized evaluations.** Systematic record keeping requires careful observation and documentation of a child's actions and language. Methods of systematic recording include anecdotal records, observation guides, and checklists/rating scales. Product collection entails producing tangible evidence of a child's new accomplishments or attempts. For the purposes of assessing learning in an outdoor play setting, photographs and videotapes are recommended. Standardized measures are tests that have been developed using rigorous empirical procedures. An individual's performance on a test is evaluated by comparing the test score to a predetermined set of norms.

Systematic Record Keeping: Anecdotal Records

An anecdote is an interesting story or tale that is relatively brief and has a satisfying conclusion. As families share the most significant aspects of their day with one another, they informally take turns telling anecdotes. As teachers, we often share with one another anecdotes that contain humorous events or expressions used by the children we teach. Writing an anecdotal record is a variation on telling an interesting anecdote. Anecdotal records contain three major components: the setting is explained, important details are included, and an obvious conclusion is offered. Like a good story, an anecdotal record provides just enough detail to make the reader feel as if she were there. Typically, anecdotal records set the stage for the reader, identify central characters, describe action in detail, describe interaction between characters, record exact quotes, and conclude with an obvious outcome or reaction among characters (Nilsen, 2001). The record itself should record *only* what is observed. Interpretations or reactions to the event can be noted in a separate section for comments. An example of an anecdotal record is presented in Figure 5–3.

The tangible forms of anecdotal records vary. Forms that have been printed in advance simplify the process because basic information such as names of children observed, name of observer, date, time, and setting can simply be filled in on the blank spaces provided. A blank space should be left where the actual observation is written followed by a section for comments that provides more space for the observer to write a subjective interpretation. Teachers also use sheets of adhesive-backed labels to make anecdotal records. The sheets can be attached to a clipboard and carried outdoors to make records of children's actions. Later, the records can easily be filed by peeling each label and sticking it to children's individual record folders or portfolio.

Since the primary purpose of anecdotal records is to provide on-going evidence of a child's development over time (Kapel, Gifford, & Kapel, 1991), multiple records must be collected. A minimum of one or two records per child each week provides enough documentation for reliable interpretation of behaviors (Nicholson & Shipstead, 1998). When reviewing anecdotal records to draw conclusions, teachers need to keep in mind findings from other data available on the child. For example, anecdotal records can be reviewed in conjunction with checklists, photographs, and standardized measures before evaluations or recommendations are made. Reviewing all information increases reliability in findings and reduces the chance of inaccurately or unfairly evaluating a child.

Figure 5–3   Anecdotal records.

Child(ren): *Daniel (4) and Cody (5)*   **Observer:** *Monique M.*

Date: *2–20*   **Time:** *10:30*   **Setting:** *Playground*

Daniel and Cody are wearing firefighter hats and announce, "We're putting out fires today." Daniel picks up the end of a (discarded) vacuum cleaner hose and points it at the playhouse. Cody rushes in and tries to pull out the two girls inside shouting, "Get out! Your house is on fire!" The girls stop their tea party role-playing and join in the new drama by screaming, "Help!" and "We can't leave the baby." One girl grabs a baby doll and all three children run from the house yelling, "Fire, fire, Mrs. McGuire."

Comments

Daniel and Cody are probably responding to our integrated unit on fire safety. Daniel showed ingenuity in using the vacuum cleaner hose (he had brought from home) as a fire hose. The girls demonstrated flexibility by suddenly stopping their own role-play to join in another. They also showed concern for others as they remembered to "save" the baby doll. The children used a familiar line from a book as they shouted, "Fire, fire, Mrs. McGuire."

Child(ren): *Golden (5)*   **Observer:** *Anita B.*

Date: *2–24*   **Time:** *10:40*   **Setting:** *Playground*

Miss Anita supervises closely and helps children as they cross the horizontal ladder. Golden approaches the apparatus saying, "I'm trying something new today." He swings out holding onto the first rung with both hands, then releases his right hand and grabs the third rung, releases his left hand and grabs the fifth rung. He continues "skipping" every other rung until he reaches the end of the horizontal ladder. Children watching and waiting for a turn applaud as Golden steps onto the adjacent platform.

Comments

Golden is physically strong and enjoys taking risks. Supervision is important to ensure he is not injured when trying new things. The children appreciate and are motivated by his physical ability.

Child(ren): *Katrina (3) and Gabrielle (3)*   **Observer:** *Anissa L.*

Date: *3–1*   **Time:** *9:30*   **Setting:** *Sandbox*

Katrina and Gabrielle are digging a hole in the middle of the sandbox. As the hole gets deeper, sand from the opening begins to spill in. "Stop doing that," says Katrina. "I'm not doing it, you are," says Gabrielle. The girls are silent and continue digging when more dry sand from the opening spills

(continued)

Figure 5–3 Continued.

into the hole. Katrina stands up and begins kicking more sand into the hole as she clenches her teeth and repeats, "You're stupid, stupid, stupid." Gabrielle begins to cry. Miss Anissa sits down next to them, holds Katrina in her lap and consoles Gabrielle. She explains and demonstrates why the sand continued to seep into the hole. Then she helps the girls dig a new hole and demonstrates how to wet the sand at the opening using a trigger spray bottle. The girls become interested in the changing color of the sand when it is wet and stop digging.

Comments

Katrina and Gabrielle both expressed their frustration at not being able to control a "fluid" material. Katrina needed to be physically reassured that it was not her fault or the fault of her friend. They either became distracted when a new feature was added to the sand play (water) and/or were happy not to return to the frustrating task of digging a hole.

Systematic Record Keeping: Observation Guides

Observation guides contain a list of predetermined questions that can be used to conduct assessments of a child's performance. Questions can be adapted from program goals or curriculum objectives. A set of five or six direct, relevant questions can provide a great deal of information about progress when used to collect assessment data for each child three to four times a year. When responses are compared over time, children's strengths and weaknesses become evident (Wellhousen & Kieff, 2001). Observation guide questions pertaining to children's outdoor play might include:

1. Does the child show enthusiasm for outdoor play?
2. What playground equipment, loose parts, outdoor learning center, or games does the child choose most often?
3. What new motor skills has the child attempted and/or mastered?
4. Is the child usually successful in his/her attempts to play with peers in an outdoor setting?
5. How does the child manage problems that occur in outdoor play settings? Does he/she attempt to

resolve them alone, with peers, or with an adult's assistance?

6. What is the child's greatest achievement during this observation period?

These six general questions provide an abundance of data that can be analyzed along with other observation records. General questions presented in an observation guide contribute to the overall assessment of the whole child.

Systematic Record Keeping: Checklists and Rating Scales

Checklists and rating scales are among the most familiar assessment methods. Both contain a list of observable behaviors, usually arranged in a logical sequence. Checklists provide a space to indicate whether or not a particular behavior is observed while rating scales require the observer to indicate the frequency and/or quality of the behavior. For example, the item "runs with control while changing direction" will be answered differently on a checklist than on a rating scale. A checklist requires simply a response of "yes" or "no," while a rating scale provides information about the frequency of the behavior (never, rarely, sometimes, or always runs with control over direction) and/or the quality of the behavior (minimal or utmost control). In most cases, rating scales are preferred because of the additional information provided. Fortunately, it is relatively easy to adapt checklists into a rating scale format. See Figure 5–4 for a checklist based on national professional standards published by NASPE (1992) and compiled by Steve Sanders, Ph.D., Tennessee Technological University.

Products: Photographs and Videotapes

Products are a method of assessment that provide tangible evidence of a child's new attempts, challenges, and accomplishments. New technology affords teachers the opportunity to photograph and videotape children at play with relatively little expense. Recyclable and used cameras, donations of fresh rolls of film, plus special offers for developing can greatly reduce costs. Digital cameras and scanners that allow for reproducing

Figure 5–4 Checklist for outdoor play.

Child's Name _____ **Date** _____

Check the appropriate column: D = Demonstrated, ND = Not Demonstrated

Skill	D	ND

Standard 1. *Demonstrates competency in many movement forms and proficiency in a few movement forms.*

	D	ND
Travels in forward and sideways directions using a variety of locomotor (non-locomotor) patterns and changes in direction quickly in response to a signal.	____	____
Demonstrates clear contrasts between slow and fast movements while traveling.	____	____
Walks and runs using mature form.	____	____
Rolls sideways without hesitating or stopping.	____	____
Tosses a ball and catches it before it bounces twice.	____	____
Kicks a stationary ball using a smooth continuous running step.	____	____
Maintains momentary stillness bearing weight on a variety of body parts.	____	____

Standard 2. *Applies movement concepts and principles to the learning and development of motor skills.*

	D	ND
Walks, runs, hops, and skips, in forward and sideways directions, and changes direction quickly in response to a signal.	____	____
Identifies and uses a variety of relationships with objects (e.g., over/under, behind, alongside, through).	____	____
Identifies and begins to utilize the technique employed (leg flexion) to soften the landing in jumping.	____	____

Standard 3. *Exhibits a physically active lifestyle.*

	D	ND
Participates regularly in vigorous physical activity.	____	____
Recognizes that physical activity is good for personal well-being.	____	____
Identifies feelings that result from participation in physical activities.	____	____

Standard 4. *Achieves and maintains a health-enhancing level of physical fitness.*

	D	ND
Sustains moderate to vigorous physical activity.	____	____
Is aware of his or her heart beating fast during physical activity.	____	____

Figure 5–4 Continued.

	D	ND

Standard 5. *Demonstrates responsible personal and social behavior in physical activity settings.*

	D	ND
Knows the rules for participating in the gymnasium and on the playground.	____	____
Works in a group setting without interfering with others.	____	____
Responds to teacher signals for attention.	____	____
Responds to rule infractions when reminded once.	____	____
Follows directions given to the class for an all-class activity.	____	____
Handles equipment safely by putting it away when not in use.	____	____
Takes turns when using a piece of equipment.	____	____
Transfers rules of the gym to "rules of the playground."	____	____

Standard 6. *Demonstrates understanding and respect for differences among people in physical activity settings.*

	D	ND
Enjoys participation alone and with others.	____	____
Chooses playmates without regard to personal differences (e.g., race, gender, disability)	____	____

Standard 7. *Understands that physical activity provides the opportunity for enjoyment, challenge, self-expression, and social interaction.*

	D	ND
Enjoys participation alone and with others.	____	____
Identifies feelings that result from participation in physical activities.	____	____
Looks forward to physical activity.	____	____

From NASPE. (1995). *Moving into the Future: National Standards for Physical Education.* St. Louis, MO: Mosby-Year Book. This checklist is based on national professional standards published by the National Association for Sport and Physical Education (NASPE). Compiled, designed, and reprinted with permission from Dr. Steve Sanders, Tennessee Technological University.

---

pictures via computers can reduce costs even further. Video cameras can be borrowed or rented periodically if one is not available through the school. Each child can bring one videotape labeled with her name to be used throughout the year. These ideas make using photographs and videotapes an affordable and enjoyable way to document children's growing abilities.

Photographs and videotapes offer a logistical way of capturing children's motor skills as well as other types of learning that take place in an outdoor setting.

A photograph or videotape of a child crossing the horizontal bars offers peers, parents, and teachers an opportunity to celebrate the accomplishment over and
over. Other skills that would otherwise be impossible
to save include building a creation in the sand box,
erecting a playhouse from hollow blocks, independently staying in motion on a swing, completing an
obstacle course, moving from a wheelchair to a transfer station with minimal assistance, tossing and catching a beanbag, and carefully filling containers at the
water table. These valuable accomplishments are often
overlooked in the assessment process because it is difficult to document the event (Kuschner, 1989; McAfee &
Leong, 1997).

Showing children tangible evidence of themselves
as they attempt new challenges or show off an accomplishment that is the result of much practice is an ideal
way to introduce children to the concept of self-
assessment. As they look at a series of photographs
taken over a period of time, or view two separate
videotapes made months apart, children can proudly
see for themselves the accomplishments achieved. This
contributes significantly to their self-awareness and
self-esteem as well as provides a source of motivation.
Woods (2000) explains how photographs also support

social development and self-awareness. "As children look and share, new discoveries emerge about themselves and others. They explore both their similarities and their differences, the qualities that make them members of the human species, and the qualities that establish their individuality within the species" (Woods, 2000, p. 82).

In addition to filing photographs in individual portfolios to be used as documentation in parent conferences, pictures can be copied and used in displays around the classroom. For example, a bulletin board can be titled, "Look What We Can Do," with individual photographs of children's outdoor accomplishments each framed by a colorful background. A brief description of the photographs, such as "Jake works in the garden," contributes to children's reading and writing development. Bulletin boards and other displays provide a gratifying way for children to celebrate their own accomplishments as well as those of their peers.

Video cameras have been used to assess early literacy development through dramatic play in the classroom (Reynolds & Milner, 1998). Since dramatic play is a major form of play in an outdoor setting, video cameras can be used to preserve the unfolding stories that occur on the playground. Children's literacy learning is enhanced as they later watch themselves on video and discuss their play (Reynolds & Milner, 1998). They enjoy seeing themselves on camera but also use the information to create future scenarios to be played out (Paley, 1990).

Sanders and Yongue (1998) suggest teachers videotape children individually as they perform various skills such as running, jumping, throwing, catching, and striking. As families view and discuss the video of their child in action, they can contribute important information to the assessment and learning process. Personally viewing a videotape of a child's abilities provides valuable information that other types of assessment cannot.

Some Tips for Photographing and Videotaping Children Photographs and videotapes are only useful if they are of good enough quality to visually show what children are doing during outdoor play. Taking good shots requires some basic know-how, patience, and practice. With a little preplanning, providing documentation of children's accomplishments through photographs and videos will become routine.

The following tips for teachers will enhance photos taken in a school setting (Woods, 2000).

- Get close enough to the subject to clearly see the action and eliminate uninteresting background.
- Feel free to "crop" or cut excess views that interfere with the subject of the photograph.
- Pictures of children "in action" are the goal as opposed to those in which children are posing.
- Black and white photographs can be inexpensively copied and therefore used in a variety of ways.

Finally, since photographs are used for assessment purposes, keep a camera loaded with film and available at all times. An ideal way to keep a camera handy outdoors is to carry it in a cause that can be worn around the waist.

Video cameras are bulky, expensive equipment as compared to cameras. If one is not readily available on a daily basis, use video cameras to periodically showcase skills individual children have learned over a period of three to four weeks. Another use is to videotape children playing and talking about what they like to do best outdoors. Tips for videotaping children outdoors include:

- Introduce video camera equipment to children prior to taping. Allow them to look through the lens and touch the camera.
- Depending on the subject of the taping, the camera can be mounted out of children's reach or attached to a tripod. In both cases, a remote control is extremely helpful.
- Prior to videotaping children for assessment purposes, walk around with the camera while it is set to record. With time, children will be accustomed to this and the novelty of the video camera will diminish, allowing for more accurate recording of behaviors.

Remember, before taking any photographs or videos of children, obtain written permission from parents and guardians. Explain why pictures and videos are being taken and how they will be used. Teachers can use this opportunity to request permission to display photos, show videotapes at group functions (such as an open house), and even submit them to local newspapers and television stations. It is important to be respectful of parents' decisions as to whether or not they will allow their child to be photographed and about how the pictures of their child can be used.

Standardized Evaluations

Standardized evaluations are very different from systematic observations and product collection. The primary difference is the specified conditions under which a test is given. In an attempt to duplicate the testing situation, test directions, time allotted, physical environment, and training of test administrators are kept as similar as possible. Also, standardized tests undergo rigorous evaluation in order to determine their dependability and to establish norms used to interpret individual test scores.

Standardized tests have received much criticism from experts in the field of early and primary education. Critics identify a number of reasons for minimizing the administration of standardized tests in the early years.

- Many standardized tests designed for young children fall short of technical standards established by the American Psychological Association (Goodwin & Goodwin, 1993; Meisels, Steele, & Quinn-Leering, 1993; Shepard & Graue, 1993).
- The use of standardized tests has become so massive it robs educational institutions of time and money that could be put to better use to benefit children (McAfee & Leong, 1997) and pressures teachers to shape instruction to fit the test (Meisels, Steele, & Quinn-Leering, 1993; Shepard & Graue, 1993).
- Results of tests are misused (National Association for the Education of Young Children, 1988).
- Tests may be biased and incapable of accurately assessing children other than those who are typically developing and from English-speaking, middle class, backgrounds(FairTest, 1990; Perrone, 1975–1978, Bagnato & Neisworth, 1991).

- The developmental nature of young children is not conducive to most testing situations (Kamii, 1990).

Professional early childhood organizations have published position papers on the subject of standardized tests. The Association for Childhood Education International (Perrone, 1975–1978) published a position paper titled *On Standardized Testing and Evaluation*, which expressed concern over the usefulness and accuracy of standardized test scores. A primary concern was the decisions being made regarding the placement of children in special education classes based on single test scores (Wortham, 1995). A decade later, the National Association for the Education of Young Children adopted its *Position Statement on Standardized Testing of Young Children 3 through 8 Years of Age* in November 1987 (NAEYC, 1988). The position paper outlines seven guidelines to be followed when administering, interpreting, and making decisions based on standardized test scores. Both of these respected organizations specifically state that *if* standardized test scores are used to evaluate young children, they should be used with caution and decisions about instruction or placement will not be made based on standardized test scores alone.

Standardized tests can supply valuable assessment information *if* the test is well-designed, fair, and accurate and *when* standardized test scores are used as just one piece of the assessment puzzle. Wortham (1995) cites distinct advantages of incorporating standardized test scores into the assessment process. First, standardized tests undergo analysis to determine if they are valid and reliable. Second, they provide uniformity in test administration. Third, the results are quantifiable scores that allow for comparison of an individual's performance to an established standard.

Even though standardized tests are typically administered under controlled indoor settings, results can still be used for planning outdoor play experiences. For example, one standardized test screens a preschooler's ability to hop on one foot and throw a bean bag. Another provides data on how well children listen and follow directions. A third test measures children's socialization skills in a group setting. Teachers can use test results to plan outdoor learning experiences, such as devising activities that promote hopping, and introducing soft objects for throwing. Games such as "Simon Says" and "Mother May I?" can be introduced as a way to encourage children to listen and follow directions. With test scores reflecting a child's social abilities, teachers are better prepared to help a shy child enter a play group and give her increased opportunities to be a leader. Even though a standardized test may not be designed as a measure of children's outdoor play abilities, the results can still be used in planning appropriate experiences.

Standardized Testing of Infants and Toddlers
The problems of testing children from birth to age two or three years are obvious, yet developmental screening instruments have been designed specifically for this age group. The Neonatal Behavioral Assessment Scale (Brazelton, 1984) is used to identify mild neurological dysfunctions and variations in temperament of newborns. The *Denver Developmental Screening Test,* Revised (Frankenburg, Dodds, Fandal, Kazuk, & Cohrs, 1975) measures gross motor, fine motor, language, and social abilities of children from birth until six years of age. The information provided from these standardized instruments is useful for early detection of neurological problems and deficiencies in other domains.

Standardized Testing of Preschool and Kindergarten Children   Many of the standardized tests administered in the preschool years can be classified as **developmental screening instruments.** These evaluations are used to provide information about whether or not a child's development is proceeding like typically developing children. If a developmental screening instrument indicates a child's development is delayed, as compared to others their age, additional testing devises are then used. Two developmental screening tests that can be used with preschoolers are the *Denver Developmental Screening Test,* Revised (Frankenburg, Dodds, Fandal, Kazuk, & Cohrs, 1975) and the *Developmental Indicators for the Assessment of Learning,* Third Edition (DIAL-III) (Mardell-Czudnowski & Goldenberg, 1998). The DIAL-III assesses motor, concept, and language skills for children aged two to six years. It is designed to screen a range of ability from severe dysfunction to potentially advanced. Further testing is recommended for children scoring at either of the two extremes of this range.

Standardized Tests for Primary Grade Children
There are numerous intelligence tests, achievement tests, and skills tests that are required of children in the primary grades. Standardized tests are also available for measuring skills and abilities children typically learn through outdoor play activities. Usually, these are administered during organized physical education classes by teachers who have been trained to administer, score, and interpret findings. One widely recognized test given annually in physical education classes throughout the United States is the President's Challenge (President's Council on Physical Fitness and Sports, 2000–2001). Requirements vary based on the age of the child and national norms have been established for children ages six to seventeen.

Test items include physical skills such as curl-ups or partial curl-ups, shuttle run, one mile run/walk,

pull-ups, and v-sit and reach. Each child's performance is compared to the set of national norms based on other children the same age and gender. Based on their performance, children may be awarded the Presidential Physical Fitness Award for an outstanding level of physical fitness, the National Physical Fitness Award for achieving a challenging level of physical fitness, the Participant Physical Fitness Award for a score that falls below the 50th percentile on one or more of the test items, or the Health Fitness Award for students who reach a healthy level of fitness.

Since the goal of the President's Challenge (President's Council on Physical Fitness and Sports, 2000–2001) is to provide motivation for life-long physical activity, provisions are outlined for accommodating students with disabilities. The following guidelines are for qualifying students with disabilities for the Presidential, National, Participant Physical Fitness, or the Health Fitness Award.

1. The instructor has reviewed the individual's records to identify medical, orthopedic, or other health problems which should be considered prior to participation in physical activities including physical fitness testing.
2. The individual has a disability or other problem that adversely affects performance on one or more test items.
3. The individual has been participating in an appropriate physical fitness program that develops and maintains cardio-respiratory endurance, muscular strength and endurance, flexibility, and body composition.
4. The instructor has administered all five test items making needed modifications or substituting alternative test items for the individual.
5. The instructor judges that the individual has been tested on all five test items and/or in each of the five fitness categories and has performed at a level equivalent to a Presidential, National, Participant Physical Fitness, or the Health Fitness Award (President's Council on Physical Fitness and Sports, 2000–2001, p. 7).

These guidelines are a good example of how some standardized measures can be modified for students with disabilities.

The American Alliance for Health, Physical Education, Recreation, and Dance (AAHPERD) endorses FITNESSGRAM® (AAHPERD, 2000) as a tool for assessing students' levels of fitness in Kindergarten through grade twelve. This assessment establishes a baseline from which students can set personal goals and check their own progress. Students are essentially competing against themselves rather than other students in their grade, school, or at a national level. Rather than emphasizing sports-related performance, FITNESSGRAM® (AAHPERD, 2000) stresses health-related physical fitness. This is important because only approximately ten percent of the student population is considered athletically talented. FITNESSGRAM® (AAHPERD, 2000) and its accompanying educational program Physical Best® strive to educate all children regardless of their abilities or disabilities (AAHPERD, 2000).

CONCLUSION

A strong case can be made for assessing children's play and learning in an outdoor setting. Assessment data collected in an outdoor setting can be used to supplement and complement more traditional evaluations of performance in a classroom situation. Through systematic record keeping, product collection, and standardized tests, teachers can create a portfolio that offers a fair assessment of what children can do. Teachers need an understanding of appropriate assessment techniques as well as a thorough knowledge of legal requirements for evaluating and planning for children, regardless of special needs.

KEY TERMS

portfolio system   systematic record keeping
individualized family service   product collection
  plan (IFSP)   standardized evaluations
individualized education   developmental screening
  plan (IEP)   instruments

THEORY INTO PRACTICE

1. Ask a teacher to tell you about the types of evaluations he uses. How is the information used to inform his

teaching? Are children's outdoor play and learning assessed?

2. Implement one of the techniques for systematic record keeping: anecdotal records, observation guide, or checklist/rating scale. What did you find useful about the technique? What was difficult about using it?

3. Review a test manual for a standardized test. Read about features of the test such as the standardization sample, reliability and dependability factors, test administration and scoring, and practical considerations (such as how long it takes to administer the test and how much training is required).

RELATED WEB SITES

www.aahperd.org
The homepage for the American Alliance for Health, Physical Education, Recreation, and Dance provides information on the organization's program and events and publications and resources.

www.indiana.edu
The President's Challenge Web site provides information on placing orders and program information. Those interested can subscribe to a monthly e-mail distribution, "fitnessfun."

www.fitness.gov
Web site address for The President's Council on Physical Fitness and Sports.

www.agsnet.com
The American Guidance Service publishes a variety of assessments for students of all ages as well as textbooks and instructional materials.

www.fairtest.org
The National Center for Fair and Open Testing (FairTest) is an advocacy organization that challenges the misuse of standardized tests. The Web site explains current projects and offers written publications.

RELATED RESOURCES

Helm, J.H., Beneke, S., & Steinheimer, K. (1997). *Windows on learning: Documenting young children's work*. New York: Teachers College Press.

Shores, E.F., & Grace, C. (1998). *The portfolio book: A step-by-step guide for teachers*. Beltsville, MD: Gryphon House.

Meisels, S.J., & Atkins-Burnett, S. (1994). *Developmental screening in early childhood: A guide* (4th ed.). Washington, DC: National Association for the Education of Young Children.

REFERENCES

American Alliance of Health, Physical Recreation, and Dance. (2000). FITNESSGRAM®. Reston, VA: American Alliance of Health, Physical Recreation, and Dance.

Bagnato, S.J., & Neisworth, J.T. (1991). *Assessment for early intervention*. New York: Guilford Press.

Bayley, N. (1969). *Bayley scales of infant development: Birth to two years*. New York: Psychological Corporation.

Bowe, F.G. (2000) *Birth to five:* Early childhood special education (2d ed.). Albany, NY: Delmar.

Brazelton, T.B. (1984). *Neonatal behavioral assessment scale* (2d ed.). Philadelphia, PA: J.B. Lippincott.

Bredekamp, S. (Ed.). (1987). *Developmentally appropriate practice in early childhood programs serving children birth through age 8*. Washington, DC: National Association for the Education of Young Children.

Bredekamp, S., & Copple, C. (Eds.). (1997). *Developmentally appropriate practice in early childhood programs* (Rev. ed.). Washington, DC: National Association for the Education of Young Children.

FairTest. (1990). Wh33at's wrong with standardized tests? *Factsheet*. Cambridge, MA: National Center for Fair and Open Testing.

Frankenburg, W., Dodds, J., Fandal, J. Kazuk, E., & Cohrs, M. (1975). *Denver developmental screening test* (Rev.) Denver, CO: University of Colorado Medical Center.

Goodwin, W.R., & Goodwin, L.D. (1993). Young children and measurement: Standardized and nonstandardized instruments in early chldhood education. In B. Spodek (Ed.), *Handbook of research on the education of young children* (pp. 441–463). New York: Macmillan.

Grace, C., & Shores, E. (1998). *The portfolio and its use*. Little Rock, AR: Southern Early Childhood Association.

Henniger, M.L. (1993/1994). Enriching the outdoor play experience. *Childhood Education, 70*(2), 87–90.

Herr, J., & Larson, Y. (2000). *Creative resources: For the early childhood classroom* (3d ed.). Albany, NY: Delmar.

Kamii, C. (Ed.). (1990). *Achievement testing in the early grades: The games grown-ups play*. Washington, DC: National Association for the Education of Young Children.

Kapel, D., Gifford, C., & Kapel, M. (1991). *American educators' encyclopedia*. New York: Greenwood Press.

Klein, M.D., Cook, R.E., & Richardson-Gibbs, A.M. (2001). *Strategies for including children with special needs in early childhood settings*. Albany, NY: Delmar.

Kuschner, D. (1989). Put your name on your painting, but . . . the blocks go back on the shelves. *Young Children, 45*(1), 49–56.

Mardell-Czudnowski, C., & Goldenberg, D.S. (1998). *DIAL-III: Developmental indicators for the assessment of learning* (3d ed.). Circle Pines, MN: American Guidance Service.

McAfee, O., & Leong, D. (1997). *Assessing and guiding young children's development and learning* (2d ed.). Boston: Allyn & Bacon.

Meisels, S.J., Steele, D.M., & Quinn-Leering, K. (1993). Testing, tracking, and retaining young children: An analysis of research and social policy. In B. Spodek (Ed.), *Handbook of research on the education of young children* (pp. 279–292). New York: Macmillan.

National Association for Sport and Physical Education (NASPE). (1992). *Developmentally appropriate physical education practices for young children. A position statement of the Council on Physical Education for Children of NASPE.* Reston, VA: AAHPERD.

National Association for the Education of Young Children. (1988). Position statement on standardized testing of young children 3 through 8 years of age. *Young Children, 43*(3), 42–47.

National Association for the Education of Young Children and The National Association of Early Childhood Specialists in State Departments of Education (NAEYC and NAECS/SDE). (1991). Guidelines for appropriate curriculum content and assessment in programs serving children ages 3 through 8. *Young Children, 46*(3), 21–38.

Nicholson, S., & Shipstead, S. (1998). *Through the looking glass: Observations in the early childhood classroom* (2d ed.). Columbus, OH: Merrill.

Nilsen, B. (2001). *Week by week: Plans for observing and recording young children* (2d ed.). Albany, NY: Delmar.

Paley, V. (1990). *The boy who would be a helicopter.* Cambridge, MA: Harvard University Press.

Perrone, V. (1975–1978). *On standardized testing and evaluation.* Wheaton: MD: Association for Childhood Education International.

President's Council on Physical Fitness and Sports. (2000–2001). *The President's challenge: Physical fitness program packet.* Bloomington, IN: U.S. Department of Health and Human Services.

Reynolds, M.R., & Milner, S. (1998). Preschoolers on camera: Using video to explore emergent literacy. *Dimensions, 26*(1), 23–24.

Sanders, S.W., & Yongue, B. (1998). Challenging movement experiences for young children. *Dimensions, 26*(1), 9–17.

Shepard, L.A., & Graue, M.E. (1993). The morass of school readiness screening: Research on test use and test validity. In B. Spodek (Ed.), *Handbook of research on the education of young children* (pp. 293–305). New York: Macmillan.

Wellhousen, K., & Kieff, J.(2001). *A constructivist approach to block play in early childhood.* Albany, NY: Delmar.

Woods, C.S. (2000). A picture is worth a thousand words—Using photographs in the classroom. *Young Children, 55*(5), 82–84.

Wortham, S. (1995). *Measurement and evaluation in early childhood education* (2d ed.). Englewood Cliffs, NJ: Merrill.

CHAPTER **6**

Playground Safety and Accessibility

Guiding Questions

1. What are the four categories for playground safety identified by the National Program for Playground Safety?
2. What is the meaning of the term "critical height"? List five common types of playground surfacing material.
3. How is the "use zone" calculated for swings and slides?
4. What are five common playground hazards? How can injuries from these hazards be prevented?
5. How does the Americans with Disabilities Act Accessibility Guidelines differentiate between ground level and elevated play components?

INTRODUCTION

Young children are naturally drawn to outdoor play activities. Outdoors they enjoy a special kind of freedom to run, jump, yell, and exhibit other behaviors that are typically not allowed in an indoor setting. Play equipment designed specifically for children's age, ability levels, and special needs provides countless opportunities for learning new skills, challenging one's own abilities, interacting with peers, and simply enjoying the outdoors. Perhaps this is why outdoor playgrounds have been a favorite activity for generations of young children.

There has been an increase in awareness of playground safety over the last two decades. Government agencies and consumer protection groups recommend specific safety standards for playgrounds. As a result, manufacturers of playground equipment scientifically test materials for safety and stability.

Playground designers are concerned with playground safety as well accessibility. Federal guidelines now specify the number of different playground components that must be accessible to children in wheelchairs. Surfacing materials must be planned carefully to ensure that children in wheelchairs can move from the school or parking area to the playground with relative ease, as well as access play equipment.

In addition to being safe and accessible, playgrounds must provide creative outdoor spaces for children to play. As our understanding of how children's play contributes to their learning progresses, so must our willingness to provide them with the appropriate environment and materials.

OVERVIEW OF PLAYGROUND SAFETY

Statistics on playground-related deaths and injuries read like grim newspaper headlines (PIRG, 1998; CPSC, 2000; AP, 2000):

- An eight-year-old girl in Neptune, New Jersey, dies after falling eight feet from the top of a horizontal ladder (monkey bars) to the hard ground.

- A seven-year-old boy in Oakland, California, falls from the horizontal ladder hitting his head on asphalt that was exposed due to a worn out rubber padding and dies in the hospital five days later.
- Three preschoolers died in separate incidents involving head entrapment. The children slid off a platform trapping their heads between a guardrail and the platform and strangled to death.
- A child's head became entrapped in a cargo net while playing at a fast food restaurant. A parent rushed to cut the net to release the child.
- There have been incidents in which children suffered second- and third-degree burns to hands, legs, and buttocks from sitting on metal stairs, decks, or slides that were exposed to the heat and sun.
- A three-year-old at a child care center was strangled to death when, in play, a child placed a rope around his neck.

Over the last two decades, incidents such as these have led to an emphasis on the safety features of outdoor play spaces for children. This is a result of alarming statistics regarding injuries and deaths on American playgrounds. According to the Public Interest Research Groups (PIRG, 1998) falls to the ground account for about seventy-five percent of all playground related injuries and about thirty-three percent of the deaths due to playground-related injuries. Children under six years of age are more likely to sustain head and facial injuries from falls because they do not have the motor coordination or cognitive skills required to intuitively break falls by putting their arms in front of their bodies. Older children are more likely to use their arms to break falls and as a result are more susceptible to upper limb fractures.

Other types of injuries result from the equipment itself. Strangulation accounts for almost half of all fatalities related to playground equipment. Strangulation is caused by either **entanglement** or **head entrapment.** Entanglement occurs when something the child is wearing, such as jacket hoods, drawstrings, scarves, mittens, clothing, or necklaces, becomes caught on equipment and wrapped around the child's neck resulting in strangulation. Head entrapment occurs when a child enters an opening in equipment (such as between guardrails or rungs on a ladder), either head first or feet first but cannot withdraw his head because the opening is too small. Openings between 3.5 inches and 9 inches present a risk for head entrapment and death by strangulation. Smaller openings prevent children's body parts from sliding through and entrapping the head. Larger openings allow the entire body, including the head, to move through the space, thus preventing strangulation.

There are many other hazards associated with playgrounds, but as young children play, they pay little or no attention to protecting themselves and those around them from injury. It is the responsibility of adults who care for and teach young children to ensure that outdoor play areas and equipment are safe and free from danger. The fact that children are attempting new physical challenges outdoors makes it impossible to eliminate all risks, but much can be done to the environment itself to reduce the number of playground related injuries and deaths.

CATEGORIES OF PLAYGROUND SAFETY

The PIRG (1998) has investigated playgrounds in the United States every two years from 1996–1998. The 1998 study found improvements in playgrounds as compared to previous years, but serious hazards were still identified. Similarly, the National Program for Playground Safety (NPPS, 2000) conducted a more recent study of America's playgrounds with more upsetting findings. Even though each state was given a separate rating (see Figure 6–1), the overall grade for playgrounds in the United States was a "C." The survey divided twenty-three criteria into four separate categories: supervision, age-appropriateness, fall surfacing, and equipment maintenance. These categories can be remembered by using the acronym *S-A-F-E*. The two lowest graded categories contributing to the majority of the 20,000 injuries and 17 deaths that occur annually on America's playgrounds are "supervision" and "age-appropriate design." However, all four categories deserve adequate attention in order to reduce current injury and death statistics and make playgrounds safer.

Figure 6–1 State-by-state report card grades for playground safety.

Alabama	C–	Montana	C+
Alaska	C+	Nebraska	C
Arizona	B+	Nevada	B
Arkansas	C–	New Hampshire	C+
California	B–	New Jersey	C–
Colorado	B	New Mexico	B–
Connecticut	C	New York	C
Delaware	B	North Carolina	C–
Florida	D–	North Dakota	C+
Georgia	B	Ohio	C+
Hawaii	C–	Oklahoma	B
Idaho	C–	Oregon	B
Illinois	C	Pennsylvania	C+
Indiana	C+	Rhode Island	C+
Iowa	C–	South Carolina	C
Kansas	C+	South Dakota	B
Kentucky	C	Tennessee	B
Louisiana	B–	Texas	B–
Maine	C	Utah	B
Maryland	B–	Vermont	C–
Massachusetts	C+	Virginia	C
Michigan	D–	Washington	C–
Minnesota	C+	Wisconsin	D+
Mississippi	C–	West Virginia	C
Missouri	C–	Wyoming	B–

Source: The National Program for Playground Safety.

Supervision for Safety

Lack of supervision is cited as a contributing factor in approximately forty percent of reported playground injuries (NPPS, 2000). The problems associated with a lack of supervision apply to community parks, backyards, child care centers, and schools for children of all ages. An all-too-familiar site when driving past schools that care for young children is a group of caregivers seated in a cluster during outdoor playtime while children are at play. This is widely recognized as an inadequate and ineffective means of supervising children, yet some teachers still equate outdoor play periods as a "break time" for teachers. Teachers do need brief periods of time away from children and opportunities to converse with other adults, but directors and supervisors need to schedule these appropriately and make clear distinctions. Otherwise, teachers will perceive

---

Figure 6–2 Newspaper article reporting death on child care playground.

Child Dies at Tuscaloosa Day Care:
Police Investigate Apparent Accident in Which Boy Was Strangled

TUSCALOOSA—The apparent strangulation death of a 3-year-old boy at a Tuscaloosa day-care center appeared to be accidental, police said, but an investigation was continuing.

Deronte Rashawn Fields died about 10:30 a.m. Friday on the playground of Jelly Belly Child Care and Development Center, authorities said. The child's brother told his parents he saw another child put a rope around Deronte's neck.

"At this time, investigators feel the boy's death could have been accidental, but a full-blown investigation is under way," said Tuscaloosa Police Chief Ken Swindle. He said some details of the child's death were not being released.

The incident happened while Deronte was in a group of seven or eight children inside a fenced-in playground at the day care, accompanied by an adult, police said.

Police interviewed adults and children at the center Friday. Attempts by The Tuscaloosa News to reach the center's owner, Lisa Foster, were unsuccessful Friday.

Deronte had turned 3 the day before. His mother, Raqual Bell, said she had planned to bring his birthday cake to the center for a party Friday. "With his smile and his laugh, Deronte was the life of the party," she said.

Reprinted with permission of The Associated Press.

---

outdoor play as a break time from responsibilities, which is a dangerous assumption. Outdoor play poses unique risks to children and attentive supervision is imperative to avoiding injury. A lack of quality supervision can quickly lead to disaster such as that described in Figure 6–2.

What *should* teachers be doing during outdoor playtime? What is considered good supervision? Obviously, adults must watch for potential dangers and intervene when children may be at risk of injury. In essence, they are watching for those "accidents waiting to happen" in order to prevent injury before it occurs. This requires vigilant observation and an understanding of individual children and their abilities. Teachers must watch for hundreds of situations that may occur during an afternoon of outdoor play, such as rough-and-tumble play that becomes too aggressive, untied shoestrings and drawstrings in clothing, or a child attempting a new climbing challenge.

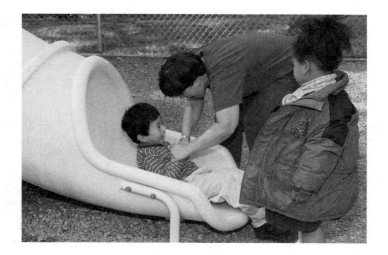

NPPS (2000) offers the following guidelines for supervising children during outdoor play.

1. An adequate ratio of adults to children should be maintained. There should be no fewer adults supervising children during outdoor play than there are indoors. Preferably, more adults should be available during outdoor play.

2. Adequate supervision can only occur when all children can be seen. There should be no blind spots such as long tunnels or crawl spaces where children can be hidden from view.

3. Teachers must watch for loose strings on clothing and shoes, which can be caught in equipment and cause serious injury such as strangulation. Drawstrings around winter coat hoods should be removed.

4. Have an emergency plan in place. In addition to having a first aid kit on hand at all times (see Appendix A), emergency phone numbers for medical assistance and for contacting parents should be readily available. All incidents involving injury must be documented.

5. Rules should be reviewed daily and enforced consistently. Children ages two to five years should have no more than three or four simple rules so they can remember them. Because there are only

a few rules, they should be fairly generic but suitable to the play yard and equipment.

Examples of simple rules include:

1. Watch out for other children as you play.
2. Use toys, equipment, and materials as they are intended.
3. Come *down* the slide only.

Beaty (1999) recommends having children set the rules when appropriate, such as deciding how many children can share an outdoor learning center. This suggestion is not appropriate when safety is at stake. Children can still participate in rule making, however, by dramatizing the correct way to follow a rule and discussing what might happen if the rule is broken. For example, two children may demonstrate how buckets and shovels are to be used in the sand center. Afterwards, the group can discuss what might have happened if the buckets had been thrown or if the sand had been poured out above children's heads. Thinking and talking about these actions and consequences help children understand and follow rules.

Teachers must be prepared for instances when children break the rules. When redirecting a child, be firm without shouting or becoming angry. Rules are meant to make all children feel safe, not threatened (Beaty, 1999). Remind children that the rules are meant to keep everyone safe and impose an appropriate consequence such as discussing the rule privately or, if the child is upset, requiring her to sit close to you for a few minutes until she regains her composure. Children should feel as if they have learned how to get along better in an outdoor play environment, rather than feeling punished.

Rules should never make up for age-inappropriate playgrounds. Frost (1992) offers the example that the rule "we will not chase a ball into the street" (p. 241) is unsuitable for a group of preschoolers on an unfenced playground next to a busy street. The correct solution is, of course, to build a fence. Rules are established and taught as a way to remind children of appropriate behavior in an environment that is designed for their needs. In addition, the CPSC (1997) suggests that adults supervising children be thoroughly familiar with determining which equipment is appropriate for the children under their supervision.

Supervision for Learning In addition to supervision for safety's sake, teachers are responsible for children's learning outdoors, just as they are in the classroom. Therefore, teachers need to understand the careful balance of involvement in children's play without interference. Deciding when and how to become involved can be difficult and depends on many factors including age of children, ability levels, prior experiences, and risk-taking behaviors.

Infants and young toddlers are almost totally dependent on adult caregivers. They may need physical assistance, such as moving a nonmobile infant to a shady area or steadying the hand of a toddler as he attempts to pour sand through a sieve. Preschoolers, on the other hand, are anxious to master new challenges and demonstrate their success to caring adults. Teachers of preschoolers have many demands for their attention as children shout, "Watch me swing! Watch me slide! Watch me run!" Sincere enthusiasm for each accomplishment secures preschoolers' confidence in new skills. Primary grade students will rely less on teachers during outdoor play, but this does not minimize their important role. Grade school teachers must be creative in introducing new equipment and ideas for games. They play a crucial role in keeping all children involved in active play, regardless of their physical ability (see Figure 5–1). Regardless of the age of their students, teachers perform an optimum role in supporting outdoor play and learning.

In order to illustrate the degrees of teacher involvement, a model designed for the block center has been adapted for the play yard (Wellhousen & Kieff, 2001) and is shown in Figure 6–3. The degree of teacher involvement is spread across a continuum ranging from "minimum" to "moderate." The left end of the continuum includes teacher behaviors that support children's play and learning in the least intrusive manner. These include initial set-up of equipment, documenting learning experiences, and providing materials to promote new and varied types of experience. The

---

Figure 6–3   Teacher involvement continuum for outdoor play.

Minimum ◄————————————————————————————► **Moderate**

> Designing play area
>> Initial set-up of equipment
>>> Document learning
>>>> Providing materials to vary experiences
>>>>> Assist with clean-up
>>>>>> Respond to requests for assistance
>>>>>>> Ask relevant questions
>>>>>>>> Maintain close physical proximity
>>>>>>>>> Engage in role play
>>>>>>>>>> Suggest an activity
>>>>>>>>>>> Take part in a game

---

middle of the continuum includes teaching strategies that require more small group and individualized attention, such as responding to requests for assistance, asking relevant questions, and assisting with clean-up. The far right of the continuum describes teacher behaviors that are the most officious. If adequate adult supervision is available to keep children safe, one adult may choose to join a game, engage in role-playing, suggest an activity, or maintain close physical proximity as a child attempts a new physical challenge. Reviewing the continuum and adding relevant adult behaviors for specific play yards helps teachers be prepared to facilitate learning as children play.

Age-Appropriate Design

According to the NPPS (2000), one of the most problematic aspects of America's playgrounds is a lack of attention to age-appropriate design. In order to design good playgrounds, adults must first decide the age category which the play area will serve. NPPS recommends playgrounds be designed with two distinct age categories in mind—ages two to five years or ages five to twelve years—and that these age guidelines be posted and enforced when children approach playground equipment. The need for this logical approach to preventing injuries through offering age appropriate equipment is made evident through two observations made at a neighborhood child care center.

Observation 1

The class of toddlers (18–24 months) shares a playground used by young preschoolers (3 year olds). Even though the director has tried to make the play yard appropriate for the toddlers by offering Little Tykes® slides, Adam, a wiry twenty-month-old, is drawn to the climbing equipment designed for older children. He constantly darts toward the larger ladder and slide, which is clearly beyond his climbing ability, requiring adults to intervene and redirect Adam to age-appropriate play equipment.

Observation 2

The after-school care group bounces out of the van and heads straight for the playground, eager to spend their pent-up energy from a long day at school. The kindergartners and small first graders still feel challenged by the preschoolers' climbing equipment but larger, older, and more agile children quickly grow bored with the climbing and sliding equipment designed for two- to five-year-olds. Janine, an dexterous first grader, climbs from the opening of the tube slide onto the top and scales her way up where she then climbs over the supporting beam of the equipment. Supervising adults rush to stop her, but she is quick. The problem is a reoccurring one.

Both examples demonstrate the problem of children playing on equipment that is not designed for their respective ages. In the first example, Adam is drawn to a piece of equipment that is beyond his physical ability while Janine, in the second example, is limited to play equipment that is too restricting for her needs. Admittedly, it is a challenge for centers and schools to accommodate both groups, but it is absolutely imperative for safety's sake.

To facilitate playground design, the CPSC (1997) specifically lists equipment that should *not* be accessible to children ages two to five years. These include chain or cable walks, free-standing arch climbers, fulcrum seesaws, long spiral slides with more than one turn, overhead rings, parallel bars, and vertical sliding poles. Young children do not typically possess the motor skills and physical abilities needed to play safely on this equipment.

The CPSC (1997) provides a list of equipment designed for preschool-age children with specific recommendations for each item. These include rung ladder and ramps, climbers, horizontal ladders, merry-go-rounds, spring rockers, single-axis swings, and tot swings. Before installing equipment or while evaluating existing playgrounds, it is strongly advised that *The Handbook for Public Playground Safety* (CPSC, 1997) be consulted.

Community parks and school playgrounds that serve children ages five to twelve need to plan an obvious layout that shows the distinct areas for each age group. The two areas can be separated visually with plants or a seating area with posted signs designating the appropriate area for each age group. Playgrounds designed specifically for the use of younger children must also post signs to guide adults and assist them in enforcing age limits for children's safety.

In addition to safety reasons, children need age-appropriate playgrounds to facilitate their overall growth and development. Outdoor play allows for a variety of experiences that are not available inside a classroom. Also, the outdoor experience adds a new dimension to activities that are usually done indoors. In order to design an age appropriate playground with safety *and* learning in mind, planners need to consider a number of different factors such as appropriately sized equipment and materials to serve children's developmental needs. Reputable playground equipment manufacturers are knowledgeable about differences in children's physical abilities and construct equipment according to age appropriate guidelines. Examples of modular playground systems intended for different age groups and additional information relating to age appropriateness of playgrounds is presented in each of the age-specific chapters (see Chapters 2, 3, and 4).

Fall Surfacing

Supplying appropriate surfacing to cushion falls is the third recommendation made by NPPS (2000) for preventing death and injuries to children during outdoor play. Falls from equipment may result in life-threatening head injuries and are the cause of the majority of emergency room visits due to playground injuries (Tinsworth & Kramer, 1990). As a result, falls to the ground were a contributing factor in about seventy-five percent of all reported playground injuries (NPPS, 2000). The PIRG

(1998) survey of 760 U.S. playgrounds revealed that eighty-seven percent of playgrounds in the study lacked adequate protective fall surfacing necessary for minimizing injuries from falls (see Figure 6–4). Resilient surfaces, such as wood chips, gravel, sand, and synthetic material, filled to an appropriate depth, reduce the frequency and severity of head injuries. Hard surfaces such as grass, packed dirt, concrete and asphalt provide no protection. For example, a short fall of only two inches onto concrete or asphalt can result in a life-threatening head injury. A fall from the same distance onto a surface of six inches of uncompressed wood chips will protect the head from any injury. Therefore, providing and maintaining appropriate playground surfacing is crucial to reducing the risk of injury and death on playgrounds.

Recommended surfacing materials are divided into two categories: loose-fill and unitary. Loose-fill materials include fine or coarse sand, fine or medium gravel, shredded wood mulch, wood chips (identified as engineered wood fibers by CPSC), and shredded tires. When installed on natural surfaces such as earth or grass (never on asphalt or concrete), loose-fill materials can adequately absorb the impact of a fall if a sufficient depth is maintained. The depth of fall surfacing material needed to prevent life-threatening injuries de-

Figure 6–4 Protective surfacing results from study of U.S. playgrounds by Public Interest Research Groups (PIRC)

% Playgrounds with adequate protective surfacing

	1994	1996	1998
loose fill of depth greater than 9 inches (wood chips, mulch, sand, etc.)	3	10	6
unitary synthetic surfacing	5	5	7
total adequate	8	15	13

% Playgrounds with inadequate protective surfacing

	1994	1996	1998
loose fill of inadequate depth of less than 9 inches	60	61	58
hard surfaces (cement, asphalt, grass, packed soil, etc.)	13	9	8
mixed hard and loose fill surfaces	19	15	22
total inadequate	92	85	87

Source: PIRC, 1998.

pends on which type of loose-fill is selected. For example, twelve inches deep of coarse sand can prevent a life-threatening head injury for a child falling six feet. But twelve inches deep of fine gravel can prevent a life-threatening head injury from a fall of up to ten feet. CPCS conducted tests to determine the shock absorbing properties of common loose-fill materials. These test comparisons are made when loose-fill materials were uncompressed because compression of loose-fill materials reduces their ability to cushion impact. It is crucial, therefore, to regularly maintain loose-fill materials by raking, sifting, turning, and loosening. This maintenance also helps collect and remove debris. Loose-fill must be replaced as needed to maintain the proper depth. A border that contains loose-fill materials is required to prevent it from scattering and minimizing its capacity to cushion falls.

Unitary materials refer to commercially developed fall surfaces such as rubber tiles, rubber mats, and poured rubber. CPSC (1997) defines unitary surfaces as "rubber mats or a combination of rubber-like materials held in place by a binder that may be poured in place at the playground site and then cured to form a unitary shock absorbing surface." Shock absorbing properties of unitary materials varies from product to product, therefore, critical heights test data should be requested from individual manufacturers along with site requirements for installment before making a selection. The comparisons between types of loose-fill materials (and recommended depths) are made in Figure 6–5.

Surface materials such as asphalt, concrete, dirt, and grass are considered inappropriate and dangerous under play equipment. As an illustration, NPPS points out that a fall from eight feet onto a dirt surface equals the life-threatening injuries a child would sustain if she hit a brick wall traveling thirty miles per hour. A comparison of the different types of playground surfacing materials is made in Figure 6–6.

Maintenance/Placement of Surface Materials

Adequate fall surfacing materials must be selected, installed, and maintained. Depths lower than required standards after installation can be the result of compaction, decomposition, or displacement of materials. A permanent marking on a piece of stationary equipment at the appropriate height serves as a reminder that

Figure 6–5   Fall height (in inches) from which a life-threatening head injury
would not be expected.

	Critical heights (in feet) of tested materials			
	Uncompressed depth		Compressed depth	
Material	6 inch	9 inch	12 inch	9 inch
wood chips*	7	10	11	10
double-shredded bark mulch	6	10	11	7
engineered wood fibers†	6	7	>12	6
fine sand	5	5	9	5
coarse sand	5	5	6	4
fine gravel	6	7	10	6
medium gravel	5	5	6	5
shredded tires‡	10–12	N/A	N/A	N/A

*This product was referred to as Wood Mulch in previous versions of this handbook. The term Wood Chips more accurately describes the product.

†This product was referred to as Uniform Wood Chips in previous versions of this handbook. In the playground industry, the product is more commonly known as Engineered Wood Fibers.

‡This data is from tests conducted by independent testing laboratories on a 6 inch depth of uncompressed shredded tire samples produced by four manufacturers. The tests reported critical heights which varied from 10 feet to greater than 12 feet. It is recommended that persons seeking to install shredded tires as a protective surface request test data from the supplier showing the critical height of the material when it was tested in accordance with ASTM F1292.

Source: U.S. Consumer Product Safety Commission (1997). *Handbook for public playground safety* (No. 325). Washington, DC: U.S. Government Printing Office.

fall surfacing materials need to be replenished. If the mark can be seen, the level of surfacing materials is too low.

Equally important to selecting and maintaining surfacing materials is determining where they will be placed. Surfacing materials must be placed around equipment from which children could fall. Virtually all equipment requires surfacing material with the exception of those that require a child to be standing or sitting at ground level during play, such as sand boxes and play houses. The appropriate depth of surfacing material should be placed directly underneath playground equipment and, in most cases, extend six feet in all directions. This guideline applies to equipment such as merry-go-rounds, spring rockers, stationary climbing equipment, and composite play structures

Figure 6–6 Comparison of playground safety materials.

Materials	Advantages	Disadvantages
loose organic materials—wood chips, park mulch, engineered wood fibers	low intial cost easy to install less attractive to pets readily available engineered wood fiber may be accessible	subject to environmental conditions decomposes subject to fungus easily displaced requires containment borders requires good drainage continuous maintenance
loose inorganic materials—sand, gravel	low initial cost easy to install nonflammable readily available	may be affected by environmental conditions combines with dirt or may compact not accessible abrasive floors, skin conceals animal excrement and debris easily displaced continuous maintenance requires containment borders
loose synthetic materials—chopped rubber, plastics	easy to install slow to decompose not subject to fungus growth nonabrasive readily available does not deteriorate less likely to compact	higher initial cost flammable may contain contaminants from processing not accessible easily displaced continuous maintenance requires containment borders requires good drainage
fixed synthetic materials—rubber tiles, poured-in-place rubber urethane combinations	easy to clean consistent shock absorbency—does not compact not attractive to pets optional colors available minimal maintenance generally accessible not displaced generally does not require containment border some materials can be installed over concrete, asphalt, stone	high initial cost may be susceptible to frost damage may be flammable requires skilled installation subject to vandalism often must be used on level surfaces

Note: Adapted from *Handbook for Public Playground Safety* (Document #325), by the U.S. Consumer Product Safety Commission, 1997. Web site: www.cpsc.gov/cpscpub/pubs/chld_sfty.html
Source: Theemes, T. (1999). *Let's go outside: Designing the early childhood playground.* Ypsilanti, MI: High/Scope Press.

(two or more play activities attached to one structure). The exception to this "six feet" guideline is the area under swings and slides where there is a larger use zone. Concrete footings around all equipment must be well-covered with the appropriate depth of surfacing.

Swings The PIRG (1998) found swings are involved in about twenty-six percent of all injuries on public playground equipment. About sixty-six percent of swing-related injuries are falls to the surface below and twenty-five percent of swing injuries are caused by impact with a moving swing. Children five and younger are most often injured by impact with a moving swing. The primary dangers associated with single-axis swings include: (1) children running in front of or behind a child swinging; (2) children being hit by the seat of a swing that has not come to a full rest; and (3) children jumping from a swing in motion. Each of these situations can cause severe injuries and efforts to maximize safety on and near swings must be taken if they are included on the playground. Swings should be located away from other high-activity areas and a low barrier placed around the perimeter of the use zone. Seats should be made from lightweight rubber or plastic rather than wood or metal. Ideally, no more than two swings should be hung together in a single bay and these should have a minimum of twenty-four inches between each swing and a minimum of thirty inches between the swing and the supporting structure (see Figure 6–7). Installing swing hangers at least twenty inches apart reduces the side-to-side motion that causes collisions between two children swinging next to each other.

Single-axis swings have a use zone of twice the height from the ground to the supporting crossbar, both in the front and back of the swing. The use zones to the sides follow the six feet guideline. The distance from the seat to surfacing material below should be no less than twelve inches for preschoolers and no less than sixteen inches for primary grade students. Multi-axis swings (such as tires hung horizontally) require a use zone of six feet *plus* the distance from the crossbar to the swing. The use zone under a multi-axis swing extends in every direction because the swing, suspended by three separate chains connected to a single swivel mechanism, pivots at 360 degrees.

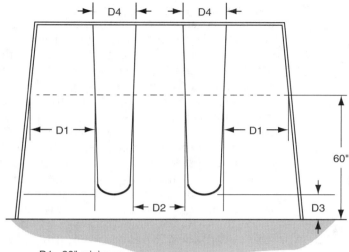

D1 = 30" minimum
D2 = 24" minimum
D3 = 12" minimum for preschool-age children
16" minimum for school-age children
24" minimum for tot swings
D4 = 20" minimum

Figure 6–7 Minimum clearances for single-axis swings.

Source: U.S. Consumer Product Safety Commission (1997). *Handbook for public playground safety* (No. 325). Washington, DC: U.S. Government Printing Office.

Multi-axis swings are to be hung alone rather than next to a second multi-axis swing or a single-axis swing. Multi-axis swings should not be attached to a composite structure. A minimum clearance of thirty inches between the supporting structures and the swing seat when rotated nearest the structure is required (see Figure 6–8). Tires are generally used as a swing seat, however, heavy truck tires are too dangerous to be used as swings. If steel-belted radials are used, regular examination is needed to protect children from dangerous protrusions. Drainage holes drilled in the underside of the tire allow water to drain. Several children tend to use multi-axis swings at once, adding to the stress placed on the hanger mechanism. Children using the swing in small groups of two or three cause only limited stress, but regular attention to the maintenance of the swing mechanism is necessary.

Swings designed for use by toddlers require a use zone in front of and behind the swing that measures twice the distance from the pivot point to the lowest point on the seat. The tot swing (intended for children four years of age and younger to use with adult assistance) should be hung so that the seat is at least 24 inches from the surfacing material. This will make it

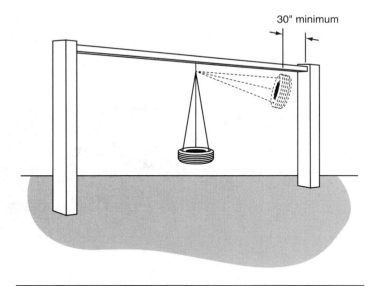

30" minimum

Figure 6–8   Multi-axis tire swing clearance.

Source: U.S. Consumer Product Safety Commission (1997). *Handbook for public playground safety* (No. 325). Washington, DC: U.S. Government Printing Office.

difficult for unsupervised toddlers to attempt to climb in the seat alone. Tot swings should not be hung alongside swings intended for older children. The swing seat should provide support to the child on all sides and be in compliance with criteria for avoiding entrapment. CPSC (1997) guidelines recommend the following types of swings be avoided.

- animal figure swings
- multiple occupancy swings (with the exception of multi-axis tire swings)
- rope swings
- swinging dual exercise rings and trapeze bars (used as athletic equipment)

Slides According to the PIRG (1998), "Slides account for almost 30 percent of all public playground equipment-related injuries. Of all injuries sustained on slides, one-half are associated with falls to the surface below the equipment and another one-fourth involve falls onto other parts of the equipment. Falls from the platform, from the top of the slide, and from the top portion of the slide chute are most common. Falls also often occur as children climb ladders that access slide structures. When compared to other types of equipment, slides tend to have higher rates of serious head injuries" (p. 4).

This quote emphasizes the dangers associated with slides, a popular piece of playground equipment. Slides are the *most frequent* cause of injury for children under the age of six. Therefore, the PIRG (1998) suggests that the top rung or platform of a slide be no higher than 4 feet for preschoolers and a maximum of 6 feet for school-age children (see Figure 6–9). Limiting the height of slides placed on playgrounds reduces risks associated with falls.

The use zone of slides is computed by adding 4 feet to the height of the slide. For example, a slide, which is 5 feet at its highest point, will require a use zone of 9 feet. Regardless of the height of the slide, however, the use zone should never measure less than 6 feet and does not need to be greater than 14 feet. The use zone includes the area at the exit and each side of the slide.

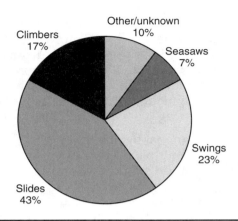

Figure 6–9 Playground equipment–related injuries sustained by children under 6.

Source: Public Interest Research Groups, 1998.

EQUIPMENT AND PLAYGROUND MAINTENANCE

There are a number of hazards common to playground equipment and playgrounds. Outdoor play areas must be properly maintained and children's apparel checked regularly to avoid injuries. Problems to be aware of include:

1. Protrusions and projections on slides and other equipment can entangle drawstrings on hoods of jackets and sweatshirts, jewelry such as necklaces, and other items worn by children, causing strangulation. Recessing or countersinking potential hazards should eliminate these. (See Related Resources at the end of this chapter for information on test kits.)
2. Sharp points, corners, and edges can puncture skin and cause lacerations.
3. Pinch, crush, and shearing points injure children by entrapping a body part such as fingers and arms and by catching on clothing.
4. Head entrapments are a danger when children attempt to crawl either headfirst or feet first through

an opening. To restrict a child's head or feet moving through the space, the opening should be less than 3.5 inches or greater than 9 inches (to permit a head to move into and out of the space). Angles formed by components should be greater than 55 degrees to avoid head entrapment. Cargo nets with the perimeter of the openings (sum of the length of the four sides) between 17 inches and 28 inches pose an entrapment and strangulation hazard.

5. Tripping hazards are all too common on playgrounds. To prevent children from tripping, anchoring devices should be installed below ground level and beneath surfacing material. Boundaries for loose-fill surfacing materials should be highly visible with an obvious change of elevation or bright color. Children wearing appropriate shoes on the playground with shoestrings vigilantly tied are less likely to trip and fall. Accessory materials such as balls, wagons, and tricycles can be kept in a specific area rather than scattered around the playground.

6. Metal surfaces on slides and platforms cause burns when they come in contact with children's bare skin, such as legs and arms. Locate these out of direct sunlight in cooler climates and avoid metal surfaces altogether in warmer regions. Platforms can alternatively be made from wood or plastic and slide beds from plastic.

7. Drawstrings on hoods of jackets and sweatshirts and at the bottom of coats, as well as jewelry and other items worn by children, put them at risk for strangulation. Drawstrings should be *removed* from the hoods of jackets and sweatshirts and children advised against wearing jewelry. Teachers can diligently inspect children for apparel that could result in strangulation when items catch on protrusions and projections. See Figure 6–10 for more information.

8. Plants used in landscaping add a pleasant ambience to playgrounds but remove plant life and other vegetation that are poisonous or pose a choking hazard. There are hundreds of varieties of toxic garden plants, vegetable plants, hedges,

bushes, trees, and vines. Check with a county extension agent, local landscape architect, or poison control center to identify toxic plants indigenous of a particular region.

9. Insects are common to most outdoor play areas; however, those that pose a serious threat to children should be eliminated. Ant beds can be treated with a chemical that is not harmful to humans or treated during a time period when children will not come into contact with the treated bed. Holes drilled in tires and other equipment allow standing water to drain, discouraging mosquito larvae and other insects.

10. Prior to 1978, lead-based paints were commonly used on playground equipment. The danger associated with old equipment covered in lead-based paint is that the paint can chip or flake off posing a serious risk for poisoning if ingested. This is particularly problematic for children six and under who may pick up lead paint chips and lead dust on their hands while playing on equipment and then put their hands in their mouths.

11. Exposed metal rusts, wood splinters, and plastic equipment cracks. Adults should vigilantly watch for these types of wear and tear on equipment and have them repaired (by sanding and painting or varnishing) before children are allowed to play on them or removed from the play area.

12. Broken glass, trash, and other debris is dangerous and unsanitary. When playgrounds are inspected for these dangerous items and cleaned up before children go out to play, accidents and contamination are avoided.

13. Broken and missing parts may cause playground equipment to work ineffectively and be a danger to children. Repairs should be reported and made immediately. These and other types of equipment maintenance are listed in Figure 6–11.

Guidelines for Drawstrings on Children's Upper Outerwear

Introduction

In February 1996, the U.S. Consumer Product Safety Commission (CPSC) issued these guidelines to help prevent children from strangling or getting entangled on the neck and waist drawstrings of upper outerwear garments, such as jackets and sweatshirts. Drawstrings on children's clothing are a hidden hazard that can lead to deaths and injuries when they catch on such items as playground equipment, bus doors, or cribs. From January 1985 through January 1999, CPSC received reports of 22 deaths and 48 non-fatal incidents involving the entanglement of children's clothing drawstrings.

In June 1997, ASTM adopted a voluntary standard that incorporated CPSC's guidelines. You can obtain a copy of ASTM F1816-97, Standard Safety Specification for Drawstrings on Children's Upper Outerwear, by calling ASTM at (610) 832-9585.

These guidelines and the voluntary standard provide consumers with information to prevent hazards with garments now in their possession and make informed purchasing choices in the future. Manufacturers and retailers should also be aware of the hazards, and should be sure garments they manufacture and sell conform to the voluntary standard.

CPSC's drawstring guidelines do not represent a standard or mandatory requirement set by the agency. And, while CPSC does not sanction them as the only method of minimizing drawstring injuries, CPSC believes that these guidelines will help prevent children from strangling by their clothing drawstrings.

Deaths and Injuries

Hood/neck drawstrings Over two-thirds of the deaths and non-fatal incidents involved hood/neck drawstrings on upper outerwear. The majority of these cases involved playground slides. Typically, as the child descended the slide, the toggle or knot on the drawstring got caught in a small space or gap at the top of the slide. Examples of catch points include a protruding bolt or a tiny space between the guardrail and the slide platform. As the child hung by the drawstring, suspended part way down the slide, the drawstring pulled the garment taut around the neck, strangling the child. Victims of these cases ranged in age from 2 through 8 years old.

In one case, a 5-year-old girl strangled after the drawstring on her jacket hood caught on the slide at her school.

One incident involved a fence. A 4-year-old girl strangled after the hood drawstring on her coat became entangled on a fence as she attempted to climb over it.

(continued)

Figure 6–10 Continued.

Two strangulations occurred in cribs. In one case, an 18-month-old child was found hanging from a corner post of his crib by the tied cord of the hooded sweatshirt he was wearing. Another little girl was hanged by the drawstring of her sweatshirt in her crib the first time she wore the sweatshirt.

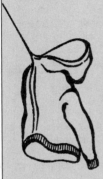

Hood and neck drawstrings can become entangled on playground equipment, crbs, and other common items.

Waist/bottom drawstrings Almost one-third of the deaths and non-fatal incidents involved drawstrings at the waist bottom of children's jackets and sweatshirts. Most of these involved children whose waist or bottom strings of their jackets caught on school bus hand-rails or in school bus doors. In most cases, the drawstring at the bottom of the jacket snagged in a small space in the hand rail as the child was getting off the bus. Without the child or bus driver realizing that the drawstring was caught on the handrail, the bus doors closed and the bus drove away, dragging the chiki. Deaths occurred when children were run over by the bus. Victims of these school bus cases ranged in age from 7 through 14 years old.

A 14-year-old boy was killed when the long, trailing drawstring on his jacket got caught in the closed door of a moving school bus and he was eventually pulled beneath the bus and run over.

Waist drawstrings can become entangled in a bus door.

Figure 6–10 Continued.

Recommended Guidelines

Hood/neck drawstrings CPSC recommends that parents or caregivers completely remove the hood and neck drawstrings from all children's upper outerwear, including jackets and sweatshirts, sized 2T to 12. CPSC technical staff has concluded that drawstrings at the neck that are shortened still may present a strangulation hazard. Therefore, CPSC recommends that consumers purchase children's upper outerwear that has alternative closures, such as snaps, buttons, Velcro, and elastic. CPSC also recommends that manufacturers and retailers provide upper outerwear with these alternative closures, rather than drawstrings at the head and neck area.

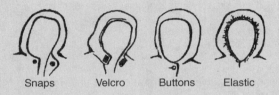

| Snaps | Velcro | Buttons | Elastic |

Waist/bottom drawstrings For upper outerwear sized 2T to 16, CPSC recommends to consumer, manufacturers, and retailers that the ends of waist/bottom drawstrings measure no more than 3 inches from where the strings extend out of the garment when it is expanded to its fullest width. Also, the drawstring should be sewn to the garment at its midpoint so the string can not be pulled to one side, making it long enough to catch on something. CPSC also recommends eliminating toggles or knots at the ends of all drawstrings. Shortening the length of drawstrings to 3 inches at the waist and bottom of children's upper outerwear reduces the risk that the strings will become entangled in objects such as school bus doors or other moving objects.

Waist/bottom drawstrings of upper outerwear should measure no more than 3 inches from where strings extend out of the garment.

Source: CPSC, 1996.

Figure 6–11   Safety checklist.

Inspect the outdoor play area daily for:

☐ adequate depths of surface material
☐ children's apparel with drawstrings, jewelry, so on
☐ debris such as broken glass, cans, trash, and animal droppings
☐ hot metal surfaces
☐ signs of insects, such as anthills, wasps' nests, or other insects
☐ standing water on the ground and in equipment

Inspect the outdoor play area regularly for:

☐ broken, bent, or warped equipment surfaces
☐ broken or missing equipment and equipment parts
☐ head entrapments
☐ loose nuts and bolts
☐ loose or broken equipment, footings, and supports
☐ open tubes or pipes that need to be capped
☐ peeling paint, lead-based paint
☐ pinch, crush, and shearing points
☐ poisonous plants
☐ protrusions and projections
☐ rotting wood (including fittings that can rot underground)
☐ sharp parts or edges
☐ splinters, rust, cracked plastic
☐ squeaky parts in need of lubrication
☐ tripping hazards such as exposed footings and tree roots
☐ worn swing chains, S-hooks, and multi-axis swing mechanisms

     Promptly report or repair any hazard or defect you identify during your inspections.

Adapted and reprinted with permission from *Scholastic Early Childhood Today* (1995). Checklist for outdoor safety. *9*(8) 22.

WEATHER-RELATED HAZARDS

Special attention to ever-changing global weather patterns and its effect on the local climate can prevent weather-related injuries. The American Sun Protection Association (2000) in conjunction with the American Cancer Research Center provides recommendations to minimize the short and long term damaging effects of the sun.

1. Avoid outdoor play during peak sun intensity hours when the sun moves higher in the sky and ultraviolet (UV) rays travel a more direct distance

to the Earth. Schedule outdoor play before 10 A.M. and after 3 P.M. (standard time) or before 11 A.M. and after 4 P.M. (daylight savings time). Another option is to utilize covered porch or deck areas during these times.

2. Monitor the UV Index forecasts via the newspaper or Web site (www.epa.gov), and plan indoor activities on days of high intensity.
3. Assess playgrounds to ensure that adequate shade is available during outdoor play times. Build permanent shade structures such as porches, picnic shelters, and canopies, and plant trees.
4. Have parents sign a release form allowing teachers to apply sunscreen to children.
5. Educate teachers, staff, and parents about sun safety and encourage them to be good role models.

Excessive temperatures can also result in burns from hot surfaces on playground equipment. Check hot surfaces such as decks, slides, and steps with the palm of the hand before allowing children to play on them.

Extremely cold temperatures and wet climates interfere with outdoor play. To increase the time children spend outdoors in these conditions, dress them in layers with hats, gloves, and boots for cold weather and raincoats and water-resistant shoes for wet weather. A warm, dry change of clothes reduces some of the problems associated with outdoor play in less than ideal weather conditions. In colder climates, outdoor play can be scheduled for the warmest (or driest) part of the day with the amount of time spent outdoors carefully monitored. Several shorter outdoor play periods may be more desirable than one long period of time.

Dehydration is also a weather-related concern. Easy access to water (especially on warmer days) is a necessity. If drinking fountains are not readily available, supply a cooler and disposable cups.

ACCESSIBILITY TO PLAYGROUNDS

The Americans with Disabilities Act Accessibility Guidelines (ADAAG) address access to newly built and altered playgrounds for children with disabilities who require adaptive equipment (ADAAG, 2000). These federally regulated guidelines pertain to public playgrounds, public and private schools, government operated and privately owned child care centers, and other facilities subject to the ADA. Family child care homes are exempt from the regulation. The complete guidelines are available from the Access Board Web site. (Refer to Related Web Sites at the end of this chapter.) A brief summary of these imperative guidelines is presented here.

Play Components

Play components are defined by the ADAAG as "manufactured or natural elements used for play, socialization, or learning." Components are categorized as **ground level** (such as swings, play houses, sand and water tables, steering wheels, spring riders, barrels, and activity panels) or **elevated level** (such as slides, tire climbers, cargo nets, steps, steering wheels on an elevated surface, overhead ladders, bilateral climbers, overhead rings, slide pole, and bridges). There are several different criteria regarding each type of component.

Ground Level Play Components The first criteria for ground level play components requires access to at least one of each type of ground level play equipment in the play area. For example, if there are four swings, three spring riders, and two activity panels, *at least one* of each type of equipment (swing, spring rider, and activity panel) must be accessible to children using adaptive equipment such as wheelchairs. Second, the ADAAG (2000) recognizes that all portions of elevated play components may not be accessible. In cases such as this, the number and variety of accessible ground level components must be increased. A chart is provided which reflects the number of ground level components required per number of elevated components available. This second criteria does not apply to play areas with no elevated structures or where access to at least 50 percent of elevated components is provided via wheelchair ramps. According to the play components requirements in Figure 6–12, if a public or school play area has equipment with ten elevated components and five of these are accessible via a transfer system only (with no ramps available), there must also be

Figure 6–12 Required play components for wheelchair accessible playgrounds.

Number of elevated components provided	Ground level components required
2–4	1
5–7	2 (at least 2 types)
8–10	3 (at least 3 types)
11–13	4 (at least 3 types)
14–16	5 (at least 3 types)
17–19	6 (at least 3 types)
20–22	7 (at least 4 types)
23–25	8 (at least 4 types)
Over 25	8 plus 1 for each additional 3 over 25, or fraction thereof (at least 5 types)

Source: Americans with Disabilities Act Access Board, 2000.

at least three accessible ground level components (of three different types). This is in addition to the "one of each type" stipulation in the first criteria cited above. So in addition to the swing, spring rider, and activity panel, described in the previous example, there also must be three additional ground level components available of three different varieties, such as a sand table, playhouse, and steering wheel.

Elevated Play Components   At least half of the total number of elevated play components is required to be accessible by ramp or transfer platform. Ramp access enables a child seated in a wheelchair to reach the elevated play components. Transfer systems provide a platform to assist children as they move from a wheelchair to a platform that makes the play component accessible through transfer steps. Access to play components can be provided by transfer systems *only* when there are less than twenty elevated play components. (Remember, in this situation at least three accessible ground level components are required, each of a different variety.) When twenty or more elevated play components exist, ramps must account for at least half of the means for accessibility and provide access to at least one-fourth of the elevated play components.

Accessible Surfacing

Surfacing to the play area from adjacent buildings and parking lots must be adequate. In addition, play area surfacing must be firm, stable, and slip resistant enough for a wheelchair while maintaining its important safety function of cushioning falls. Engineered wood fibers installed at the appropriate depth meet these criteria as well as unitary surfacing materials such as poured-in-place rubber surfaces and rubber tiles. A combination of surfaces used along routes to play components and in use zones may be the best solution to this critical feature of play areas.

Variation in surfacing can be used to designate different areas of the playground for children with limited vision. Rubber matting indicates climbing equipment while grassy areas direct a child to a sand table. Bold black and white stripes painted on the ground or on signs near certain pieces of equipment provide additional cues. Barriers such as landscape borders or railroad ties alert children to areas that could be dangerous to them, such as a bike path or swing set.

Manufactured Playground Equipment

Manufacturers of playground components are fully aware of the need for accessible equipment, such as the specially designed swings in Figure 6–13. Grounds for Play® (Strickland & Dempsey, 2000), a company based in Austin, Texas, designs comprehensive outdoor play environments and offers a variety of equipment designed for children with special needs, including:

- *Corner chairs.* The chair attaches to the inside corners of a sandbox and enables a child to sit in the sandbox with back and side support.
- *Texture floors and pathways.* Different sections of flooring offer a variety of textures for children to touch and feel as they sit, walk, or crawl along.
- *Panels.* There is a wide variety of panels available that stimulate visual, auditory, or tactile stimulation including the mirror, chime, sound cylinder, texture, shape spinner, color spinner, and visual discrimination panel.

Figure 6–13 Commercial playground equipment is available for children with special needs.

- *Sand house.* Children in wheelchairs can pull up to the surface and engage in sand play.
- *Wheelchair platform swings.* Specially designed swings allow children in wheelchairs to safely enjoy the to-and-fro sensation of a swing.
- *Pull slide.* A transfer system leads to a slide with horizontal bars overhead. Children can use their arms to raise and lower themselves up and down the slide.
- *Accessible picnic table.* Children in wheelchairs can pull up to the table and enjoy the company of nondisabled children sitting across from them. The flat surface provides a place to do art activities, enjoy a book, or play a game.
- *Fall zone access ramp.* This ramp enables children in wheelchairs to move from one surface to another.

These are a few examples of the types of equipment that are available for children with special needs.

CHARACTERISTICS OF CREATIVE OUTDOOR PLAY SPACES

Outdoor play spaces should be safe and accessible to all children. But this expectation is only the foundation for the types of experiences children need to thrive in an outdoor play setting. Playgrounds should go beyond the minimum requirements for accessibility to ensure all children reap the benefits of the outdoor play experience. Henniger (1994) identified four key characteristics of creative play spaces which apply to all children regardless of their ability: healthy risk taking, graduated challenges, promoting a variety of play types, and children manipulating the environment. Each of these characteristics are described in greater detail with examples for adapting outdoor play situations for children with special needs. Additional suggestions for modifying playground equipment are made in Appendix B.

Healthy Risk Taking

Taking risks is a natural part of learning new skills and confidently handling new challenges. Safe, well-supervised playgrounds are the ideal place for children to take risks because there are fewer opportunities for injury. It is suggested that children crave physical challenges to such a degree that if these experiences are not made safely available to them they will create their own risk-taking situations, which could be less desirable and more dangerous. Risk taking behavior in a supervised outdoor setting may include climbing to a new height, running to avoid being tagged as "it," or riding down a moderately steep hill in a wagon.

Children with communication disorders have a difficult time expressing their wants and needs. On the playground, nonverbal children can use augmentive or alternative communication (AAC) devises to communicate. Drawings or photographs of playground equipment and activities can be used to help children convey where they want to go on the playground and what new challenges they might want to try.

Graduated Challenges

As children play outdoors, their motor and communication skills, cognitive abilities, and social-emotional development are gradually changing and improving. The creative outdoor play area accommodates their changing needs and abilities. This can be accomplished in part by providing equipment with varying degrees of difficulty or by adapting multiuse materials as children change. Equipment such as balance beams and swings which can be adapted by adults to meet children's changing needs is ideal (Esbensen, 1987).

Children with disabilities who are capable of using only upper body strength, benefit physically from equipment (such as a tunnel) fitted with side-mounted grips to help children pull themselves along (Theemes, 1999). For example, a series of tunnels of different lengths provides a graduated challenge to children as their upper body strength increases. A basketball ball hoop that can be adjusted to different heights offers a graduated challenge to children who are just learning the skill of shooting baskets as well as those seated in a wheelchair.

Promoting a Variety of Play Types

Although the playground is historically associated with physical fitness (Frost & Wortham, 1988), contemporary researchers find that outdoor play stimulates learning in other areas as well, including social interaction (Kraft, 1989) and dramatic play (Henniger, 1985). Outdoor play enhances the level of cognitive functioning through each of the four major types of play: **functional play,** *pretend play, constructive play,* and *games with rules* (Piaget, 1962; Smilansky, 1968). These types of play are distinguished by the child's motivation and action. An infant repeatedly banging a rattle against the tray of her activity center is engaged in functional play while a preschooler "painting" a fence with a wide brush dipped in an empty paint can is involved in pretend play. A kindergartner balancing a board between two overturned milk crates is demonstrating constructive play while her older sister bouncing a ball to a friend during a game of four-square, indicates her understanding of games with rules. Each of these types of play offers a unique and important benefit to children. Therefore, opportunities to be involved in each type of play should be made readily available to children outdoors as well as in the classroom.

Playground equipment can easily be added to the outdoor play area or adapted to promote these four different types of play. For example, a steering wheel mounted on a post or piece of stationary play equipment promotes pretend play. Mounting the wheel at a lower level on the post and adding a devise that makes a sound when the steering wheel is turned accommodates children who are in a wheelchair and/or those with visual impairments (Theemes, 1999). Sand tables at wheelchair height can be used in place of sandboxes that are traditionally built-in at ground level. The tables should be sturdy enough for children with poor balance to lean on them for support (Theemes, 1999).

Adults can help children think of ways to adapt games with rules to include peers who may be disabled. For example, children who are hearing impaired can play "Duck, Duck, Goose" if a beanbag is dropped in the lap of the child chosen to run rather than simply saying the word, "goose." Movement games such as "Hokey Pokey" can be lead by a classmate, freeing the teacher to sign directions to a child who is hearing impaired, or touch the designated body part for a young child who is visually impaired and just learning to associate the label with the correct body part.

Children Manipulating the Play Environment

Manipulating objects and interacting with people in their world is how children learn best (Kamii & DeVries, 1978; Piaget, 1952). Early childhood teachers who readily see these benefits set up indoor play environments to reflect this philosophy. However, with the exception of sand and water play and tricycles (Frost, Bowers, & Wortham, 1990), opportunities for children to manipulate the outdoor environment are limited (Henniger, 1994). This can be easily remedied by including **loose parts,** or accessory materials that are manipulated by children. Examples of loose parts include outdoor blocks, boards, crates, sawhorses, and cable spools as well as classroom materials that are usually used indoors such as puzzles, books, and art supplies (Frost & Wortham, 1985). Children in wheelchairs or on walkers can assist with carrying loose parts if a bag or basket is attached to their adaptive devise. A tray securely attached to a wheelchair or a table that allows children to roll the chair underneath provides a place to create artistic pictures, work a puzzle, or read a book.

As a rule, children with special needs require repetition of an experience several times in order to learn from it. They need time and opportunity to become familiar with materials and discover different ways to interact with them. Therefore, loose parts and other activities offered outdoors should not be changed too often (Klein, Cook & Richardson-Gibbs, 2001). For example, the same materials can be left in an outdoor art center over a period of several days. An obstacle course will remain intact until children have a chance to "master" it. If a discovery walk is planned, it needs to be repeated frequently for children to learn all they can from the experience.

ADAPTATIONS FOR CHILDREN WITH SPECIAL NEEDS

The key to including all children regardless of their abilities is to adapt the environment to their special needs. Adapting outdoor play spaces can be a particularly challenging goal. Kieff and Casbergue (2000) draw on the work of several experts in the field of special education (Cook, Tessier, & Armbruster, 1987; Fewell & Kaminski, 1988; Morris & Schultz, 1989; Wesley, 1992; Wolery & Wilbert, 1994) and offer suggestions to enhance the outdoor play experiences of children with special needs.

Children with physical challenges need to be positioned so they can attain maximum range of reach, motion, muscle control, and visual contact. Encourage children with physical challenges to use their own means of getting around to different play areas while providing assistance when needed. Adapted equipment specifically designed for outdoor play should be furnished. Children with limited upper body strength or control, can use lightweight objects for throwing and catching or engage in activities that can be done with lower body parts such as legs or feet.

Children with a hearing disability need to be positioned so they are facing other children. This helps peers get the attention of the child with a hearing disability and facilitates communication and social interaction. Teachers can use sign language and spoken words to acknowledge what the child is doing and to help the child communicate with others.

Children with a visual disability need open play areas. Dividing play spaces visually with walls, fences, or equipment blocks the child's visual field and leads to isolation. Mark locations of major play structures or areas with audible clues such as wind chimes or bells, as well as danger spots such as swings and slide exits (Gober, 1998). Favorite playmates may also wear objects that provide audible clues. Lead the child through the outdoor play area to assist in orienting her to major play areas and verbally orient the child by describing where different playmates are located and what they are playing. Children with limited understanding need encouragement to participate in outdoor activities such as running, jumping, and climbing to stimulate motor skill development. Adapt activities to help the child achieve success and provide challenges with differing degrees of difficulty such as balance beams of different lengths and simple obstacle courses. Introduce noncompetitive games (see Chapter 4) to relieve the stress of having to perform up to the standard of more capable peers.

CONCLUSION

There are many factors to consider when ensuring that playgrounds are safe places for children to play. Adults must be vigilant in the upkeep of playgrounds and in the supervision of children at play. The acronym S-A-F-E reminds us to ensure that children have proper *supervision,* age-*appropriate* equipment, protective *fall* surfacing, and continuous *equipment* maintenance. Familiarity with all playground hazards is the key to minimizing injury and eliminating unnecessary deaths. Weather conditions must also be taken into consideration when providing safe environments for children to play.

New accessibility guidelines specifying federal regulations for making play areas available to all children regardless of ability are available. Building new playgrounds according to these guidelines and refitting older playgrounds will ensure that all children benefit from outdoor play.

Simply making playgrounds safe and accessible according to minimum standards is not enough to ensure that children are truly benefiting from outdoor play. In addition, creative outdoor play spaces must take into account children of all abilities who need opportunities for healthy risk taking, graduated challenges, a variety of types of play, and manipulating play objects.

KEY TERMS

entanglement
head entrapment
play components
ground level

elevated level
functional play
loose parts

THEORY INTO PRACTICE

1. Inspect an existing playground for safety hazards cited throughout this chapter. Is the equipment appropriate to the age of children for which it is intended? Are the fall zones large enough? What type of surfacing is used and is it maintained at the appropriate depth? Cite other safety hazards observed.

2. Observe families at a local park. Describe how they supervise their children at play. List all injuries and explain if they could have been prevented through closer supervision or changes made to the play area.
3. Analyze an outdoor playground and determine what changes need to be made in order for it to be compliant with federal regulations as determined by the ADAAG.

RELATED WEB SITES

www.access-board.gov
Overview of the Americans with Disabilities Act Accessibility Guidelines for public and private play areas.

www.americansun.org
American Sun Protection Association provides tips, information, and links to organizations that offer free curriculum materials on sun safety.

www.cpsc.gov
Homepage for Consumer Product Safety Commission. Access warnings concerning playground hazards as well as other products that endanger children.

www.pirg.org
U.S. Public Interest Research Group homepage. Resource guide on children's environmental health issues.

www.boundlessplayground.org
Boundless Playground is a nonprofit organization that helps communities create accessible playgrounds for children with special needs.

www.uni.edu/playground
The National Program for Playground Safety Web site gives updates on latest news regarding safety information, statistics, and advocacy projects.

RELATED RESOURCES

Apogee Communications Group. (1998). *Infant and toddler emergency first aid video. Vol. 1: Accidents.* Boulder, CO: Author.

Klein, M.D., Cook, R.E., & Richardson-Gibbs, A.M. (2001). *Strategies for including children with special needs in early childhood settings.* Albany, NY: Delmar.

National Program for Playground Safety. (1997). *Sammy's playground pointers video.* Cedar Falls, IA: National Program for Playground Safety

Video Active Productions. (2000). *Safe active play: A guide to avoiding play area hazards.* Washington, DC: National Association for the Education of Young Children.

Wallach, F. (1999). *Playground audit guide.* Lewisburg, PA: PlayDesigns®. (Safety Audit Kits are available from PlayDesigns®, 1000 Buffalo Road, Lewisburg, PA 17837-9795. 800-327-7571.)

REFERENCES

American Sun Protection Association. (2000). *Sun safety information for schools and child care centers.* www.aspa.amc.org

Americans with Disabilities Act Access Guidelines. (2000). *Accessibility guidelines for play areas: An overview.* www.access-board.gov

Associated Press. (2000). *Child dies at Tuscaloosa day care.* Mobile, AL: Mobile Press Register.

Beaty, J. (1999). *Prosocial guidance for the young child.* Upper Saddle River, NJ: Merrill.

Cook, R.E., Tessier, A., & Armbruster, V.B. (1987). *Adapting early childhood curricula for children with special needs.* Columbus, OH: Merrill.

Esbensen, S.B. (1987). *An outdoor classroom.* Ypsilanti, MI: High/Scope Press.

Fewell, R.R., & Kaminski, R. (1988). Play skills development and instruction for young children with handicaps. In S.L. Odom & M.B. Karnes (Eds.), *Early intervention for children and infants with handicaps* (pp. 145–158). Baltimore: Paul H. Brooks.

Frost, J.L. (1992). *Play and playscapes.* Albany, NY: Delmar.

Frost, J.L., & Wortham, S. (1988). The evolution of American playgrounds. *Young Children, 43*(5), 19–28.

Frost, J.L., Bowers, L., & Wortham, S. (1990). The state of American preschool playgrounds. *Journal of Physical Education, Recreation, and Dance, 61*(8), 18–23.

Gober, B. (1998). All the right moves. *Scholastic Early Childhood Today, 12*(7), 36–38.

Henniger, M.L. (1994). Planning for outdoor play. *Young Children, 49*(4), 10–15.

Henniger, M.L. (1985). Preschool children's play behaviors in an indoor and outdoor environment. In J.L. Frost & S. Sunderlin (Eds.), *When children play* (pp. 145–149). Wheaton, MD: Association for Childhood Education International.

Kamii, C., & DeVries, R. (1978). *Physical knowledge in preschool education.* Englewood Cliffs, NJ: Prentice Hall.

Keiff, J., & Casbergue, R. (2000). *Playful learning and teaching: Integrating play into preschool and primary programs.* Boston, MA: Allyn & Bacon.

Klein, M.D., Cook, R.E., & Richardson-Gibbs, A.M. (2001). *Strategies for including children with special needs in early childhood settings.* Albany, NY: Delmar.

Kraft, R.E. (1989). Children at play. Behavior of children at recess. *Journal of Physical Education, Recreation, and Dance, 60*(4), 21–24.

Morris, L.R., & Schultz, L. (1989). *Creative play activities for children with disabilities.* Champaign, IL: Human Kinetics.

National Program for Playground Safety. (2000). *Safety information.* www.uni.edu/playground

Piaget, J. (1952). *The origins of intelligence.* New York: International Universities Press.

Piaget, J. (1962). *Play, dreams, and imitation in childhood.* New York: W.W. Norton.

Public Interest Research Groups. (1998). Playing it safe: Results of the investigation: The nation's playgrounds pose hidden hazards. www.pirg.org

Smilansky, S. (1968). *The effect of sociodramatic play on disadvantaged preschool children.* New York: Wiley.

Strickland, E., & Dempsey, J. (2000). *Grounds for play: Creative play environments.* Austin, TX: Grounds for Play.

Theemes, T. (1999). *Let's go outside! Designing the early childhood playground.* Ypsilanti, MI: High/Scope Press.

Tinsworth, D.K., & Kramer, J.T. (1990). *Playground equipment-related injuries and deaths.* Washington, DC: U.S. Consumer Product Safety Commission.

U.S. Consumer Product Safety Commission. (1997). *Handbook for public playground safety* (No. 325). Washington DC: U.S. Government Printing Office.

Wellhousen, K., & Kieff, J. (2001). *A constructivist approach to block play in early childhood.* Albany, NY: Delmar.

Wesley, P. (1992). *Mainstreaming young children: A training series for child care providers.* Chapel Hill, NC: University of North Carolina, Frank Porter Graham Child Development Center.

Wolery, M., & Wilbert, J. (Eds.) (1994). *Including children with special needs in early childhood programs.* Washington, DC: National Association for the Education of Young Children.

CHAPTER 7

Residential and Community Outdoor Play Areas

Guiding Questions

1. *How does the acronym S-A-F-E (supervision, age-appropriateness, fall surfacing, and equipment maintenance) relate to residential playgrounds? (Review Chapter 6.)*
2. *What are two ways individuals within a community can work together to create a playground?*
3. *What are the unique advantages of residential and community playgrounds?*
4. *What are three outdoor family activities common to your geographic region? How might these compare with another part of the United States?*

INTRODUCTION

One justification for diminishing or eliminating outdoor play periods in schools is that children have ample opportunities to play outdoors when school is not in session. Sadly, in some homes and communities, this is not the case. Many types of residences do not lend themselves to a traditional *backyard* playground and parents' concerns for their children's safety may limit outdoor play in neighborhoods. In addition, many community playgrounds, a viable option for families without a backyard or safe neighborhood, have fallen into disrepair and create more opportunities for injury than for beneficial play.

Fortunately, a new movement among communities throughout the United States is addressing the problems associated with a lack of safe, developmentally appropriate playgrounds. Concerned citizens are finding ways to create exciting, new playgrounds for their community with assistance from for-profit design firms, nonprofit agencies, and a volunteer labor force. Community playgrounds built by organized volunteers have a positive impact on communities beyond the initial goal of helping children: namely, a new sense of pride in the community and its residents.

RESIDENTIAL PLAYGROUNDS

Take a few moments to reflect on your childhood and time spent outdoors. It may bring back memories of warm, carefree, summer days playing kickball in the street, climbing trees, or exploring new territory on bicycles. Others may remember winter sports such as sledding, skiing, and building snow forts. For many of us, time spent outdoors brings back images of our own backyard playgrounds. The playground typically consisted of a metal A-frame structure with swings, a glider, and slide attached. Although our memories may be fond ones, those insubstantial structures of a generation ago are considered highly unsafe by today's standards.

Along with pleasant memories of playing outdoors, many of us will recall incidents involving minor or serious injuries as well. For instance, the author recalls a sudden kick to the mouth as she ran in front of a neighborhood friend on a swing. The extent of the injury was only a lost tooth, but current statistics tell us that the injury could have been much more serious. Today, there is a wide variety of backyard play equipment available to families. The metal A-frame swing set still exists and continues to pose risks to children. Swings and other axis-supported apparatus are placed too close together, frames may tip or fall over if not adequately anchored, pinch points, protrusions, and rust become a problem over time, and rarely is there any type of cushioning for falls in place. Fortunately, more innovative and safer play systems have recently been introduced.

Today, families can choose from several options including: (1) complete kits that contain all materials needed, (2) partial kits that supply hardware, plastic play components, and drawings (but require lumber to be purchased separately), (3) commercial companies that sell a variety of play set configurations and provide installation, and (4) books with detailed designs for building play sets, tree houses, forts, and other outdoor structures. Play sets are now referred to as *play systems* and their sales have become a multimillion dollar industry (Fleishman, 2001). The average dollar amount parents spend for a backyard play system is between $2,000 and $2,500, which is twice as much as they were spending only a few years ago. But parents are also getting more for their money with larger play systems sporting the basic swings, ladders, slides, and playhouse *plus* extras such as crawl tunnels, climbing walls, telescopes, steering wheels, speaking tubes, and electronic two-way communication systems (Fleishman, 2001).

In addition to play systems, outdoor accessory equipment is widely available for young children including sandboxes, wading pools, sports equipment, stand-alone play houses, tree slides, wagons, and wheeled vehicles. Small-scale, freestanding platforms and slide sets are made from sturdy but lightweight plastic and designed for very young children. Bucket-style swings for toddlers can replace strap swings. A balanced combination of play systems and accessory equipment offers a safe, fun, and exciting place to learn and play.

SAFETY ON RESIDENTIAL PLAYGROUNDS

There are many options for equipment that provide a wide range of challenges for children of different ages. Unfortunately, it is easy for well-meaning, enthusiastic parents and grandparents eager to provide outdoor fun to forget the elements of basic safety. Recall the acronym S-A-F-E (supervision, age-appropriateness, fall surfacing, and equipment maintenance) explained in Chapter 6. Even though the backyard is not a public playground and therefore not subject to the guidelines of the Consumer Product Safety Commission (CPSC), families still have the responsibility of keeping the children who play at their residence safe. Each of these elements will be reviewed specifically with the residential playground in mind.

Supervision

Many adults are under the assumption that a backyard playground offers a place for children to play independently without interference from adult authority. While free play without adult intrusion is important, it should never take precedence over safety. Therefore, supervision of children in the backyard playground is essential to ensuring their safety. The National Playground Safety Institute (NPSI) publishes "The Dirty Dozen," a list of twelve common playground hazards (see Related Resources). Among these is a lack of supervision. The document states,

> A play area should be designed so that it is easy for a parent or caregiver to observe the children at play. Young children are constantly challenging their own abilities, very often not being able to recognize potential hazards. It is estimated that over forty percent of all playground injuries are directly related to lack of supervision in some way. Parents must supervise their children in some way on the playground!

Age-Appropriate Design

The National Program for Playground Safety (Hudson & Thompson, 1998) recommends that playgrounds be designed with two distinct age categories in mind: ages two to five years and ages five to twelve years. This can create quite a dilemma for families with children whose ages overlap these two categories. However, adjustments can be made to facilitate different age groups even on a residential playground as the following example illustrates.

The Phillips family has four children ranging in age from two years old to nine years old. It was impossible to find one play set that could safely accommodate all children. So they solved the problem by erecting a combination swing/slide/trapeze set designed for children five to twelve years old. The strap-style seats were easily removed and a bucket style seat designed for infants and toddlers hung in its place. Then they supplemented with playground components designed for children five and under, such as a Little Tykes® slide, a playhouse, sandbox, and many accessories including balls, beanbags, and buckets. With appropriate supervision, the family spent many hours (and years) enjoying their outdoor playground.

Fall Surfacing

According to the Public Interest Research Group (PIRG, 1998), falls onto hard surfaces below playground equipment (such as packed dirt, grass, and concrete) account for approximately 75 percent of all playground-related injuries and 3 percent of the playground-related deaths. These shocking statistics justify the strict CPSC (1997) guideline for protective surfacing under and around all public playground equipment. The types and appropriate depths of surfacing vary, with the most common being loose-fill materials such as sand, gravel, wood chips, and mulch. (See Figure 6–5 for more information on protective surfacing materials.) This safety feature is probably the most overlooked aspect of the residential playground. Adults must understand that even with attentive supervision, falls can still occur. Without adequate protective surfaces, there is a risk of split-second falls with potentially disastrous results. Consider the following scenario:

Three-year-old Shaquana asked her mommy to push her in the backyard swing. She obviously enjoyed the rush of air as she swung back and forth begging her mother to push her even higher. As the swing pivoted to its highest position, Shaquana, always a risk-taker, wondered how it would feel to let go of the chain. In an instant she slipped out of the swing onto the surface below. Fortunately, the area around the play set was covered in pea gravel, nine inches-deep, and Shaquana was not injured.

Protective surfacing materials, such as the pea gravel in the previous scenario, must be replenished when the depth drops below appropriate requirements. Landscape timbers, railroad ties, half-buried horizontal tree trunks, and commercially designed materials can be used to keep loose-fill materials in place.

Equipment Maintenance

Just like public playground equipment, residential playgrounds must be well planned, inspected regularly, and repairs completed immediately. The size and number of pieces of equipment should be proportionate to the space available. Equipment should be installed in an area that allows for good visibility and security but away from obstacles such as areas where vehicles are parked, utility poles, and wires. Keep in mind your children's size and age when purchasing equipment

Figure 7–1   Residential playground.

and follow the manufacturer's guidelines for installation. Ensure that equipment is installed in a level area and that it is anchored to prevent tipping. Each piece of equipment should have an adequate fall zone covered with resilient surfacing materials such as mulch, sand, or pea gravel. Check your child's play attire, avoiding necklaces, clothing with drawstrings, and helmets. Additional problems to watch for include splintering wood, rust, peeling paint, protrusions, sharp points, and potential head entrapments. A safety checklist applicable to all playgrounds is provided in Figure 6–11.

Each safety feature identified by the CPSC (1997) and other organizations is crucial to keeping children safe at school, at parks, *and* at home. Never assume that adherence to one feature, such as supervision, takes the place of another, such as adequate protective surfacing. All safety features work in conjunction to prevent serious and fatal injuries. Figure 7–1 illustrates a residential playground with all these safety feature addressed.

LOOSE PARTS

Adaptable outdoor accessories, commonly referred to as loose parts, play a crucial role in creating a varied and stimulating residential playground. The materials selected will depend on the age and interests of the child. Refer to Figure 4–2 for a list of possible loose parts. A complete discussion of loose parts appropriate for primary grade students can be found in Chapter 4. A collection of loose parts can be created from toys and other objects found around the house, garage, or neighborhood. The collection may include balls of a variety of sizes and types, planks, milk crates, blankets, shovel and pail, leaves, pinecones, and sticks. The variety of loose parts available to children is limited only by their imaginations! The following vignette illustrates the infinite possibilities of play with loose parts. Spencer and his collection of loose parts are pictured in Figure 7–2a and b.

Six-year-old Spencer enjoys the pretend play scenes that can be created from loose parts. A set of toy traffic cones initiated his role-play that resulted in months of outdoor play in which he set up pretend roadblocks, traffic detours, and obstacle courses. Gradually he acquired authentic traffic cones, a barrel used during local road construction, and a role of yellow plastic tape printed with the words, "police line—do not cross." Wheeled vehicles such as a wagon, peddle car, and bicycle enhanced his play. From time to time Spencer incorporated written language with items such as a discarded award plaque, printed road signs made of cardboard, and homemade signs with invented symbols. With determination and authority he "read" aloud each sign explaining the current instructions for maneuvering through his maze of loose parts.

There are important similarities and differences between residential and public playgrounds. Both must be safe for children and every effort should be made to minimize the risk of injury. They both offer variety in the types of gross motor play experiences as well as opportunities to incorporate loose parts.

The residential playground offers some advantages over those used publicly. It can be customized to the age, ability, and interests of the children who use it. Materials used in pretend play scenarios can be left intact allowing the play to develop further over time. As children develop new interests and skills, equipment and materials (both permanent and temporary) can be introduced. The backyard playground can evolve over time and continually meet the needs of growing, developing children.

Figure 7–2a Spencer plays outdoors using his collection of loose parts.

Figure 7–2b   Spencer's collection of loose parts takes shape.

COMMUNITY PLAYGROUNDS

Communities play an important role in providing safe, age-appropriate playground equipment and recreational activities. Families depend on community parks and playgrounds as a way to provide children with outdoor play experiences and the opportunity to meet and socialize with other children. Community playgrounds are an absolute necessity for the growing number of families who do not have a residential or backyard playground. Families who reside in apartments, condominiums, patio homes, and other residences with limited outdoor space rely on community play areas as a means of recreation. Families in some upscale residential communities are finding that legal restrictions do not permit outdoor play equipment (even when there is a generous backyard area) because it detracts from the appearance of the neighborhood. Fortunately, most of these neighborhood associations establish a communal playground for the residents as an alternative. Even when outdoor play space and equipment is readily available by walking out the back door, children and parents still access community parks as a way to offer new physical and social play experiences with a wider variety of playground equipment and peers. Regardless of a family's place of residence, community playgrounds provide children with additional opportunities for outdoor play experiences.

When we look around our communities at the playgrounds available to children, we typically see a piece of property provided by the city with commercially designed equipment that has been selected, purchased, assembled, and maintained by city employees. Playgrounds in some innovative communities, however, are taking on a whole different look. The following case study describes the development of a playground in the small community of Bay Minette, Alabama. The town offered only one outdated, unsafe playground for its youngest residents. But through the innocent remark of one child and the labor of thousands, an exciting playground emerged, as did a new sense of community pride. Figure 7–3a, b, and c show pictures of this event.

Figure 7–3a   Community hard at work on playground (photo series from case study).

Case Study: A Community-Built Playground

After a morning playing at a community-built park thirty-five miles from his home, a young boy asked his mother, "Why can't we have a park like that?" Her son's question motivated Connie Williams to finally address a problem that had been discussed in her community for years. The existing public playground was outdated, sparse, in disrepair, and unsafe. A new play-

Figure 7–3b   Children hard at play.

ground was needed and she made the first courageous move to make it happen. Connie did some preliminary groundwork and found the name of the designers who assisted with the community park she and her son had visited. She contacted the company to obtain basic information regarding cost, time, and commitment. Connie then went to the city council meeting, presented the information, and asked the city for land to build a community park. An affirmative decision was reached immediately and the project had officially begun. A train theme for the park was agreed upon because the community was first established as a result of the train making regular stops at the local depot.

Figure 7–3c Completed community-built playground.

Representatives from Leather and Associates®, an architectural design firm with many years of experience designing community playgrounds, met with children at local elementary schools. They asked the children what should be included on the playground and then incorporated their ideas into the overall plans. Unique ideas such as a puppet theatre and air mister were included in the plan that was finalized and presented to committees the same afternoon. The designers ensured that the playground also met the latest safety and accessibility standards as outlined by CPSC and the American Disabilities Act Accessibility Guidelines (ADAAG, 2000).

Committees were formed for each phase of the project and included: fund raising, purchasing materials, tool committee, children's community outreach, obtaining donated materials, providing meals during the work week, and gathering volunteers. The architectural design firm provided committees with information and guidance.

The financial goal was to collect $100,000 in ten months. An aggressive fund raising campaign included events and activities such as a pig roast, golf tournament, plant sale, t-shirt sale and dress-down day at local businesses, hand tiles painted by children, and a component sale in which donors were publicly recognized for buying specific pieces of playground equipment. The fund raising effort resulted in a collection of $70,000 and the city donated the final $30,000.

Organizers held a "Name the Park" contest, in which citizens submitted their suggestions, shortly before build week in order to garner more attention for the project. The winning name was "Imagination Station," suitable for the theme of the park and the community's history.

When the work week arrived, volunteers donated time, labor, expertise, and enthusiasm to the project over a five day period from the hours of 7 A.M. to 9 P.M. Local churches planned meals and fed the 150 volunteers that worked during the weekdays and the 500 volunteers that offered their services over the weekend. According to Tina Covington, a tireless volunteer and writer for the local newspaper, "Even the skeptics of the project proudly approved." She also recalls the tremendous community spirit and pride that arose out of the project. This came from personally getting to know neighbors who had previously been only acquaintances and from citizens physically laboring side by side regardless of their race, age, gender, or economic status. The final result was an exciting public playground and a united community. The final stage in the project was to develop a membership for "Friends of the Park" who will fund and oversee the maintenance, upkeep, and future additions to the new playground.

The mother in this case study was not experienced in building community playgrounds but she played a crucial role in the development of this tremendous project. She took the first step by making a few contacts, gathering basic information, and presenting the idea to her local city council. A major focus of the playground designers in this case study was to help communities get organized, reach goals, and organize a large volunteer labor force. This was but one example of how citizens of all ages can enjoy a new community playground.

Options for Community Builds

Many communities choose a *barn-raising* approach to building playground equipment with lumber. Directors of these projects should consider using redwood, cedar, and cypress. Although these hardwoods cost more, they do not have to be treated with a mixture of chemicals that often contain chromated copper arsenate (CCA) in order to protect them from rot and insects. Lumber treated with CCA can leak arsenic into the ground, resulting in a poisoning hazard. The extent of the danger of CCA in play equipment is undecided.

Other community groups may opt for manufactured equipment (see Appendix C for a list of companies) while still involving the community in other important aspects of creating the playground. A sense of community pride can still be achieved while reducing costs with a volunteer labor force. For example, when volunteers plan, design, and build playgrounds, it eliminates the cost of playground installation that may equal up to one-half the cost of the equipment. Organizers seeking this option can benefit from the services of KaBOOM!™, a national nonprofit organization created to assist communities and businesses with a shared goal of building a playground. KaBOOM!™ corporate partners support about sixty playground projects a year through financial and in-kind assistance and by recruiting volunteers. In addition, KaBOOM!™ provides (1) basic information on building safe, age-appropriate playgrounds, (2) extensive advise on completing a community-build playground including a weekly timeline for planning (see Figure 7–4, "Community Build Roadmap"), (3) a database that matches funding, in-kind and/or human resource support from a corporate sponsor, business, or individual donor with community groups, and (4) publications and resources.

Organizing Committees A KaBOOM!™ (2000) publication titled "Getting Started Kit®" recommends beginning the project with a team of nine individuals designated as the Playground Committee. Two of these members serve as co-chairs who coordinate and oversee the entire project. The remaining seven members are each team captains of seven different committees including Recruitment Team, Children's Team,

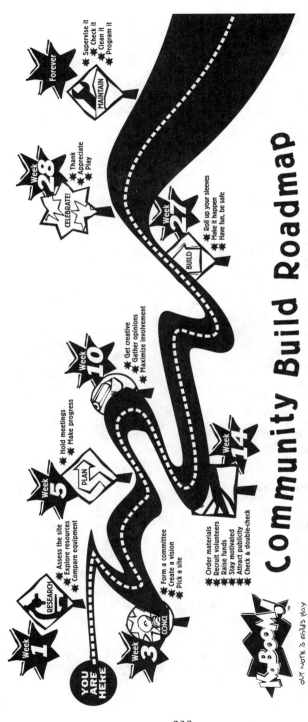

Figure 7-4 Community build roadmap.

Rendered with permission from KaBOOM!™ (www.kaboom.org).

Construction Team, Fundraising Team, Food Team, Public Relations Team, and Safety Team. Explanations for each of these teams are given in Figure 7–5. Each team captain recruits two to five members to assist with responsibilities for their assigned team. Because of the wide variety of responsibilities among the different teams, all types of skills are needed, not just volunteers with construction skills.

Figure 7–5   Playground planning committee positions.

Two Co-Chairs   The Co-chairs are the coordinators and leaders of the entire playground project. Co-chairs should have adequate time available to lead this project, and be organized and resourceful.

Recruitment Team Captain   This captain is responsible for recruiting volunteers to build the playground. It is an exciting and challenging task that demands a "people person" who isn't afraid to ask others to lend a helping hand.

Children's Team Captain   This captain will develop ways for children to participate in the project from the beginning to the end. He/she should be creative, responsible and good with children.

Construction Team Captain   We're sure you know someone in your community who can build anything and can lead groups of people. The goal of this team captain is to prepare for and facilitate the building of the playground, acquiring the tools and materials needed.

Fundraising Team Captain   This captain in is charge of raising money for the project at grassroots and corporate levels. The more money raised by the community, the more people will feel invested in the project. The Fundraising Captain also acts as a treasurer and tracks the project's budget.

Food Team Captain   The way to a volunteer's heart is through the stomach! This captain is responsible for launching an all-out effort to feed the volunteers on Build Day, which can include breakfast, lunch, snacks and lots of water. Someone who can solicit in-kind donations from local grocers or restaurants with ease should be considered.

Public Relations Team Captain   This person will generate all the press and publicity that lets the wider community, city or state support your project and celebrate your accomplishments.

Safety Team Captain   This captain plays an essential role on Build Day. He/she creates an environment on the playground work site where everyone can work hard without worrying about unsafe conditions or accidents. This individual is someone who can work with all age groups, is understanding, and is not afraid to speak up for safety's sake.

Reprinted with permission from KaBOOM!™ (www.kaboom.org).

Selecting a Site and Other Considerations   Selecting a site for the community build playground is easily accomplished if old, outdated apparatus is simply being replaced with new, safe, and accessible equipment. However, establishing the physical site for an entirely new playground can prove to be a challenge. KaBOOM!™ emphasizes the need to carefully analyze potential sites in order to minimize additional costs and maximize safety. Asking a few questions in advance will prevent problems once the project is underway.

1. Who owns the land?
2. How big is the site?
3. Is the site ready or will it need leveling or other preparation?
4. What man-made elements (buried or overhead utilities, sewage pipes, sprinkler system) are on the site now?
5. What natural elements are on the site?
6. What is the space being used for now and how was it used previously?
7. Where is the site in relation to possible obstacles or hazards?
8. What amenities are available to the site?

When designing playgrounds and selecting equipment KaBOOM!™ cautions communities to consider a number of factors including age-appropriateness, accessibility, materials, and surfacing. (See Chapter 6 for an in-depth discussion of these factors.) **Play value** is another factor to consider. This refers to the number and different types of activities a playground component provides. See Figure 7–6 for examples of different kinds of play. Personnel from KaBOOM!™, representatives from the playground equipment manufacturer, and committee volunteers can collectively make these important decisions.

Case Study: KaBOOM!™ and Small Community Build a School Playground

Elsanor Elementary School was in dire in need of a new playground. Generations of children have used

Figure 7–6   Kinds of play.

Kind of play	Activity	Benefits
active	net climbers, balance beams, climbing walls, chain, bridges, overhead climbers, chinning bars, slides, track rides, swings	coordination/balance, upper body strength, motion
creative	theme panels, storefront panels, playhouses, steering wheels, telescopes	stimulates imagination and fosters creativity
cooperative	double slides, climbing walls, teeter totters, tire swings	encourages healthy social interaction
sensory	panels with bells and/or chimes, talk tubes	develops auditory sense and skills

Reprinted with permission from KaBOOM!™ (www.kaboom.org).

the outdated and hazardous playground equipment on the school grounds. The community realized a contemporary, safe playground would benefit not only the students, but serve as a community recreation area during weekends and holidays.

Teachers and local citizens worked together to devise a plan for creating a new playground. They enlisted the assistance of KaBOOM!™, a national, nonprofit organization, that assisted the team in obtaining Home Depot as a corporate sponsor. Local contributions helped ease the financial burden of the project. The newspaper articles in Figure 7–7 explain the need for the project and "before and after" photographs of the playground.

Figure 7–7   School playground renovation.

Elsanor Playground Project Under Way: Educators and Residents Seek to Raise $10,000 to Match $20,000 Grant to Add Equipment at School

ELSANOR—Around the base of the little merry-go-round, thousands of young feet have worn a circular path over the decades.

"Like some of the other equipment on the playground of Elsanor Elementary School, no one on campus today is quite sure how old the merry-go-round is, but children have been playing on it for more than a generation," said Principal Becky Lundberg.

Lunberg continued, "I've had parents of some of these children come up and say, 'I played on that when I was going to school here.'" Nearby are sling-seated swings that school officials also said have been used for

Figure 7–7 Continued.

Guy BusBY/Register

BEFORE: Elsanor Elementary students get ready to push a merry-go-round on the school playground. Clockwise from left are Shana Morrison, Flona Morrison, C.J. Cooper, Chelsea Dawkins, Kaltlyn Dawkins and Katie Cooper. Students, teachers and community members are raising money for new playground equipment for the school.

as long as anyone now working on the 75-year-old campus can recall. A teacher commented that she recalled playing on the same type of swings in the 1960s.

With community support, the school has added some newer equipment—a brightly colored slide and a set of green monkey bars stand out against the dull gray older items. "New equipment is expensive, however, and help will be needed for more improvements," Lundberg said.

Educators and residents are hoping to replace some of the old equipment and expand the playground with help from a national nonprofit group, local contributors and a corporate sponsor—Home Depot. They hope to get help from KaBOOM!™, a Chicago-based organization set up to help communities build playgrounds.

Through the program, the community could get equipment, materials and labor worth $20,000 to improve the playground. In order to get that equipment and material, however, residents and educators in the small unincorporated community have to raise $10,000 in matching funds in the next two months, said Tammy Morrison, one of the project organizers for Elsanor Elementary.

"We can get $20,000 toward the playground, but we're going to have to find a way to come up with $10,000," Morrison said. "We're going to be looking for ways to raise that money in the next few weeks."

Under the terms of the grant, the money must be raised by the beginning of November. Construction must be completed by the end of December.

One fund-raising activity will be the sale of brick pavers with the names of contributors engraved on the bricks, she said. The pavers will be placed around the playground to recognize people who helped make the facility possible.

(continued)

Figure 7–7 Continued.

Morrison said a new playground is needed in the growing community.

"We've added some things but we're growing so fast," she said. "We're up to 258 students. Last year, we had 240. We're growing by leaps and bounds and we're going to need to do something."

If the money is raised, the equipment and appearance of the playground will be up to the children it will serve, Morrison said.

Representatives from KaBOOM!™ and Home Depot will meet with Elsanor students and teachers on Sept. 13 to discuss the design of the facility. Children will be asked to submit drawings showing what they would like to see on their new playground.

Maritza Rosario of KaBOOM!™ said organization officials will use the children's ideas and community recommendations to draw up three designs that they will then ask students to vote on.

Rosario said children are the main reason behind the organization and projects such as the playground in Elsanor.

"The kids are going to grow there physically, socially and emotionally," she said. "A playground is a free place where children can grow and take part in unstructured activity that allows them to develop on their own."

Rosario said KaBOOM!™ is a national organization dedicated solely to building playgrounds in areas where such facilities might not otherwise be constructed, such as rural and inner-city communities. The organization is also extending its programs beyond the national borders and is helping build a playground in the war-ravaged African nation of Rwanda.

Rosario said this is the first KaBOOM!™ project in South Alabama of which she is aware.

The group locates corporate sponsors willing to provide money for playground projects and puts them in touch with communities needing assistance, Rosario said. In this case, Home Depot was looking for a project in the Mobile area and Elsanor school officials had applied and their application had been approved.

She said community commitment is a key to the program. One reason for the need for matching funds is to make certain there is enough support to show the playground will be kept up once the facility is finished.

"The entire process depends on the support of the community," she said. "When Home Depot leaves when KaBOOM!™ leaves the playground will still be there and it will be up to the community to look after it."

Lundberg said the playground is important for the entire community, not just the school and its students.

"Between Robertsdale and Pensacola, there isn't a town, so the children don't have anywhere to go," she said. "This is going to be for the entire community. If we can do something like this, it's going to be a benefit for all the children and everyone in the community."

Figure 7–7 Continued.

Elsanor Elementary Sports New Playground Equipment

A dedication ceremony was held at Elsanor Elementary School last week after new playground equipment was installed during a community construction day. Residents built the playground in a day with assistance from Home Depot and KaBOOM!™, a Chicago-based organization set up to help communities build playgrounds. The new $30,000 facility, paid with a grant from KaBOOM!™ and local funds, replaced equipment that had been used in the unincorporated central Baldwin community for several decades.

AFTER: A tunnel leads from a landing to a sliding board on part of the Elsanor Elementary playground (*above*). Ladders and passage-ways (*right*) make up a portion of the new playground equipment at Elsanor Elementary School.

CONCLUSION

Residential and community playgrounds offer valuable new experiences to young children. However, adhering to guidelines designed to keep children safe on playgrounds must always be the first priority. Residential playgrounds can evolve with the interests and abilities of specific children in mind. Community playgrounds offer a variety of new experiences and opportunities to interact with peers in an outdoor setting. Every community, regardless of its size, economic make-up, obstacles and amenities needs to provide a safe, exciting place for children to play outdoors. With the help of community volunteers and profit and nonprofit organizations, the goal of establishing a new playground is an achievable goal.

KEY TERM

play value

THEORY INTO PRACTICE

1. Examine a residential playground. Look for safety features such as age-appropriateness, type and depth of fall surfacing, and equipment in need of maintenance. Describe how the backyard playground compared with those of your childhood.
2. List the loose parts available in the residential playground examined in the previous activity. What additional loose parts would you recommend based on the ages, ability-levels, and interests of the children using the playground?
3. Visit a playground built by the local community. Interview a contact person who was involved in the process and ask relevant questions about the project, such as, how did it begin, how were volunteers organized, and what were the costs? Summarize your findings.

RELATED WEB SITE

www.kaboom.org
KaBOOM!™ homepage provides all the information needed to organize a community built playground as well as advice on raising funds.

RELATED RESOURCES

National Program for Playground Safety. (1996). *Inspection guide for parents.* Cedar Falls, IA: National Program for Playground Safety.

National Program for Playground Safety. (1999). *Building SAFE playgrounds.* Cedar Falls, IA: National Program for Playground Safety.

REFERENCES

Americans with Disabilities Act Access Guidelines. (2000). *Accessibility guidelines for play areas: An overview.* www.access-board.gov

Busby, G. (2000, September 3). Elsanor playground project underway. *Mobile Register,* pp. 1, 10.

Busby, G. (2000, November 27). Elsanor elementary sports new playground equipment. *Mobile Register,* p. 1.

Fleishman, S. (2001, May 11). Swing sets get bigger, pricier. *Mobile Register,* pp. 1D, 4D.

Hudson, S., & Thompson, D. (1998). *The SAFE playground handbook.* Cedar Falls, IA: The National Program for Playground Safety.

KaBOOM!™. (2000) Getting started kit®. Washington, DC: KaBOOM!™

National Recreation and Park Association. (1995). *The dirty dozen: Are they hiding in your child's playground?* Ashburn, VA: National Recreation and Park Association.

Public Interest Research Groups. (1998). Playing it safe: Results of the investigation: The nation's playgrounds pose hidden hazards. www.pirg.org

U.S. Consumer Product Safety Commission. (1997). *Handbook for public playground safety* (No. 325). Washington DC: U.S. Government Printing Office.

APPENDIX A

First Aid Kit

It is recommended that well-equipped first aid kits be easily accessible to adults (but not children) when outdoors or on a field trip. Individual items should be wrapped separately to keep them sanitary and placed in a box with a lid, such as a traditional style lunchbox or a back pack when on field trips.

The following items are to be included:

adhesive bandages and butterfly closures
antiseptic cream
bandage tape
bee sting kit
calamine lotion
clean cloth
commercial cold pack or plastic bag
cotton
disposable latex gloves
emergency contact information (parents and
     emergency services)
eye dressing or pads
flashlight with batteries

gauze pads
nonstick sterile pads
pen or pencil and notepad
petroleum jelly
rolled flexible or stretch gauze
rubbing alcohol
safety pins
scissors
sealed packages of cleansing wipes
small plastic cup
small splints
soap
special items for children with specific health problems
thermometer
tongue depressors
triangular bandages
tweezers

Adapted from Scholastic Early Childhood Today, August/September 1998.
Reprinted with permission.

APPENDIX B

Modifying Outdoor Play Equipment

Equipment	Description	Benefits	S	P	E	C*	Modifications for integrated play
Play and work tables	Plain or with textured surfaces.	Allow room for quiet individual or group activities. Facilitate adult-child interaction.	X	X	X	X	Backrests on benches for extra support. Room for wheelchair at table height.
Sand table	A container for sand mounted at table height.	Provides sensory stimulation. Encourages language, imagination, problem solving, and creative individual or group play.	X	X	X	X	Room for wheelchair at table height. Indentations around table will enable children with poor balance to lean on table for support.
Play counter	A countertop mounted under a platform or at the side of a ramp or playhouse. May be part of a play sink or stove stop.	Encourages role play, imagination, and social interaction. Can also be used for drawing or as a ledge to play with other toys.	X	X	X	X	Appropriate height for wheelchair.
Playhouse	Child-sized house or other enclosed space. Adults should be able to see into it.	Encourages dramatic play and social interaction. Allows children to act out different roles in a safe, supportive atmosphere.	X		X	X	Accessible and large enough to accommodate a child in a wheelchair and peers.
Steering wheel	Mounted on a post, side of wall, or play equipment.	Promotes imaginative play.		X		X	Mounted at wheelchair height. Sounds added so that children with visual impairments can locate.

Equipment	Description	S	P	E	C	Modifications
Tunnel	Plastic molded passageway for crawling through and hiding in.		X			Ceiling or side-mounted grips for children to pull their bodies along.
Wide slide	Double the usual width so that a child can slide down alongside another person.	X	X			Accessible for child in wheelchair, with space to transfer from wheelchair to slide.
Tire swing	Tire used as seat, suspended from beam at a single point. Can seat one or more children.	X	X		X	No modifications needed.
Spring-based seesaw	Seesaw supported by spring rather than fulcrum. Allows children of different sizes to ride together.	X	X	X		Seats made of a nonslip surface will assist with transfer from wheelchair.
Spring toys	Single-seated rides made in animal or vehicle shapes, mounted on a sturdy coil spring.	X	X			Back supports and adequate foot holds to provide support. Accessible seating area for transfer out of wheelchair.
Swing	Soft strap or harness seat supported at two points to overhead beam.	X	X			Sound-locating device will cue location and timing of swing for safety of children with visual impairments.

Challenges children to move their bodies in a different way.

Encourages socialization and cooperation.

Improves balance, stimulates vestibular sense, and promotes language and cooperative play.

Can be used by one or more children; promotes social skills. Strengthens upper body and balance.

Promote upper-body strength and balance; stimulate vestibular sense. Offer place for observation and relaxation/quieting down.

Stimulates vestibular sense and promotes balance and coordination. Individual or group play activity.

* S = Social P = Physical E = Emotional C = Cognitive

253

Equipment	Description	Benefits	S	P	E	C*	Modifications for integrated play
Balance beams/pods	Narrow wooden beams or small pod-shaped platforms raised slightly off ground for walking on.	Promote balance, coordination, and gross-motor planning skills. Can be used as a prop for games or as part of obstacle courses.		X		X	Nonslip surface or railings to help children with poor balance.
Manipulative play panel	A counter or panel where knobs, gears, binoculars, dials, or a tick-tack-toe board are mounted.	Improves fine-motor skills and can be cognitively challenging.		X		X	Mounted at different heights to ensure wheelchair access. Add auditory activities and contrasting colors.
Overhead ladder	Horizontal overhead bars at heights appropriate for age and size of children.	Improves gross-motor planning, coordination, and upper-body development.		X		X	Accessible from wheelchair.
Basketball hoop	Adjustable plastic or steel hoop and frame.	Improves eye-hand coordination and upper-body strength.	X	X		X	Adjustable height allows younger or seated children to play. Movable frame allows for placement in different areas.
Chinning bars	Can be horizontal or inclined. Most appropriate for elementary-aged children.	Improve upper-body development.		X			Mounted at different heights.

254

Equipment	Description	Developmental benefits	S	P	E	C	Adaptations*
Nets	Can be made of cargo chain, rope, or tires. Constructed between platforms or as access devices to climbers.	Challenge balance, eye-hand coordination, and gross-motor planning skills. Strengthen both lower and upper body.	X	X	X	X	Alternate ways to access.
Tube and half tube slides	Enclosed slide allowing children to slide independently. May frighten very young children.	Provide vestibular stimulation.		X		X	Different ways to access.
Stairs	Access to slides, climbers, or platforms; best if wide enough for two children to go up and down simultaneously.	Improve gross-motor planning and lower-body development.		X			Bilateral-support railings for young children and those in need of support.
Ladders	Provide access to climbers or platforms. May be inclined or straight.	Improve eye-hand coordination, upper- and lower-body strength, and motor-planning skills. Straight vertical ladder requires more advanced skills.		X			Wide enough to permit children to pass each other. Ramped access as alternative.
Bridge	Constructed of wood, tires, rope, or chain. Connects platforms or parts of play equipment. Can be stable or move with child's movements.	Challenges balance and coordination. Can be incorporated into dramatic play activities.		X			Handrails for safety. Visual and auditory cues for spatial orientation. Wheelchair accessible and usable.

* S = Social P = Physical E = Emotional C = Cognitive

Equipment	Description	Benefits	S	P	E	C*	Modifications for integrated play
Talking tubes	Metal or plastic cone-shaped receptacles that transmit sound. Mounted on posts or within a structure.	Promote language and social interaction.	X		X	X	Adjustable mouthpiece for accessibility at different heights.
Music instruments	Wind chimes, percussion instruments, bell sounded by hand or with a stick.	Improve auditory discrimination skills and encourage creative expression. Can promote group interaction.	X	X	X	X	Placed on appropriate surface and at accessible heights.
Water play table	Water and appropriate toys in bucket; open-container table; or set of sieves, pulleys, and bowls.	Calming for many children. Encourages problem solving, language, tactile awareness, and imaginative play.	X	X	X	X	Indentations around table to accommodate wheelchairs and assist children with poor balance.

* S = Social P = Physical E = Emotional C = Cognitive

Reprinted with permission from Theemes, T. *Let's go outside! Designing the early childhood playground.* Ypsilanti, MI: High Scope Press.

APPENDIX C

Manufacturers of Playground Equipment

Childcraft Education Corp.
P.O. Box 3239
Lancaster, PA 17604
800-631-5652
www.childcrafteducation.com

Community Playthings
P.O. Box 901, Rte. 213
Rifton, NY 12471
800-777-4244

Constructive Playthings
13201 Arrington Rd.
Grandview, MO 64030-2886
800-448-4115
www.cptoys.com

Grounds for Play
1401 East Dallas St.
Mansfield, TX 76063
800-552-PLAY
www.groundsforplay.com

Howell Playground
1714 East Fairchild St.
P.O. Box 1
Danville, IL 61834-0001
217-442-0482
www.world-playground.com

Miracle Recreation Equipment
  Company
P.O. Box 420
Monett, MO 65708
800-523-4202
www.miracle-recreation.com

PlayDesigns
1000 Buffalo Rd.
Lewisburg, PA 17837-9795
800-327-7571
www.playdesigns.com

Progressive Playgrounds Inc.
56 Main St.
P.O. Box 313
Califon, NJ 07830
800-799-7529
www.progressiveplaygrounds.com

APPENDIX D

Food Pyramid

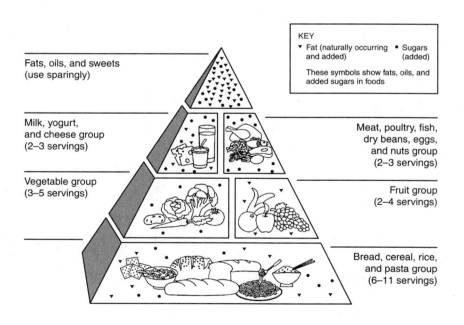

Fats, oils, and sweets
(use sparingly)

KEY
▼ Fat (naturally occurring   • Sugars
and added)   (added)

These symbols show fats, oils, and
added sugars in foods

Milk, yogurt,
and cheese group
(2–3 servings)

Meat, poultry, fish,
dry beans, eggs,
and nuts group
(2–3 servings)

Vegetable group
(3–5 servings)

Fruit group
(2–4 servings)

Bread, cereal, rice,
and pasta group
(6–11 servings)

Appendix E

Playground Safety Organizations

American Society for Testing
  and Materials (ASTM)
100 Bar Harbor Dr.
W. Conshohocken, PA 19428-2959
610-832-9585
www.astm.org

International Play Equipment
  Manufacturers Association
  (IPEMA)
8300 Colesville Rd., Suite 250
Silver Spring, MD 20910
800-395-5550
www.ipema.org

National Program for Playground
  Safety
School of Health, Physical
  Education and Leisure Services
The University of Northern Iowa
Cedar Falls, IA 50614-0618
800-554-7529
www.uni.edu/playground

National Recreation and Park
  Association
22377 Belmont Ridge Rd.
Ashburn, VA 20148-4501
703-858-2148
www.activeparks.org

U.S. Consumer Product Safety
  Commission (CPSC)
Washington, DC 20207
800-638-2772
www.cpsc.gov

APPENDIX F

Professional Organizations Supporting Young Children

American Alliance for Health, Physical Education, Recreation, and Dance (AAHPERD)
1900 Association Dr.
Reston, VA 20191

Association for Childhood Education International
The Olney Professional Building
17904 Georgia Ave., Suite 215
Olney, MD 20832
800-423-3563
www.acei.org
ACEIED@aol.com

Council for Exceptional Children
1110 N. Glebe Rd.
Suite 300
Arlington, VA 22201-5704
888-CEC-SPED
www.cec.sped.org

Early Childhood Music and Movement Association
10691 Livingston Dr.
Northglenn, CO 80234

National Association for the Education of Young Children (NAEYC)
1509 16th St., NW
Washington, DC 20036-1426
800-424-2460
www.naeyc.org
membership@naeyc.org

Southern Early Childhood Association (SECA)
P.O. Box 55930
Little Rock, AR 72215-5930
510-663-0353
www.SECA50.org
SECA@aristotle.net

# APPENDIX G

Playground Rating System

Instructions:
Rate each item on a scale from 0–5. High score possible on Section I is 100 points, Section II is 50 points and Section III is 50 points, for a possible grand total of 200 points. Divide the grand total score by 2 to obtain a final rating.

Section I. What does the playground contain?

Rate each item for degree of existence and function on a scale of 0–5 (0 = not existent; 1 = some elements exist but not functional; 2 = poor; 3 = average; 4 = good; 5 = all elements exist, excellent (function).

_____ 1. A hard-surfaced area with space for games and a network of paths for wheeled toys

_____ 2. Sand and sand play equipment

_____ 3. Dramatic play structures (playhouse, car or boat with complementary equipment, such as adjacent sand and water and housekeeping equipment)

_____ 4. A superstructure with room for many children at a time and with a variety of challenges and exercise options (entries, exits, and levels)

_____ 5. Mound(s) of earth for climbing and digging

_____ 6. Trees and natural areas for shade, nature study, and play

_____ 7. Zoning to provide continuous challenge; linkage of areas, functional physical boundaries, vertical and horizontal treatment (hills and valleys)

_____ 8. Water play areas, with fountains, pools and sprinklers

_____ 9. Construction area with junk materials such as tires, crates, planks, boards, bricks and nails; tools should be provided and demolition and construction allowed

_____ 10. An old (or built) vehicle, airplane, boat, car that has been made safe, but not stripped of its play value (should be changed or re-located after a period of time to renew interest)

_____ 11. Equipment for active play: a slide with a large platform at the top (slide may be built into side of a hill); swings that can be used safely in a variety of ways (soft material for seats); climbing trees (mature dead trees that are horizontally positioned); climbing nets

_____ 12. A large soft area (grass, bark mulch, etc.) for organized games

_____ 13. Small semi-private spaces at the child's own scale: tunnels, niches, playhouses, hiding places

_____ 14. Fences, gates, walls, and windows that provide security for young children and are adaptable for learning/play

_____ 15. A garden and flowers located so that they are protected from play, but with easy access for children to tend them; gardening tools are available

_____ 16. Provisions for the housing of pets; pets and supplies available

_____ 17. A transitional space from outdoors to indoors. This could be a covered play area immediately adjoining the playroom that will protect the children from the sun and rain and extend indoor activities to the outside.

_____ 18. Adequate protected storage for outdoor play equipment, tools for construction and garden areas, and maintenance tools. Storage can be separate: wheeled toys stored near the wheeled vehicle track; sand equipment near the sand enclosure; tools near the construction area. Storage can be in separate structures next to the building or fence. Storage should aid in children's picking up and putting equipment away at the end of each play period.

_____ 19. Easy access from outdoor play areas to coats, toilets, and drinking fountains; shaded areas and benches for adults and children to sit within the outdoor play area

_____ 20. Tables and support materials for group activities (art, reading, etc.)

Section II. Is the playground in good repair and relatively safe?

Rate each item for condition and safety on a scale of 0–5 (0 = not existent; 1 = exists but extremely hazardous; 2 = poor; 3 = fair; 4 = good; 5 = excellent condition and relatively safe yet presents challenge).

_____ 1. A protective fence (with lockable gates) next to hazardous areas (streets, deep ditches, water, etc.)

_____ 2. Eight to ten inches of noncompacted sand, wood mulch (or equivalent) under all climbing and moving equipment, extending through fall zones and secured by retaining wall

_____ 3. Size of equipment appropriate to age group served; climbing heights limited to 6–7 feet

_____ 4. Area free of litter (e.g., broken glass, rocks), electrical hazards, high voltage power lines, sanitary hazards

_____ 5. Moving parts free of defects (e.g., no pinch and crush points, bearing not excessively worn)

_____ 6. Equipment free of sharp edges, protruding elements, broken parts, toxic substances, bare metal exposed to sun

_____ 7. Swing seats constructed of soft or lightweight material (e.g., rubber, canvas)

_____ 8. All safety equipment in good repair (e.g., guard rails, signs, padded areas, protective covers)

_____ 9. No openings that can entrap a child's head (approximately 3½–9 inches); adequate space between equipment

_____ 10. Equipment structurally sound; no bending, warping, breaking, sinking, etc.; heavy fixed and moving equipment secured in ground and concrete footings recessed in ground; check for underground rotting, rusting, termites, in support members

---

Section III. What should the playground do?

Rate each item for degree and quality on a scale of 0–5 (0 = not existent; 1 = some evidence but virtually nonexistent; 2 = poor; 3 = fair; 4 = good; 5 = excellent). Use the space provided for comments.

_____ 1. Encourages play:
Inviting, easy access
Open, flowing, and relaxed space
Clear movement from indoors to outdoors
Appropriate equipment for the age group(s)

_____ 2. Stimulates the child's senses:
Change and contrasts in scale, light, texture, and color
Flexible equipment
Diverse experiences

_____ 3. Nurtures the child's curiosity;
Equipment that the child can change
Materials for experiments and construction
Plants and animals

_____ 4. Supports the child's basic social and physical needs:
Comfortable to the child
Scaled to the child
Physically challenging

_____ 5. Allows interaction between the child and the resources:
Systematic storage that defines routines
Semi-enclosed spaces to read, work a puzzle, or be alone

_____ 6. Allows interaction between the child and other children:
Variety of spaces
Adequate space to avoid conflicts
Equipment that invites socialization

_____ 7. Allows interaction between the child and adults:
Easy maintenance
Adequate and convenient storage
Organization of spaces to allow general supervision
Rest areas for adults and children

_____ 8. Complements the cognitive forms of play engaged in by the child:
Functional, exercise, gross-motor, active
Constructive, building, creating
Dramatic, pretend, make-believe
Organized games, games with rules

_____ 9. Complements the social forms of play engaged in by the child:
Solitary, private, meditative
Parallel, side-by-side
Cooperative interrelationships

_____ 10. Promotes social and intellectual development:
Provides graduated challenge
Integrates indoor/outdoor activities
Involves adults in children's play
Regular adult-child planning
The play environment is dynamic—continuously changing

Reprinted with permission from Frost, J. (1992). *Play and playscapes*. Albany, NY: Delmar.

Glossary

babbling Infant vocalizations that resemble adultlike speech.

causality Understanding cause and effect or the connection between an action and consequence.

child-centered curriculum The concept of developing curriculum around the interests of children.

complexity The extent to which a play unit encourages active manipulation and alteration by children. Categorized as simple, complex, and super.

concrete operational thought More sophisticated reasoning than preoperational thought, including a better understanding of cause and effect and other thought processes.

constructive play Creating a product.

cooperation Interacting socially within a group, often to organize an event or activity.

developmental screening instruments Provide information about whether or not a child's development is proceeding like typically developing children.

dynamic systems theory A premise connecting essential brain organization and learning to movement.

egocentrism The young child's inability to understand another's perspective.

elevated level Play components that are not accessible from ground level.

entanglement   An article of clothing or other object worn by a child becomes caught on playground equipment, resulting in strangulation.

expressive jargon   Infant babbling in a long string of complex sounds complete with intonation.

functional play   Repetitive actions for the purpose of pleasure.

fundamental movement phase   The period when children are learning movement skills that are the foundation for learning more complex skills in later phases of development.

games with rules   A type of play emerging during the primary grades in which children enjoy devising their own or following predetermined sets of rules.

gross motor skills   Skills requiring the use of large muscles such as those in the legs, arms, and trunk.

ground level   Play components that are not elevated.

head entrapment   Child's head cannot be withdrawn through playground equipment, resulting in strangulation.

individualized education program (IEP)   Contains the terms of the special education and related services a child with a disability will receive.

individualized family service plan (IFSP)   A written document that outlines the early intervention services to be received by an infant or toddler with a disability and may also include the family.

loose parts   Accessory materials used in outdoor play that are manipulated by children.

multiple intelligences   Theory devised by Howard Gardner emphasizing eight distinct intellectual capabilities.

naturalistic intelligence   One of the eight multiple intelligences recognized by Gardner. This intelligence is used to learn about features of the natural world.

negotiation   Conflict resolution technique in which the importance of finding a satisfying compromise is emphasized.

object permanence   A child now has the ability to mentally picture an object even when it is not in sight.

persona doll story   Projecting a problem and developing a story around an inanimate object such as a doll, puppet, or stuffed animal to assist children with problem solving.

perspective-taking   Conflict resolution technique in which children express their own thoughts as well as hear another child's point of view.

pincer grip   The ability to pick up small objects using the thumb and forefinger.

play components   "Manufactured or natural elements used for play, socialization, or learning" (ADAAG, 2000).

play units   A single, designated area containing objects for play that may or may not have tangible boundaries.

play value   The number and different types of activities/experiences a playground component provides.

portfolio system A collection of documents that have been reviewed and interpreted for the purpose of assessment and planning.

potential units Empty spaces that are surrounded by tangible boundaries.

pragmatics Approaching different situations with the most practical and convincing communication strategy.

preoperational thought The period or stage before children are capable of using logic to solve problems.

pretend play Transforming objects and one's self into make believe roles.

product collection A method of assessment that provides tangible evidence of a child's new attempts, challenges, and accomplishments.

productive language Infant vocalization that is used as a means of communication.

progressivism An educational approach emphasizing the child and his or her interests rather than an instructor-driven curriculum.

receptive language Infants' ability to understand language before they begin talking.

self-regulation Conflict resolution technique in which aggressive situations are deescalated.

separation anxiety Fear of being separated from a familiar caregiver.

standardized evaluations A form of assessment that undergoes rigorous evaluation to ensure consistency in all aspects of test administration and interpretation of scores.

stranger anxiety A fear of unknown people.

systematic record keeping Requires careful observation and documentation of a child's action and language.

telegraphic speech Early speech containing only words to communicate meaning.

traditional approach A term used to describe kindergarten teaching practices that were originally described as "progressive."

variety Playground equipment and materials that offer different types of experiences.

Index